I0528480

www.ingramcontent.com/pod-product-compliance
Lightning Source LLC
Chambersburg PA
CBHW051320120626
46547CB00015B/2328

דברים

THE
ISRAEL
BIBLE

DEUTERONOMY

EDITED BY

Rabbi Tuly Weisz

ISRAEL 365

The Israel Bible: Deuteronomy

First Edition, 2021

The Israel Bible was produced by Israel365 in cooperation with Teach for
Israel and is used with permission from Teach for Israel. All rights reserved.
The English translation was adapted by Israel365 from the JPS Tanakh.
Copyright © 1985 by the Jewish Publication Society. All rights reserved.

Cover image used under license from Shutterstock.com

ISBN 978-1-957109-30-5

A CIP catalogue record for this title is available from the British Library

The Israel Bible: Deuteronomy is a holy book that contains
the name of God and should be treated with respect.

Table of Contents

Introduction

The Hebrew Bible is commonly known as the *Tanakh* which stands for *Torah* (the Five Books of Moses), *Neviim* (the Prophets) and *Ketuvim* (the Writings). The *Tanakh* consists of 24 books that are considered by Jews to be the word of God. While these books have been referred to as the "Old Testament," many Jews reject this label since it implies the replacement of the Hebrew Bible with something newer and prefer the more authentic Jewish name.

The *Tanakh* is not only the most important book known to man, it is God's word that is perfect and absolute. It is therefore a daunting undertaking to publish an edition of the *Tanakh*, and the responsibilities are awesome. There is no room for error or carelessness in dealing with the eternal word of God. Further, upon embarking on such a serious initiative, we ask ourselves if our efforts are gratuitous. Considering the many editions of the Bible in print, is there truly a need for yet another one?

While there are numerous Bibles in circulation today, its most central aspect – the Land of Israel – has often been overlooked. References to Israel appear on nearly every page, and the city of Jerusalem is specifically referred to hundreds of times throughout the Bible. The essential link between Israel and *Torah* is emphasized repeatedly in verses such as, "For instruction (*Torah*) shall come forth from *Tzion*, the word of *Hashem* from *Yerushalayim*" (Micah 4:2).

The miraculous return of the People of Israel to the Land of Israel in our own generation provides the perfect moment for a new volume to fill this void in biblical literature. *The Israel Bible* includes many special features elucidating God's focus on Israel throughout *Tanakh* and there are many additional, multimedia features available on our website **www.theisraelbible.com**.

Ordering and Presentation – In presenting *The Israel Bible*, our goal is to spread awareness of the biblical significance of the Land of Israel as well as the Jewish people's eternal connection to the land, based on the text of the *Tanakh*, the Hebrew Bible. We aim to honor "the God, the People and the Land of Israel" from an Orthodox Jewish perspective. To that end, *The Israel Bible* follows the traditional Jewish ordering of the books and the customary Hebrew division of chapters. Therefore, for example, we count 24 books of *Tanakh* with *Sefer Divrei Hayamim* (Chronicles) appearing last. It is our hope that our rich content will speak to all Jews and non-Jews who appreciate Israel as the God given land of the Jewish people.

English Translation – Throughout history, Jews have studied the Bible in Hebrew, as any form of translation would miss much of the nuance of the original holy tongue in which *Torah* has been transmitted since the days of Moses. However, as many Jews settled in America in the 19th Century, the need for an English translation became necessary. To be sure, there were already English translations prepared over the centuries by Christians, but in the words of the original editors of the Jewish Publication Society (JPS), "The Jew cannot afford to have his Bible translation prepared for him by others. He cannot have it as a gift, even as he cannot borrow his soul from others."

JPS set out in the late 1800s to publish an authoritative English translation "in the spirit of Jewish tradition." It was compiled over decades by some of the leading Jewish scholars of the time. They formed committees and subcommittees to compare existing English versions, considering medieval and modern Jewish commentators. The monumental JPS translation, originally published in 1917, has been updated in recent years, and *The Israel Bible* is proud to utilize the 1984 New Jewish Publication Society (NJPS) version with its modern, clear language, as well as its wide-ranging acceptance as an accurate and high-quality translation. We applied the NJPS translation verbatim, except for a select list of nouns which we replaced with their traditional Hebrew names. This is true even when we found the NJPS translation to be different than the popular translation of a word or phrase and when the NJPS switched the order of the text for the sake of clarity (see, for example, Ezekiel 24:22–24).

Hebrew Transliteration – To give our readers an authentic *Tanakh* experience, every verse that has commentary is transliterated from Hebrew into English. The Hebrew alphabet chart includes our standards for transliteration and pronunciation of Hebrew verses, enabling readers of *The Israel Bible* to decipher key biblical passages in the holy language. Readers can hear the entire Bible read in Hebrew on our website **www.theisraelbible.com**.

There are various standards when it comes to transliterating Hebrew words into English letters. While we have relied primarily on the classical Hebrew transliteration, we have occasionally deviated for the sake of simplicity, clarity and to reflect common usage.

In addition to whole verses, we have also transliterated many proper nouns in the English translation so that our readers can learn the names of key biblical figures and locations in their Hebrew form. As a rule, we chose to transliterate names of people that were central in the establishment and functioning of the nation of Israel, as well as significant places in the Holy Land. Therefore, regarding Adam's sons, for example, only *Shet* (Seth) is transliterated since it was from him that *Noach* (Noah), and ultimately *Avraham* (Abraham), descended. For this reason, there might be verses or sections of *The Israel Bible* that contains multiple names and only some of them are transliterated.

For the same reason, we have transliterated the names of the books of *Tanakh* when referring to them in our introductions and commentary. When referencing a specific chapter or verse, however, we use the English names of the books in our citations for clarity. We also transliterated ideas and concepts that are central to Judaism such as *Shabbat* (Sabbath), the names of the Jewish holidays and the *Beit Hamikdash* (Temple), as well as biblical measurements. Finally, the name of God is transliterated. Out of respect, Orthodox Jews generally refer to the Lord as *Hashem*, which literally means 'the Name.' Referring to God as *Hashem* reminds us that we feel close to Him but also recognize our distance at the same time. To stress this moniker, we transliterated both the Tetragrammaton as well as the name *Elohim* as *Hashem*.

Study Notes – Our unique commentary was compiled by Orthodox Jewish scholars who live in Israel. It is an anthology in the sense that most of the commentary is not original, but draws from traditional teachings of early Jewish Sages and modern rabbinic commentators. We also include quotations from individuals who have played a significant part in the past century of modern Israeli history including Israeli prime ministers, poets and military leaders.

Our commentary can be broken into four categories, three of which are identified by an icon at the beginning of the study note:

Israel lessons are indicated with an icon bearing the map of Israel and focus on the Land of Israel and the modern State of Israel.

Jewish lessons are indicated with a *Torah* scroll and teach a concept in Judaism or a classic idea from rabbinic thought.

Hebrew lessons are represented by an icon bearing the letter *aleph* and focus on the meaning of a Hebrew word or phrase.

All other comments are considered general comments and are not assigned an icon.

Supplemental Material – In addition to our unique translation and original commentary, *The Israel Bible* offers supplementary material to enrich the learning experience of our readers. Before every book of *Tanakh*, we provide an introduction, as well as information, generally in the form of a map, a chart or a list, which is central to the specific book.

Maps – As the purpose of *The Israel Bible* is to highlight the biblical significance of the Land of Israel, significant time was spent researching and preparing maps to bring the physical contours of the holy land to life with great accuracy. However, since there is a lack of information regarding the precise locations of certain ancient cities, some of the places on our maps are approximate or subject to debate. In these cases, we followed the opinion that we are most comfortable with, but acknowledge that there is room for disagreement. We continue to produce new maps, which are available on our website **www.theisraelbible.com/maps**.

Torah **Readings** – The *Torah* is not just a work that is studied privately, it is also read out loud in synagogue. Every *Shabbat* and holiday a portion of the *Torah* is read, as well as a related section from *Neviim*, the prophets, called the *haftarah*. We included the blessings recited before and after the reading of the *Torah*, a list of the weekly *Torah* portions and their corresponding *haftarot*, and a chart of the *Torah* readings for special days with their corresponding *haftarot*. Readers can always find the current week's *Torah* portion by visiting **www.theisraelbible.com/weekly-torah-portion**. In this volume, we indicate where a new *Torah* portion begins by highlighting the Hebrew verse number with a gray box so readers can follow along with the communal *Torah* readings. Furthermore, we have included prayers for the State of Israel and the soldiers of the Israel Defense Forces (IDF) that are generally recited following the *Torah* reading in synagogue. It is our constant prayer that God watch over the State of Israel and the members of the IDF, who defend Israel every hour of every day.

In 1948, the State of Israel was created providing a modern answer to Isaiah's ancient question, "Is a nation born all at once?" (Isaiah 66:8). *The Israel Bible* was first published in the 70th year of God's miraculous restoration of the People of Israel to the Land of Israel. Jewish wisdom teaches that 70 is a significant number: *Moshe* (Moses) translated the *Torah* into 70 languages for all 70 nations of the world. From our very origins, the Jewish people were meant to be a light unto the 70 nations, spreading God's truth to the masses.

In the seven decades since the modern rebirth of the State of Israel, God's plan has been unfolding with unprecedented speed, dramatic highs and heart-breaking lows. Never has Israel been at the forefront of the world's attention as it is in our generation. Efforts to vilify the Jewish State seem to spread every day across the globe. At the same time, so does the growing movement of millions of non-Jewish biblical Zionists who stand with the nation of Israel as an expression of their commitment to God's word. As we seek to understand the clash of these two conflicting worldviews, the need for *The Israel Bible* has never been so important.

Standing on the great shoulders of those who came before us and emanating from the land that has always served as the birthplace for the Bible, we conclude with a heartfelt prayer: May the Almighty bless our efforts in offering this *Tanakh* to influence the hearts, minds and actions of its readers. In this way, it is our hope to spread God's name so that the publication of *The Israel Bible* brings us one step closer to the final redemption of Israel and the entire world.

Rabbi Tuly Weisz
Editor, *The Israel Bible*

Foreword

The mandate to study God's word daily is interestingly not found in the Five Books of Moses (Pentateuch), but rather in the first book of our prophetic writings: "Let not this Book of the Teaching cease from your lips, but recite it day and night, so that you may observe faithfully all that is written in it. Only then will you prosper in your undertakings and only then will you be successful" (Joshua 1:8). Charged with bringing the Israelites into the land covenantally promised to Abraham, Isaac and Jacob, God ensures Joshua of His protection if the nation observes His ways as dictated in the Divine constitution known as the *Torah*.

In Jewish tradition, Joshua (1:8) is directly linked with Deuteronomy (11:14), "You shall gather in your new grain and wine, and oil."[1] Our Sages deduced from this scriptural combination the importance of merging *Torah* study with a profession. Completely dedicating oneself to the study of *Torah* without having the financial means to sustain this lifestyle can lead one to eventually straying from observance of God's will. Poverty and crime can have an intimate relationship.

We must also be careful that our work does not affect our daily study of Scripture. The addiction of becoming a workaholic and not making *Torah* study a priority can also lead one into temptations that can violate our personal relationship with Him as well as our fellow human beings. The goal is to achieve a healthy balance between our study of God's word and our daily work.

The Deuteronomic verse quoted above is part of the second section of the Shema[2] that discusses the concept of reward and punishment. Sanctifying God by fulfilling His commandments results in the Land of Israel practically benefitting from rains that occur in the right season and reaping the abundance from the fields. However, if the nation follows pagan gods and practices, the consequences are devastating – famine and death. The Land of Israel is intrinsically linked with the keeping of the *Torah*. Covenant Land comes with covenant responsibility.

---

1. Talmud Bavli Berachot 35b
2. Consisting of three sections within the Five Books of Moses (Deut. 6:4–8; 11:13–22 and Numbers 15:37–42), the *Shema* is proclamation of accepting God's Kingdom in our lives, loyalty to His commandments and remembering His redemptive act of liberating us from Egypt. Jews recite the *Shema* twice a day as stated in Deut. 6:7.

Born into slavery, Joshua is now leading His people into the Promised Land. More than 500 years separates him from his ancestral forefather Abraham. The historical narratives that took place between Abraham leaving everything behind to follow God in Genesis 12 and the death of Moses in the last chapter of Deuteronomy are filled with intrigue, suspense, joy, sorrow and hope. What began as a family is now a nation actualizing its mission to be a kingdom of priests to the world. However, for the Israelites to succeed in the Land of Israel, they must see the *Torah* as the only compass to direct their lives.

The biblical episodes after our first entry into the land are well known. Our ancestors' triumphs and sins are all on public record. We learned the harsh reality of Leviticus (18:28) "So let not the land spew you out for defiling it as it spewed out the nation that came before you." Twice, we lost the privilege to be stewards of the Land of Israel and to fulfill our nation state mandate to be a light to the world. However, when the annals of history were ready to archive the Jewish people after the Holocaust, God kept His covenantal promise and gathered us from the four corners of the globe to come home. The year 1948 was a game changer. Biblical prophecies were and are being realized. We are now living in the birth pangs of the messianic era.

In our morning prayers, we recite a series of blessings over the *Torah* that include petitioning God to have a sweet tooth for His word, to study it without any ulterior motive and to have Him to teach it to us. They are some congregations that invoke the following liturgical prayer after the completion of these blessings: *May the Torah be my faith and El Shaddai my help. Blessed be the name of His glorious kingdom forever and all time.*

According to Jewish tradition, the neglect of not blessing the *Torah* before engaging in its study was one of the reasons for the destruction of the Temple.[3] This is deduced from the redundancy of words in Jeremiah (9:12) that talks about Israel not following God: "...Because they forsook the teaching I had set before them. They did not obey Me and they did not follow it [did not make a blessing before studying it]." Our inability to properly cherish God's greatest gift to the world, the *Torah*, led to our eventual exile from our land.

On Israel's Independence Day, Jews around the world recite Psalms 113–118 to express our gratitude to God for His Divine hand in helping establish the State of Israel. We have learned from our past and realize the privilege to see firsthand the land, people and *Torah* operating all together in our generation.

---

3. Babylonian Talmud Nedarim 81a

When Rabbi Tuly Weisz approached me about his intent to publish *The Israel Bible* that would highlight commentary about the special relationship between the land and people, I saw this project as another way to publicly demonstrate our appreciation to God for having the State of Israel. In addition, it is another educational tool to ensure biblical literacy. If we are to truly enjoy the Land of Israel, it is incumbent upon us to continually study the *Torah*. Isaiah once prophesied that the Jewish people would return to Zion with songs, "crowned with everlasting joy" (35:10). *The Israel Bible* provides us the lyrical content to express our joy in living in the land that God calls holy.

Rabbi Shlomo Riskin
Chief Rabbi of Efrat
Founder of the Center for Jewish-Christian
Understanding & Cooperation (cjcuc)

Introduction to Sefer Devarim
The Book of Deuteronomy

Introduction and commentary by Shira Schechter

While Jews believe that all twenty-four books comprising the *Tanakh* (Hebrew Bible) are the word of *Hashem*, there is a distinction between the first five, the books of *Moshe*, and the others. Known in Hebrew as *Chumash* (חומש), meaning 'five', *Sefer Bereishit* (Genesis), *Sefer Shemot* (Exodus), *Sefer Vayikra* (Leviticus), *Sefer Bamidbar* (Numbers) and *Sefer Devarim* (Deuteronomy) are on a higher level of holiness than the rest of the Bible, since *Hashem* communicated each word of these books directly to *Moshe*. In contrast, the nineteen books of the *Neviim* (Prophets) and *Ketuvim* (Writings) are based on God's prophetic communications to His individual messengers, but are written in their own language. This underscores the idea that *Moshe's* prophecy was unparalleled, based on his particularly close relationship with the Almighty, as the Bible states explicitly, "Never again did there arise in *Yisrael* a prophet like *Moshe* – whom *Hashem* singled out, face to face" (Deuteronomy 34:10). As such, the Book of Deuteronomy, or *Sefer Devarim*, marks the conclusion of the Torah portion of the *Tanakh*, and with it the end of God's direct word to *Moshe*. It must therefore be mined carefully for its precious lessons.

Written in the last weeks of *Moshe's* life, *Sefer Devarim* is a summary of his final lessons to the people in the wilderness, before they enter the Land of Israel. Hundreds of commandments are taught or reviewed, some with minor differences that teach important lessons. The quantity and diversity of the various commandments does not distract from one primary theme that is repeated multiple times throughout *Sefer Devarim*: The primacy of *Eretz Yisrael*. In one of the most beautiful and incisive descriptions, *Moshe* describes the Land of Israel as being unlike any other place on earth:

> For the land that you are about to enter and possess is not like the land of Egypt from which you have come. There, the grain you sowed had to be watered by your own labors, like a vegetable garden; but the land you are about to cross into and possess, a land of hills and valleys, soaks up its water from the rains of heaven. It is a land which *Hashem* your God

looks after, on which *Hashem* your God always keeps His eye, from year's beginning to year's end. (Deuteronomy 11:10–12)

The Israel Bible elucidates the uniqueness of the land featured repeatedly in the Book of *Devarim*, a land where God's presence is fully manifest, and where our relationship with Him is more profound and more complete. May our study of *Sefer Devarim* contribute to our own deeper love for *Hashem* and the Land of Israel.

Map of the Cities of Refuge

This map features the cities of refuge set aside by *Moshe* and *Yehoshua* as described in *Sefer Devarim* (4:41–43) and *Sefer Yehoshua* (20:7). A city of refuge is a place where someone who murdered unintentionally can seek asylum. God commanded the Israelites to set aside six Levitical cities in the Land of Israel to be cities of refuge. Three of those cities were to be on the west side of the Jordan River, and three on the east side (Numbers 35:9–15).

The three cities of refuge on the east of the Jordan River, set aside by *Moshe*, were:

1. **Bezer** in the land of *Reuven*
2. **Ramoth-Gilead** in the land of *Gad*
3. **Golan** in the land of *Menashe*

The three cities of refuge on the west side of the Jordan River, set aside by *Yehoshua*, were:

4. **Kedesh** in the land of *Naftali*
5. **Shechem** in the land of *Efraim*
6. **Kiryat Arba/Chevron** in the land of *Yehuda*

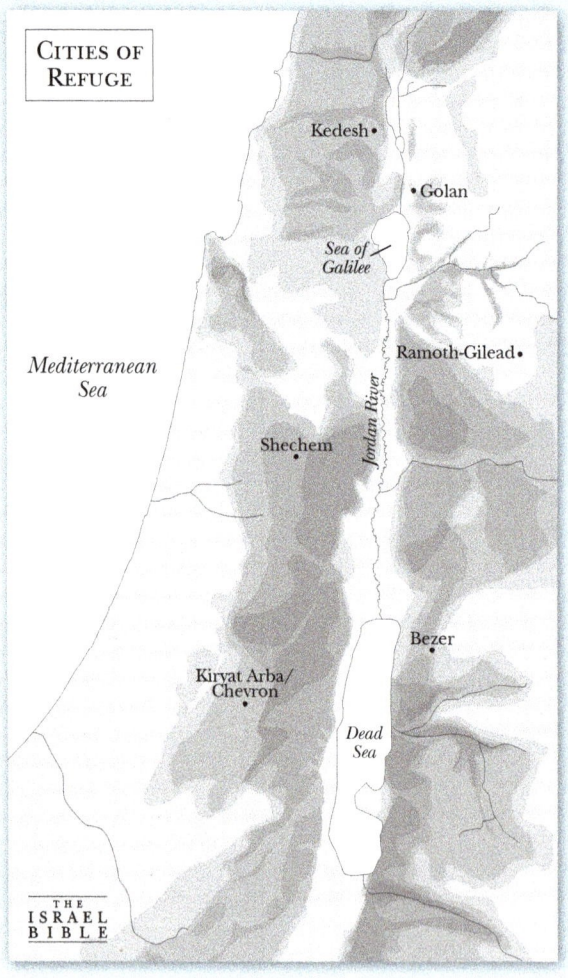

1 ¹ These are the words that *Moshe* addressed to all *Yisrael* on the other side of the *Yarden*. Through the wilderness, in the Arabah near Suph, between Paran and Tophel, Laban, Hazeroth, and Di-zahab,

אֵ֣לֶּה הַדְּבָרִ֗ים אֲשֶׁ֨ר דִּבֶּ֤ר מֹשֶׁה֙ אֶל־
כָּל־יִשְׂרָאֵ֔ל בְּעֵ֖בֶר הַיַּרְדֵּ֑ן בַּמִּדְבָּ֡ר
בָּֽעֲרָבָה֩ מ֨וֹל ס֜וּף בֵּֽין־פָּארָ֧ן וּבֵֽין־תֹּ֛פֶל
וְלָבָ֥ן וַחֲצֵרֹ֖ת וְדִ֥י זָהָֽב:

AY-leh ha-d'-va-REEM a-SHER di-BER mo-SHEH el kol yis-ra-AYL
b'-AY-ver ha-yar-DAYN ba-mid-BAR ba-a-ra-VAH MOL SUF bayn
pa-RAN u-vayn TO-fel v'-la-VAN va-kha-tzay-ROT v'-DEE za-HAV

² it is eleven days from Horeb to Kadesh-barnea by the Mount Seir route.

בּ אַחַ֨ד עָשָׂ֥ר יוֹם֙ מֵֽחֹרֵ֔ב דֶּ֖רֶךְ הַר־שֵׂעִ֑יר
עַ֖ד קָדֵ֥שׁ בַּרְנֵֽעַ:

³ It was in the fortieth year, on the first day of the eleventh month, that *Moshe* addressed the Israelites in accordance with the instructions that *Hashem* had given him for them,

גּ וַיְהִי֙ בְּאַרְבָּעִ֣ים שָׁנָ֔ה בְּעַשְׁתֵּֽי־עָשָׂ֥ר
חֹ֖דֶשׁ בְּאֶחָ֣ד לַחֹ֑דֶשׁ דִּבֶּ֤ר מֹשֶׁה֙ אֶל־
בְּנֵ֣י יִשְׂרָאֵ֔ל כְּכֹ֠ל אֲשֶׁ֨ר צִוָּ֧ה יְהֹוָ֛ה אֹת֖וֹ
אֲלֵהֶֽם:

⁴ after he had defeated Sihon king of the Amorites, who dwelt in Heshbon, and King Og of Bashan, who dwelt at Ashtaroth [and]

דּ אַחֲרֵ֣י הַכֹּת֗וֹ אֵ֚ת סִיחֹן֙ מֶ֣לֶךְ הָֽאֱמֹרִ֔י
אֲשֶׁ֥ר יוֹשֵׁ֖ב בְּחֶשְׁבּ֑וֹן וְאֵ֗ת ע֚וֹג מֶ֣לֶךְ
הַבָּשָׁ֔ן אֲשֶׁר־יוֹשֵׁ֥ב בְּעַשְׁתָּרֹ֖ת בְּאֶדְרֶֽעִי:

⁵ On the other side of the *Yarden*, in the land of Moab, *Moshe* undertook to expound this Teaching. He said:

הּ בְּעֵ֥בֶר הַיַּרְדֵּ֖ן בְּאֶ֣רֶץ מוֹאָ֑ב הוֹאִ֣יל מֹשֶׁ֔ה
בֵּאֵ֛ר אֶת־הַתּוֹרָ֥ה הַזֹּ֖את לֵאמֹֽר:

⁶ *Hashem* our God spoke to us at Horeb, saying: You have stayed long enough at this mountain.

וּ יְהֹוָ֧ה אֱלֹהֵ֛ינוּ דִּבֶּ֥ר אֵלֵ֖ינוּ בְּחֹרֵ֣ב לֵאמֹ֑ר
רַב־לָכֶ֥ם שֶׁ֖בֶת בָּהָ֥ר הַזֶּֽה:

⁷ Start out and make your way to the hill country of the Amorites and to all their neighbors in the Arabah, the hill country, the Shephelah, the *Negev*, the seacoast, the land of the Canaanites, and the Lebanon, as far as the Great River, the river Euphrates.

זּ פְּנ֣וּ | וּסְע֣וּ לָכֶ֗ם וּבֹ֨אוּ הַ֥ר הָֽאֱמֹרִי֮ וְאֶל־
כָּל־שְׁכֵנָיו֒ בָּעֲרָבָ֥ה בָהָ֛ר וּבַשְּׁפֵלָ֥ה וּבַנֶּ֖גֶב
וּבְח֣וֹף הַיָּ֑ם אֶ֤רֶץ הַֽכְּנַעֲנִי֙ וְהַלְּבָנ֔וֹן עַד־
הַנָּהָ֥ר הַגָּדֹ֖ל נְהַר־פְּרָֽת:

⁸ See, I place the land at your disposal. Go, take possession of the land that *Hashem* swore to your fathers, *Avraham*, *Yitzchak*, and *Yaakov*, to assign to them and to their heirs after them.

חּ רְאֵ֛ה נָתַ֥תִּי לִפְנֵיכֶ֖ם אֶת־הָאָ֑רֶץ בֹּ֚אוּ
וּרְשׁ֣וּ אֶת־הָאָ֔רֶץ אֲשֶׁ֣ר נִשְׁבַּ֣ע יְהֹוָ֡ה
לַאֲבֹ֣תֵיכֶ֣ם לְאַבְרָהָ֧ם לְיִצְחָ֣ק וּֽלְיַעֲקֹ֛ב
לָתֵ֣ת לָהֶ֔ם וּלְזַרְעָ֖ם אַחֲרֵיהֶֽם:

r'-AY na-TA-tee lif-nay-KHEM et ha-A-retz BO-u ur-SHU et ha-A-retz
a-SHER nish-BA ah-do-NAI la-a-VO-tay-KHEM l'-av-ra-HAM l'-yitz-KHAK
ul-ya-a-KOV la-TAYT la-HEM ul-zar-AM a-kha-ray-HEM

*Three generations celebrate *Pesach* together in Israel*

1:1 These are the words that *Moshe* addressed to all *Yisrael* *Sefer Devarim* contains *Moshe's* farewell speeches to the People of Israel. They are camped on the banks of the Jordan River, finally ready to cross over and inherit the land that *Hashem* promised to their forefathers. Since *Moshe* is not allowed to enter the land, he takes this opportunity to impart to them the thoughts, laws and ideas that he wants them to consider as they prepare for their entry into the land. *Moshe* makes sure to speak to the entire nation, as the Land of Israel belongs to everyone. Young and old, rich and poor – everyone can find his or her place in this special land.

9 Thereupon I said to you, "I cannot bear the burden of you by myself.

ט וָאֹמַר אֲלֵכֶם בָּעֵת הַהִוא לֵאמֹר לֹא־אוּכַל לְבַדִּי שְׂאֵת אֶתְכֶם:

10 *Hashem* your God has multiplied you until you are today as numerous as the stars in the sky.

י יְהֹוָה אֱלֹהֵיכֶם הִרְבָּה אֶתְכֶם וְהִנְּכֶם הַיּוֹם כְּכוֹכְבֵי הַשָּׁמַיִם לָרֹב:

11 May *Hashem*, the God of your fathers, increase your numbers a thousandfold, and bless you as He promised you.

יא יְהֹוָה אֱלֹהֵי אֲבוֹתֵכֶם יֹסֵף עֲלֵיכֶם כָּכֶם אֶלֶף פְּעָמִים וִיבָרֵךְ אֶתְכֶם כַּאֲשֶׁר דִּבֶּר לָכֶם:

12 How can I bear unaided the trouble of you, and the burden, and the bickering!

יב אֵיכָה אֶשָּׂא לְבַדִּי טָרְחֲכֶם וּמַשַּׂאֲכֶם וְרִיבְכֶם:

13 Pick from each of your tribes men who are wise, discerning, and experienced, and I will appoint them as your heads."

יג הָבוּ לָכֶם אֲנָשִׁים חֲכָמִים וּנְבֹנִים וִידֻעִים לְשִׁבְטֵיכֶם וַאֲשִׂימֵם בְּרָאשֵׁיכֶם:

14 You answered me and said, "What you propose to do is good."

יד וַתַּעֲנוּ אֹתִי וַתֹּאמְרוּ טוֹב־הַדָּבָר אֲשֶׁר־דִּבַּרְתָּ לַעֲשׂוֹת:

15 So I took your tribal leaders, wise and experienced men, and appointed them heads over you: chiefs of thousands, chiefs of hundreds, chiefs of fifties, and chiefs of tens, and officials for your tribes.

טו וָאֶקַּח אֶת־רָאשֵׁי שִׁבְטֵיכֶם אֲנָשִׁים חֲכָמִים וִידֻעִים וָאֶתֵּן אֹתָם רָאשִׁים עֲלֵיכֶם שָׂרֵי אֲלָפִים וְשָׂרֵי מֵאוֹת וְשָׂרֵי חֲמִשִּׁים וְשָׂרֵי עֲשָׂרֹת וְשֹׁטְרִים לְשִׁבְטֵיכֶם:

16 I charged your magistrates at that time as follows, "Hear out your fellow men, and decide justly between any man and a fellow Israelite or a stranger.

טז וָאֲצַוֶּה אֶת־שֹׁפְטֵיכֶם בָּעֵת הַהִוא לֵאמֹר שָׁמֹעַ בֵּין־אֲחֵיכֶם וּשְׁפַטְתֶּם צֶדֶק בֵּין־אִישׁ וּבֵין־אָחִיו וּבֵין גֵּרוֹ:

17 You shall not be partial in judgment: hear out low and high alike. Fear no man, for judgment is *Hashem*'s. And any matter that is too difficult for you, you shall bring to me and I will hear it."

יז לֹא־תַכִּירוּ פָנִים בַּמִּשְׁפָּט כַּקָּטֹן כַּגָּדֹל תִּשְׁמָעוּן לֹא תָגוּרוּ מִפְּנֵי־אִישׁ כִּי הַמִּשְׁפָּט לֵאלֹהִים הוּא וְהַדָּבָר אֲשֶׁר יִקְשֶׁה מִכֶּם תַּקְרִבוּן אֵלַי וּשְׁמַעְתִּיו:

18 Thus I instructed you, at that time, about the various things that you should do.

יח וָאֲצַוֶּה אֶתְכֶם בָּעֵת הַהִוא אֵת כָּל־הַדְּבָרִים אֲשֶׁר תַּעֲשׂוּן:

19 We set out from Horeb and traveled the great and terrible wilderness that you saw, along the road to the hill country of the Amorites, as *Hashem* our God had commanded us. When we reached Kadesh-barnea,

יט וַנִּסַּע מֵחֹרֵב וַנֵּלֶךְ אֵת כָּל־הַמִּדְבָּר הַגָּדוֹל וְהַנּוֹרָא הַהוּא אֲשֶׁר רְאִיתֶם דֶּרֶךְ הַר הָאֱמֹרִי כַּאֲשֶׁר צִוָּה יְהֹוָה אֱלֹהֵינוּ אֹתָנוּ וַנָּבֹא עַד קָדֵשׁ בַּרְנֵעַ:

20 I said to you, "You have come to the hill country of the Amorites which *Hashem* our God is giving to us.

כ וָאֹמַר אֲלֵכֶם בָּאתֶם עַד־הַר הָאֱמֹרִי אֲשֶׁר־יְהֹוָה אֱלֹהֵינוּ נֹתֵן לָנוּ:

21 See, *Hashem* your God has placed the land at your disposal. Go up, take possession, as *Hashem*, the God of your fathers, promised you. Fear not and be not dismayed."

כא רְאֵה נָתַן יְהֹוָה אֱלֹהֶיךָ לְפָנֶיךָ אֶת־הָאָרֶץ עֲלֵה רֵשׁ כַּאֲשֶׁר דִּבֶּר יְהֹוָה אֱלֹהֵי אֲבֹתֶיךָ לָךְ אַל־תִּירָא וְאַל־תֵּחָת:

r'-AY na-TAN a-do-NAI e-lo-HE-kha l'-fa-NE-kha et ha-A-retz
a-LAY RAYSH ka-a-SHER di-BER a-do-NAI e-lo-HAY
a-vo-TE-kha LAKH al tee-RAH v'-al tay-KHAT

22 Then all of you came to me and said, "Let us send men ahead to reconnoiter the land for us and bring back word on the route we shall follow and the cities we shall come to."

כב וַתִּקְרְבוּן אֵלַי כֻּלְּכֶם וַתֹּאמְרוּ נִשְׁלְחָה אֲנָשִׁים לְפָנֵינוּ וְיַחְפְּרוּ־לָנוּ אֶת־הָאָרֶץ וְיָשִׁבוּ אֹתָנוּ דָּבָר אֶת־הַדֶּרֶךְ אֲשֶׁר נַעֲלֶה־בָּהּ וְאֵת הֶעָרִים אֲשֶׁר נָבֹא אֲלֵיהֶן:

23 I approved of the plan, and so I selected twelve of your men, one from each tribe.

כג וַיִּיטַב בְּעֵינַי הַדָּבָר וָאֶקַּח מִכֶּם שְׁנֵים עָשָׂר אֲנָשִׁים אִישׁ אֶחָד לַשָּׁבֶט:

24 They made for the hill country, came to the wadi Eshcol, and spied it out.

כד וַיִּפְנוּ וַיַּעֲלוּ הָהָרָה וַיָּבֹאוּ עַד־נַחַל אֶשְׁכֹּל וַיְרַגְּלוּ אֹתָהּ:

25 They took some of the fruit of the land with them and brought it down to us. And they gave us this report: "It is a good land that *Hashem* our God is giving to us."

כה וַיִּקְחוּ בְיָדָם מִפְּרִי הָאָרֶץ וַיּוֹרִדוּ אֵלֵינוּ וַיָּשִׁבוּ אֹתָנוּ דָבָר וַיֹּאמְרוּ טוֹבָה הָאָרֶץ אֲשֶׁר־יְהֹוָה אֱלֹהֵינוּ נֹתֵן לָנוּ:

va-yik-KHU v'-ya-DAM mi-p'-REE ha-A-retz va-yo-RI-du
ay-LAY-nu va-ya-SHI-vu o-TA-nu da-VAR va-YO-m'-RU to-VAH
ha-A-retz a-sher a-do-NAI e-lo-HAY-nu no-TAYN LA-nu

26 Yet you refused to go up, and flouted the command of *Hashem* your God.

כו וְלֹא אֲבִיתֶם לַעֲלֹת וַתַּמְרוּ אֶת־פִּי יְהֹוָה אֱלֹהֵיכֶם:

27 You sulked in your tents and said, "It is because *Hashem* hates us that He brought us out of the land of Egypt, to hand us over to the Amorites to wipe us out.

כז וַתֵּרָגְנוּ בְאָהֳלֵיכֶם וַתֹּאמְרוּ בְּשִׂנְאַת יְהֹוָה אֹתָנוּ הוֹצִיאָנוּ מֵאֶרֶץ מִצְרָיִם לָתֵת אֹתָנוּ בְּיַד הָאֱמֹרִי לְהַשְׁמִידֵנוּ:

28 What kind of place are we going to? Our kinsmen have taken the heart out of us, saying, 'We saw there a people stronger and taller than we, large cities with walls sky-high, and even Anakites.'"

כח אָנָה אֲנַחְנוּ עֹלִים אַחֵינוּ הֵמַסּוּ אֶת־ לְבָבֵנוּ לֵאמֹר עַם גָּדוֹל וָרָם מִמֶּנּוּ עָרִים גְּדֹלֹת וּבְצוּרֹת בַּשָּׁמָיִם וְגַם־בְּנֵי עֲנָקִים רָאִינוּ שָׁם:

29 I said to you, "Have no dread or fear of them.

כט וָאֹמַר אֲלֵכֶם לֹא־תַעַרְצוּן וְלֹא־תִירְאוּן מֵהֶם:

30 None other than *Hashem* your God, who goes before you, will fight for you, just as He did for you in Egypt before your very eyes,

ל יְהֹוָה אֱלֹהֵיכֶם הַהֹלֵךְ לִפְנֵיכֶם הוּא יִלָּחֵם לָכֶם כְּכֹל אֲשֶׁר עָשָׂה אִתְּכֶם בְּמִצְרַיִם לְעֵינֵיכֶם:

31 and in the wilderness, where you saw how *Hashem* your God carried you, as a man carries his son, all the way that you traveled until you came to this place.

לא וּבַמִּדְבָּר אֲשֶׁר רָאִיתָ אֲשֶׁר נְשָׂאֲךָ יְהֹוָה אֱלֹהֶיךָ כַּאֲשֶׁר יִשָּׂא־אִישׁ אֶת־בְּנוֹ בְּכָל־ הַדֶּרֶךְ אֲשֶׁר הֲלַכְתֶּם עַד־בֹּאֲכֶם עַד־ הַמָּקוֹם הַזֶּה:

Clusters of grapes
near *Beit Shemesh*

1:25 It is a good land that *Hashem* our God is giving to us. The spies committed a grave sin by rejecting the Land of Israel. But despite their rejection of the land, even they could not deny its beauty and its bounty. The spies carried back a cluster of grapes, a fig and a pomegranate. Upon their return, they reported "We came to the land you sent us to; it does indeed flow with milk and honey, and this is its fruit" (Numbers 13:27). How magnificent is *Eretz Yisrael* – even those who slight it cannot help but be struck by its grandeur!

32 Yet for all that, you have no faith in *Hashem* your God,

לב וּבַדָּבָר הַזֶּה אֵינְכֶם מַאֲמִינִם בַּיהֹוָה אֱלֹהֵיכֶם:

33 who goes before you on your journeys – to scout the place where you are to encamp – in fire by night and in cloud by day, in order to guide you on the route you are to follow."

לג הַהֹלֵךְ לִפְנֵיכֶם בַּדֶּרֶךְ לָתוּר לָכֶם מָקוֹם לַחֲנֹתְכֶם בָּאֵשׁ לַיְלָה לַרְאֹתְכֶם בַּדֶּרֶךְ אֲשֶׁר תֵּלְכוּ־בָהּ וּבֶעָנָן יוֹמָם:

34 When *Hashem* heard your loud complaint, He was angry. He vowed:

לד וַיִּשְׁמַע יְהֹוָה אֶת־קוֹל דִּבְרֵיכֶם וַיִּקְצֹף וַיִּשָּׁבַע לֵאמֹר:

35 Not one of these men, this evil generation, shall see the good land that I swore to give to your fathers

לה אִם־יִרְאֶה אִישׁ בָּאֲנָשִׁים הָאֵלֶּה הַדּוֹר הָרָע הַזֶּה אֵת הָאָרֶץ הַטּוֹבָה אֲשֶׁר נִשְׁבַּעְתִּי לָתֵת לַאֲבֹתֵיכֶם:

36 none except *Kalev* son of Jephunneh; he shall see it, and to him and his descendants will I give the land on which he set foot, because he remained loyal to *Hashem*.

לו זוּלָתִי כָּלֵב בֶּן־יְפֻנֶּה הוּא יִרְאֶנָּה וְלוֹ־אֶתֵּן אֶת־הָאָרֶץ אֲשֶׁר דָּרַךְ־בָּהּ וּלְבָנָיו יַעַן אֲשֶׁר מִלֵּא אַחֲרֵי יְהֹוָה:

37 Because of you *Hashem* was incensed with me too, and He said: You shall not enter it either.

לז גַּם־בִּי הִתְאַנַּף יְהֹוָה בִּגְלַלְכֶם לֵאמֹר גַּם־אַתָּה לֹא־תָבֹא שָׁם:

38 *Yehoshua* son of Nun, who attends you, he shall enter it. Imbue him with strength, for he shall allot it to *Yisrael*.

לח יְהוֹשֻׁעַ בִּן נוּן הָעֹמֵד לְפָנֶיךָ הוּא יָבֹא שָׁמָּה אֹתוֹ חַזֵּק כִּי־הוּא יַנְחִלֶנָּה אֶת־יִשְׂרָאֵל:

39 Moreover, your little ones who you said would be carried off, your children who do not yet know good from bad, they shall enter it; to them will I give it and they shall possess it.

לט וְטַפְּכֶם אֲשֶׁר אֲמַרְתֶּם לָבַז יִהְיֶה וּבְנֵיכֶם אֲשֶׁר לֹא־יָדְעוּ הַיּוֹם טוֹב וָרָע הֵמָּה יָבֹאוּ שָׁמָּה וְלָהֶם אֶתְּנֶנָּה וְהֵם יִירָשׁוּהָ:

40 As for you, turn about and march into the wilderness by the way of the Sea of Reeds.

מ וְאַתֶּם פְּנוּ לָכֶם וּסְעוּ הַמִּדְבָּרָה דֶּרֶךְ יַם־סוּף:

41 You replied to me, saying, "We stand guilty before *Hashem*. We will go up now and fight, just as *Hashem* our God commanded us." And you all girded yourselves with war gear and recklessly started for the hill country.

מא וַתַּעֲנוּ וַתֹּאמְרוּ אֵלַי חָטָאנוּ לַיהֹוָה אֲנַחְנוּ נַעֲלֶה וְנִלְחַמְנוּ כְּכֹל אֲשֶׁר־צִוָּנוּ יְהֹוָה אֱלֹהֵינוּ וַתַּחְגְּרוּ אִישׁ אֶת־כְּלֵי מִלְחַמְתּוֹ וַתָּהִינוּ לַעֲלֹת הָהָרָה:

42 But *Hashem* said to me, "Warn them: Do not go up and do not fight, since I am not in your midst; else you will be routed by your enemies."

מב וַיֹּאמֶר יְהֹוָה אֵלַי אֱמֹר לָהֶם לֹא תַעֲלוּ וְלֹא־תִלָּחֲמוּ כִּי אֵינֶנִּי בְּקִרְבְּכֶם וְלֹא תִּנָּגְפוּ לִפְנֵי אֹיְבֵיכֶם:

43 I spoke to you, but you would not listen; you flouted *Hashem*'s command and willfully marched into the hill country.

מג וָאֲדַבֵּר אֲלֵיכֶם וְלֹא שְׁמַעְתֶּם וַתַּמְרוּ אֶת־פִּי יְהֹוָה וַתָּזִדוּ וַתַּעֲלוּ הָהָרָה:

44 Then the Amorites who lived in those hills came out against you like so many bees and chased you, and they crushed you at Hormah in Seir.

מד וַיֵּצֵא הָאֱמֹרִי הַיֹּשֵׁב בָּהָר הַהוּא לִקְרַאתְכֶם וַיִּרְדְּפוּ אֶתְכֶם כַּאֲשֶׁר תַּעֲשֶׂינָה הַדְּבֹרִים וַיַּכְּתוּ אֶתְכֶם בְּשֵׂעִיר עַד־חָרְמָה:

45 Again you wept before *Hashem*; but *Hashem* would not heed your cry or give ear to you.

מה וַתָּשֻׁבוּ וַתִּבְכּוּ לִפְנֵי יְהֹוָה וְלֹא־שָׁמַע יְהֹוָה בְּקֹלְכֶם וְלֹא הֶאֱזִין אֲלֵיכֶם:

Deuteronomy

46 Thus, after you had remained at Kadesh all that long time,

מו וַתֵּשְׁבוּ בְקָדֵשׁ יָמִים רַבִּים כַּיָּמִים אֲשֶׁר יְשַׁבְתֶּם:

2 1 we marched back into the wilderness by the way of the Sea of Reeds, as *Hashem* had spoken to me, and skirted the hill country of Seir a long time.

ב א וַנֵּפֶן וַנִּסַּע הַמִּדְבָּרָה דֶּרֶךְ יַם־סוּף כַּאֲשֶׁר דִּבֶּר יְהֹוָה אֵלָי וַנָּסָב אֶת־הַר־שֵׂעִיר יָמִים רַבִּים:

2 Then *Hashem* said to me:

ב וַיֹּאמֶר יְהֹוָה אֵלַי לֵאמֹר:

3 You have been skirting this hill country long enough; now turn north.

ג רַב־לָכֶם סֹב אֶת־הָהָר הַזֶּה פְּנוּ לָכֶם צָפֹנָה:

4 And charge the people as follows: You will be passing through the territory of your kinsmen, the descendants of Esau, who live in Seir. Though they will be afraid of you, be very careful

ד וְאֶת־הָעָם צַו לֵאמֹר אַתֶּם עֹבְרִים בִּגְבוּל אֲחֵיכֶם בְּנֵי־עֵשָׂו הַיֹּשְׁבִים בְּשֵׂעִיר וְיִירְאוּ מִכֶּם וְנִשְׁמַרְתֶּם מְאֹד:

5 not to provoke them. For I will not give you of their land so much as a foot can tread on; I have given the hill country of Seir as a possession to Esau.

ה אַל־תִּתְגָּרוּ בָם כִּי לֹא־אֶתֵּן לָכֶם מֵאַרְצָם עַד מִדְרַךְ כַּף־רָגֶל כִּי־יְרֻשָּׁה לְעֵשָׂו נָתַתִּי אֶת־הַר שֵׂעִיר:

6 What food you eat you shall obtain from them for money; even the water you drink you shall procure from them for money.

ו אֹכֶל תִּשְׁבְּרוּ מֵאִתָּם בַּכֶּסֶף וַאֲכַלְתֶּם וְגַם־מַיִם תִּכְרוּ מֵאִתָּם בַּכֶּסֶף וּשְׁתִיתֶם:

7 Indeed, *Hashem* your God has blessed you in all your undertakings. He has watched over your wanderings through this great wilderness; *Hashem* your God has been with you these past forty years: you have lacked nothing.

ז כִּי יְהֹוָה אֱלֹהֶיךָ בֵּרַכְךָ בְּכֹל מַעֲשֵׂה יָדֶךָ יָדַע לֶכְתְּךָ אֶת־הַמִּדְבָּר הַגָּדֹל הַזֶּה זֶה אַרְבָּעִים שָׁנָה יְהֹוָה אֱלֹהֶיךָ עִמָּךְ לֹא חָסַרְתָּ דָּבָר:

8 We then moved on, away from our kinsmen, the descendants of Esau, who live in Seir, away from the road of the Arabah, away from Eilat and Ezion-geber; and we marched on in the direction of the wilderness of Moab.

ח וַנַּעֲבֹר מֵאֵת אַחֵינוּ בְנֵי־עֵשָׂו הַיֹּשְׁבִים בְּשֵׂעִיר מִדֶּרֶךְ הָעֲרָבָה מֵאֵילַת וּמֵעֶצְיֹן גָּבֶר וַנֵּפֶן וַנַּעֲבֹר דֶּרֶךְ מִדְבַּר מוֹאָב:

9 And *Hashem* said to me: Do not harass the Moabites or provoke them to war. For I will not give you any of their land as a possession; I have assigned Ar as a possession to the descendants of Lot. –

ט וַיֹּאמֶר יְהֹוָה אֵלַי אַל־תָּצַר אֶת־מוֹאָב וְאַל־תִּתְגָּר בָּם מִלְחָמָה כִּי לֹא־אֶתֵּן לְךָ מֵאַרְצוֹ יְרֻשָּׁה כִּי לִבְנֵי־לוֹט נָתַתִּי אֶת־עָר יְרֻשָּׁה:

*va-YO-mer a-do-NAI ay-LAI al ta-TZAR et mo-AV v'-al tit-GAR
BAM mil-kha-MAH KEE lo e-TAYN l'-KHA may-ar-TZO
y'-ru-SHAH KEE liv-nay LOT na-TA-tee et AR y'-ru-SHAH*

 2:9 I have assigned Ar as a possession to the descendants of Lot The people of Moab are descendants of Lot, nephew of *Avraham*. When *Avraham* went to Egypt to escape the famine, he told the Egyptians that *Sara* was his sister, instead of his wife, in order to save his life. The Sages of the *Midrash* explain that Lot, who was with them, maintained his silence and preserved the secret. As an expression of gratitude for this act of nobility, the children of *Avraham* are forbidden from attacking the children of Lot generations later, even for the purpose of expanding the borders of Israel.

View of the Dead Sea and the Moab mountain range from Kibbutz *Ein Gedi*, Israel

10 It was formerly inhabited by the Emim, a people great and numerous, and as tall as the Anakites.

י הָאֵמִים לְפָנִים יָשְׁבוּ בָהּ עַם גָּדוֹל וְרַב וָרָם כָּעֲנָקִים:

11 Like the Anakites, they are counted as Rephaim; but the Moabites call them Emim.

יא רְפָאִים יֵחָשְׁבוּ אַף־הֵם כָּעֲנָקִים וְהַמֹּאָבִים יִקְרְאוּ לָהֶם אֵמִים:

12 Similarly, Seir was formerly inhabited by the Horites; but the descendants of Esau dispossessed them, wiping them out and settling in their place, just as *Yisrael* did in the land they were to possess, which *Hashem* had given to them. –

יב וּבְשֵׂעִיר יָשְׁבוּ הַחֹרִים לְפָנִים וּבְנֵי עֵשָׂו יִירָשׁוּם וַיַּשְׁמִידוּם מִפְּנֵיהֶם וַיֵּשְׁבוּ תַּחְתָּם כַּאֲשֶׁר עָשָׂה יִשְׂרָאֵל לְאֶרֶץ יְרֻשָּׁתוֹ אֲשֶׁר־נָתַן יְהוָה לָהֶם:

13 Up now! Cross the wadi Zered! So we crossed the wadi Zered.

יג עַתָּה קֻמוּ וְעִבְרוּ לָכֶם אֶת־נַחַל זָרֶד וַנַּעֲבֹר אֶת־נַחַל זָרֶד:

14 The time that we spent in travel from Kadesh-barnea until we crossed the wadi Zered was thirty-eight years, until that whole generation of warriors had perished from the camp, as *Hashem* had sworn concerning them.

יד וְהַיָּמִים אֲשֶׁר־הָלַכְנוּ מִקָּדֵשׁ בַּרְנֵעַ עַד אֲשֶׁר־עָבַרְנוּ אֶת־נַחַל זֶרֶד שְׁלֹשִׁים וּשְׁמֹנֶה שָׁנָה עַד־תֹּם כָּל־הַדּוֹר אַנְשֵׁי הַמִּלְחָמָה מִקֶּרֶב הַמַּחֲנֶה כַּאֲשֶׁר נִשְׁבַּע יְהוָה לָהֶם:

15 Indeed, the hand of *Hashem* struck them, to root them out from the camp to the last man.

טו וְגַם יַד־יְהוָה הָיְתָה בָּם לְהֻמָּם מִקֶּרֶב הַמַּחֲנֶה עַד תֻּמָּם:

16 When all the warriors among the people had died off,

טז וַיְהִי כַאֲשֶׁר־תַּמּוּ כָּל־אַנְשֵׁי הַמִּלְחָמָה לָמוּת מִקֶּרֶב הָעָם:

17 *Hashem* spoke to me, saying:

יז וַיְדַבֵּר יְהוָה אֵלַי לֵאמֹר:

18 You are now passing through the territory of Moab, through Ar.

יח אַתָּה עֹבֵר הַיּוֹם אֶת־גְּבוּל מוֹאָב אֶת־עָר:

19 You will then be close to the Ammonites; do not harass them or start a fight with them. For I will not give any part of the land of the Ammonites to you as a possession; I have assigned it as a possession to the descendants of Lot. –

יט וְקָרַבְתָּ מוּל בְּנֵי עַמּוֹן אַל־תְּצֻרֵם וְאַל־תִּתְגָּר בָּם כִּי לֹא־אֶתֵּן מֵאֶרֶץ בְּנֵי־עַמּוֹן לְךָ יְרֻשָּׁה כִּי לִבְנֵי־לוֹט נְתַתִּיהָ יְרֻשָּׁה:

20 It, too, is counted as Rephaim country. It was formerly inhabited by Rephaim, whom the Ammonites call Zamzummim,

כ אֶרֶץ־רְפָאִים תֵּחָשֵׁב אַף־הִוא רְפָאִים יָשְׁבוּ־בָהּ לְפָנִים וְהָעַמֹּנִים יִקְרְאוּ לָהֶם זַמְזֻמִּים:

21 a people great and numerous and as tall as the Anakites. *Hashem* wiped them out, so that [the Ammonites] dispossessed them and settled in their place,

כא עַם גָּדוֹל וְרַב וָרָם כָּעֲנָקִים וַיַּשְׁמִידֵם יְהוָה מִפְּנֵיהֶם וַיִּירָשֻׁם וַיֵּשְׁבוּ תַחְתָּם:

22 as He did for the descendants of Esau who live in Seir, when He wiped out the Horites before them, so that they dispossessed them and settled in their place, as is still the case.

כב כַּאֲשֶׁר עָשָׂה לִבְנֵי עֵשָׂו הַיֹּשְׁבִים בְּשֵׂעִיר אֲשֶׁר הִשְׁמִיד אֶת־הַחֹרִי מִפְּנֵיהֶם וַיִּירָשֻׁם וַיֵּשְׁבוּ תַחְתָּם עַד הַיּוֹם הַזֶּה:

23 So, too, with the Avvim who dwelt in villages in the vicinity of *Azza*: the Caphtorim, who came from Crete, wiped them out and settled in their place. –

כג וְהָעַוִּים הַיֹּשְׁבִים בַּחֲצֵרִים עַד־עַזָּה כַּפְתֹּרִים הַיֹּצְאִים מִכַּפְתּוֹר הִשְׁמִידֻם וַיֵּשְׁבוּ תַחְתָּם:

²⁴ Up! Set out across the wadi Arnon! See, I give into your power Sihon the Amorite, king of Heshbon, and his land. Begin the occupation: engage him in battle.

כד קוּמוּ סְּעוּ וְעִבְרוּ אֶת־נַחַל אַרְנֹן רְאֵה נָתַתִּי בְיָדְךָ אֶת־סִיחֹן מֶלֶךְ־חֶשְׁבּוֹן הָאֱמֹרִי וְאֶת־אַרְצוֹ הָחֵל רָשׁ וְהִתְגָּר בּוֹ מִלְחָמָה:

²⁵ This day I begin to put the dread and fear of you upon the peoples everywhere under heaven, so that they shall tremble and quake because of you whenever they hear you mentioned.

כה הַיּוֹם הַזֶּה אָחֵל תֵּת פַּחְדְּךָ וְיִרְאָתְךָ עַל־פְּנֵי הָעַמִּים תַּחַת כָּל־הַשָּׁמָיִם אֲשֶׁר יִשְׁמְעוּן שִׁמְעֲךָ וְרָגְזוּ וְחָלוּ מִפָּנֶיךָ:

²⁶ Then I sent messengers from the wilderness of Kedemoth to King Sihon of Heshbon with an offer of peace, as follows,

כו וָאֶשְׁלַח מַלְאָכִים מִמִּדְבַּר קְדֵמוֹת אֶל־סִיחוֹן מֶלֶךְ חֶשְׁבּוֹן דִּבְרֵי שָׁלוֹם לֵאמֹר:

²⁷ "Let me pass through your country. I will keep strictly to the highway, turning off neither to the right nor to the left.

כז אֶעְבְּרָה בְאַרְצֶךָ בַּדֶּרֶךְ בַּדֶּרֶךְ אֵלֵךְ לֹא אָסוּר יָמִין וּשְׂמֹאול:

²⁸ What food I eat you will supply for money, and what water I drink you will furnish for money; just let me pass through

כח אֹכֶל בַּכֶּסֶף תַּשְׁבִּרֵנִי וְאָכַלְתִּי וּמַיִם בַּכֶּסֶף תִּתֶּן־לִי וְשָׁתִיתִי רַק אֶעְבְּרָה בְרַגְלָי:

²⁹ as the descendants of Esau who dwell in Seir did for me, and the Moabites who dwell in Ar – that I may cross the *Yarden* into the land that *Hashem* our God is giving us."

כט כַּאֲשֶׁר עָשׂוּ־לִי בְּנֵי עֵשָׂו הַיֹּשְׁבִים בְּשֵׂעִיר וְהַמּוֹאָבִים הַיֹּשְׁבִים בְּעָר עַד אֲשֶׁר־אֶעֱבֹר אֶת־הַיַּרְדֵּן אֶל־הָאָרֶץ אֲשֶׁר־יְהֹוָה אֱלֹהֵינוּ נֹתֵן לָנוּ:

³⁰ But King Sihon of Heshbon refused to let us pass through, because *Hashem* had stiffened his will and hardened his heart in order to deliver him into your power – as is now the case.

ל וְלֹא אָבָה סִיחֹן מֶלֶךְ חֶשְׁבּוֹן הַעֲבִרֵנוּ בּוֹ כִּי־הִקְשָׁה יְהֹוָה אֱלֹהֶיךָ אֶת־רוּחוֹ וְאִמֵּץ אֶת־לְבָבוֹ לְמַעַן תִּתּוֹ בְיָדְךָ כַּיּוֹם הַזֶּה:

³¹ And *Hashem* said to me: See, I begin by placing Sihon and his land at your disposal. Begin the occupation; take possession of his land.

לא וַיֹּאמֶר יְהֹוָה אֵלַי רְאֵה הַחִלֹּתִי תֵּת לְפָנֶיךָ אֶת־סִיחֹן וְאֶת־אַרְצוֹ הָחֵל רָשׁ לָרֶשֶׁת אֶת־אַרְצוֹ:

³² Sihon with all his men took the field against us at Jahaz,

לב וַיֵּצֵא סִיחֹן לִקְרָאתֵנוּ הוּא וְכָל־עַמּוֹ לַמִּלְחָמָה יָהְצָה:

³³ and *Hashem* our God delivered him to us and we defeated him and his sons and all his men.

לג וַיִּתְּנֵהוּ יְהֹוָה אֱלֹהֵינוּ לְפָנֵינוּ וַנַּךְ אֹתוֹ וְאֶת־בנו [בָּנָיו] וְאֶת־כָּל־עַמּוֹ:

³⁴ At that time we captured all his towns, and we doomed every town – men, women, and children – leaving no survivor.

לד וַנִּלְכֹּד אֶת־כָּל־עָרָיו בָּעֵת הַהִוא וַנַּחֲרֵם אֶת־כָּל־עִיר מְתִם וְהַנָּשִׁים וְהַטָּף לֹא הִשְׁאַרְנוּ שָׂרִיד:

³⁵ We retained as booty only the cattle and the spoil of the cities that we captured.

לה רַק הַבְּהֵמָה בָּזַזְנוּ לָנוּ וּשְׁלַל הֶעָרִים אֲשֶׁר לָכָדְנוּ:

³⁶ From Aroer on the edge of the Arnon valley, including the town in the valley itself, to *Gilad*, not a city was too mighty for us; *Hashem* our God delivered everything to us.

לו מֵעֲרֹעֵר אֲשֶׁר עַל־שְׂפַת־נַחַל אַרְנֹן וְהָעִיר אֲשֶׁר בַּנַּחַל וְעַד־הַגִּלְעָד לֹא הָיְתָה קִרְיָה אֲשֶׁר שָׂגְבָה מִמֶּנּוּ אֶת־הַכֹּל נָתַן יְהֹוָה אֱלֹהֵינוּ לְפָנֵינוּ:

37 But you did not encroach upon the land of the Ammonites, all along the wadi Jabbok and the towns of the hill country, just as *Hashem* our God had commanded.

לז רַק אֶל־אֶרֶץ בְּנֵי־עַמּוֹן לֹא קָרָבְתָּ כָּל־יַד נַחַל יַבֹּק וְעָרֵי הָהָר וְכֹל אֲשֶׁר־צִוָּה יְהֹוָה אֱלֹהֵינוּ:

3 ¹ We made our way up the road toward Bashan, and King Og of Bashan with all his men took the field against us at Edrei.

א וַנֵּפֶן וַנַּעַל דֶּרֶךְ הַבָּשָׁן וַיֵּצֵא עוֹג מֶלֶךְ־הַבָּשָׁן לִקְרָאתֵנוּ הוּא וְכָל־עַמּוֹ לַמִּלְחָמָה אֶדְרֶעִי:

² But *Hashem* said to me: Do not fear him, for I am delivering him and all his men and his country into your power, and you will do to him as you did to Sihon king of the Amorites, who lived in Heshbon.

ב וַיֹּאמֶר יְהֹוָה אֵלַי אַל־תִּירָא אֹתוֹ כִּי בְיָדְךָ נָתַתִּי אֹתוֹ וְאֶת־כָּל־עַמּוֹ וְאֶת־אַרְצוֹ וְעָשִׂיתָ לּוֹ כַּאֲשֶׁר עָשִׂיתָ לְסִיחֹן מֶלֶךְ הָאֱמֹרִי אֲשֶׁר יוֹשֵׁב בְּחֶשְׁבּוֹן:

³ So *Hashem* our God also delivered into our power King Og of Bashan, with all his men, and we dealt them such a blow that no survivor was left.

ג וַיִּתֵּן יְהֹוָה אֱלֹהֵינוּ בְּיָדֵנוּ גַּם אֶת־עוֹג מֶלֶךְ־הַבָּשָׁן וְאֶת־כָּל־עַמּוֹ וַנַּכֵּהוּ עַד־בִּלְתִּי הִשְׁאִיר־לוֹ שָׂרִיד:

⁴ At that time we captured all his towns; there was not a town that we did not take from them: sixty towns, the whole district of Argob, the kingdom of Og in Bashan

ד וַנִּלְכֹּד אֶת־כָּל־עָרָיו בָּעֵת הַהִוא לֹא הָיְתָה קִרְיָה אֲשֶׁר לֹא־לָקַחְנוּ מֵאִתָּם שִׁשִּׁים עִיר כָּל־חֶבֶל אַרְגֹּב מַמְלֶכֶת עוֹג בַּבָּשָׁן:

⁵ all those towns were fortified with high walls, gates, and bars – apart from a great number of unwalled towns.

ה כָּל־אֵלֶּה עָרִים בְּצֻרוֹת חוֹמָה גְבֹהָה דְּלָתַיִם וּבְרִיחַ לְבַד מֵעָרֵי הַפְּרָזִי הַרְבֵּה מְאֹד:

⁶ We doomed them as we had done in the case of King Sihon of Heshbon; we doomed every town – men, women, and children –

ו וַנַּחֲרֵם אוֹתָם כַּאֲשֶׁר עָשִׂינוּ לְסִיחֹן מֶלֶךְ חֶשְׁבּוֹן הַחֲרֵם כָּל־עִיר מְתִם הַנָּשִׁים וְהַטָּף:

⁷ and retained as booty all the cattle and the spoil of the towns.

ז וְכָל־הַבְּהֵמָה וּשְׁלַל הֶעָרִים בַּזּוֹנוּ לָנוּ:

⁸ Thus we seized, at that time, from the two Amorite kings, the country beyond the *Yarden*, from the wadi Arnon to Mount *Chermon*

ח וַנִּקַּח בָּעֵת הַהִוא אֶת־הָאָרֶץ מִיַּד שְׁנֵי מַלְכֵי הָאֱמֹרִי אֲשֶׁר בְּעֵבֶר הַיַּרְדֵּן מִנַּחַל אַרְנֹן עַד־הַר חֶרְמוֹן:

⁹ Sidonians called *Chermon* Sirion, and the Amorites call it Senir

ט צִידֹנִים יִקְרְאוּ לְחֶרְמוֹן שִׂרְיֹן וְהָאֱמֹרִי יִקְרְאוּ־לוֹ שְׂנִיר:

¹⁰ all the towns of the Tableland and the whole of *Gilad* and Bashan as far as Salcah and Edrei, the towns of Og's kingdom in Bashan.

י כֹּל עָרֵי הַמִּישֹׁר וְכָל־הַגִּלְעָד וְכָל־הַבָּשָׁן עַד־סַלְכָה וְאֶדְרֶעִי עָרֵי מַמְלֶכֶת עוֹג בַּבָּשָׁן:

¹¹ Only King Og of Bashan was left of the remaining Rephaim. His bedstead, an iron bedstead, is now in Rabbah of the Ammonites; it is nine *amot* long and four *amot* wide, by the standard *amah*!

יא כִּי רַק־עוֹג מֶלֶךְ הַבָּשָׁן נִשְׁאַר מִיֶּתֶר הָרְפָאִים הִנֵּה עַרְשׂוֹ עֶרֶשׂ בַּרְזֶל הֲלֹה הִוא בְּרַבַּת בְּנֵי עַמּוֹן תֵּשַׁע אַמּוֹת אָרְכָּהּ וְאַרְבַּע אַמּוֹת רָחְבָּהּ בְּאַמַּת־אִישׁ:

¹² And this is the land which we apportioned at that time: The part from Aroer along the wadi Arnon, with part of the hill country of *Gilad* and its towns, I assigned to the Reubenites and the Gadites.

יב וְאֶת־הָאָרֶץ הַזֹּאת יָרַשְׁנוּ בָּעֵת הַהִוא מֵעֲרֹעֵר אֲשֶׁר־עַל־נַחַל אַרְנֹן וַחֲצִי הַר־הַגִּלְעָד וְעָרָיו נָתַתִּי לָראוּבֵנִי וְלַגָּדִי:

13 The rest of *Gilad*, and all of Bashan under Og's rule – the whole Argob district, all that part of Bashan which is called Rephaim country – I assigned to the half-tribe of *Menashe*.

יג וְיֶתֶר הַגִּלְעָד וְכָל־הַבָּשָׁן מַמְלֶכֶת עוֹג נָתַתִּי לַחֲצִי שֵׁבֶט הַמְנַשֶּׁה כֹּל חֶבֶל הָאַרְגֹּב לְכָל־הַבָּשָׁן הַהוּא יִקָּרֵא אֶרֶץ רְפָאִים:

14 *Yair* son of *Menashe* received the whole Argob district (that is, Bashan) as far as the boundary of the Geshurites and the Maacathites, and named it after himself: Havvoth-jair – as is still the case.

יד יָאִיר בֶּן־מְנַשֶּׁה לָקַח אֶת־כָּל־חֶבֶל אַרְגֹּב עַד־גְּבוּל הַגְּשׁוּרִי וְהַמַּעֲכָתִי וַיִּקְרָא אֹתָם עַל־שְׁמוֹ אֶת־הַבָּשָׁן חַוֹּת יָאִיר עַד הַיּוֹם הַזֶּה:

15 To Machir I assigned *Gilad*.

טו וּלְמָכִיר נָתַתִּי אֶת־הַגִּלְעָד:

16 And to the Reubenites and the Gadites I assigned the part from *Gilad* down to the wadi Arnon, the middle of the wadi being the boundary, and up to the wadi Jabbok, the boundary of the Ammonites.

טז וְלָרֵאוּבֵנִי וְלַגָּדִי נָתַתִּי מִן־הַגִּלְעָד וְעַד־נַחַל אַרְנֹן תּוֹךְ הַנַּחַל וּגְבֻל וְעַד יַבֹּק הַנַּחַל גְּבוּל בְּנֵי עַמּוֹן:

17 [We also seized] the Arabah, from the foot of the slopes of Pisgah on the east, to the edge of the *Yarden*, and from Chinnereth down to the sea of the Arabah, the Dead Sea.

יז וְהָעֲרָבָה וְהַיַּרְדֵּן וּגְבֻל מִכִּנֶּרֶת וְעַד יָם הָעֲרָבָה יָם הַמֶּלַח תַּחַת אַשְׁדֹּת הַפִּסְגָּה מִזְרָחָה:

18 At that time I charged you, saying, "*Hashem* your God has given you this country to possess. You must go as shock-troops, warriors all, at the head of your Israelite kinsmen.

יח וָאֲצַו אֶתְכֶם בָּעֵת הַהִוא לֵאמֹר יְהוָה אֱלֹהֵיכֶם נָתַן לָכֶם אֶת־הָאָרֶץ הַזֹּאת לְרִשְׁתָּהּ חֲלוּצִים תַּעַבְרוּ לִפְנֵי אֲחֵיכֶם בְּנֵי־יִשְׂרָאֵל כָּל־בְּנֵי־חָיִל:

va-a-TZAV et-KHEM ba-AYT ha-HEE lay-MOR a-do-NAI e-lo-hay-KHEM na-TAN la-KHEM et ha-A-retz ha-ZOT l'-rish-TAH kha-lu-TZEEM ta-av-RU lif-NAY a-khay-KHEM b'-nay yis-ra-AYL kol b'-nay KHA-yil

19 Only your wives, children, and livestock – I know that you have much livestock – shall be left in the towns I have assigned to you,

יט רַק נְשֵׁיכֶם וְטַפְּכֶם וּמִקְנֵכֶם יָדַעְתִּי כִּי־מִקְנֶה רַב לָכֶם יֵשְׁבוּ בְּעָרֵיכֶם אֲשֶׁר נָתַתִּי לָכֶם:

20 until *Hashem* has granted your kinsmen a haven such as you have, and they too have taken possession of the land that *Hashem* your God is assigning them, beyond the *Yarden*. Then you may return each to the homestead that I have assigned to him."

כ עַד אֲשֶׁר־יָנִיחַ יְהוָה לַאֲחֵיכֶם כָּכֶם וְיָרְשׁוּ גַם־הֵם אֶת־הָאָרֶץ אֲשֶׁר יְהוָה אֱלֹהֵיכֶם נֹתֵן לָהֶם בְּעֵבֶר הַיַּרְדֵּן וְשַׁבְתֶּם אִישׁ לִירֻשָּׁתוֹ אֲשֶׁר נָתַתִּי לָכֶם:

3:18 You must go as shock-troops, warriors all The tribes of *Reuven* and *Gad* requested to settle on the eastern side of the *Yarden* in the lands conquered from Sihon and Og, rather than join their brethren on the western side. *Moshe* granted this request on condition that *Reuven* and *Gad* would fight alongside the other tribes in the conquest of the land. Here, *Moshe* reminds *Reuven* and *Gad* of their agreement. And, indeed, when *Yehoshua* succeeds *Moshe* and leads the nation into their land, he calls upon these tribes to fulfill their promise. The men of *Reuven* and *Gad* answer their call to duty and fight in the army until the battles are over. As in the days of *Yehoshua*, today the State of Israel calls upon all of its citizens to serve in the Israel Defense Forces. Military service typically lasts for three years, between the ages of eighteen to twenty-one, followed by several weeks of reserve duty each year until the age of forty-five. Similarly, Israel turns to those living outside the State for different, but also important, contributions to its vitality, growth and security.

IDF soldiers raising a handmade flag in *Eilat*, 1949

²¹ I also charged *Yehoshua* at that time, saying, "You have seen with your own eyes all that *Hashem* your God has done to these two kings; so shall *Hashem* do to all the kingdoms into which you shall cross over.

כא וְאֶת־יְהוֹשׁוּעַ צִוֵּיתִי בָּעֵת הַהִוא לֵאמֹר עֵינֶיךָ הָרֹאֹת אֵת כָּל־אֲשֶׁר עָשָׂה יְהוָה אֱלֹהֵיכֶם לִשְׁנֵי הַמְּלָכִים הָאֵלֶּה כֵּן־יַעֲשֶׂה יְהוָה לְכָל־הַמַּמְלָכוֹת אֲשֶׁר אַתָּה עֹבֵר שָׁמָּה:

²² Do not fear them, for it is *Hashem* your God who will battle for you."

כב לֹא תִּירָאוּם כִּי יְהוָה אֱלֹהֵיכֶם הוּא הַנִּלְחָם לָכֶם:

²³ I pleaded with *Hashem* at that time, saying,

כג וָאֶתְחַנַּן אֶל־יְהוָה בָּעֵת הַהִוא לֵאמֹר:

²⁴ "O *Hashem*, You who let Your servant see the first works of Your greatness and Your mighty hand, You whose powerful deeds no god in heaven or on earth can equal!

כד אֲדֹנָי יְהוִה אַתָּה הַחִלּוֹתָ לְהַרְאוֹת אֶת־עַבְדְּךָ אֶת־גָּדְלְךָ וְאֶת־יָדְךָ הַחֲזָקָה אֲשֶׁר מִי־אֵל בַּשָּׁמַיִם וּבָאָרֶץ אֲשֶׁר־יַעֲשֶׂה כְמַעֲשֶׂיךָ וְכִגְבוּרֹתֶךָ:

²⁵ Let me, I pray, cross over and see the good land on the other side of the *Yarden*, that good hill country, and the Lebanon."

כה אֶעְבְּרָה־נָּא וְאֶרְאֶה אֶת־הָאָרֶץ הַטּוֹבָה אֲשֶׁר בְּעֵבֶר הַיַּרְדֵּן הָהָר הַטּוֹב הַזֶּה וְהַלְּבָנוֹן:

e-b'-rah NA v'-er-EH et ha-A-retz ha-to-VAH a-SHER b'-AY-ver ha-yar-DAYN ha-HAR ha-TOV ha-ZEH v'-ha-l'-va-NON

²⁶ But *Hashem* was wrathful with me on your account and would not listen to me. *Hashem* said to me, "Enough! Never speak to Me of this matter again!

כו וַיִּתְעַבֵּר יְהוָה בִּי לְמַעַנְכֶם וְלֹא שָׁמַע אֵלָי וַיֹּאמֶר יְהוָה אֵלַי רַב־לָךְ אַל־תּוֹסֶף דַּבֵּר אֵלַי עוֹד בַּדָּבָר הַזֶּה:

²⁷ Go up to the summit of Pisgah and gaze about, to the west, the north, the south, and the east. Look at it well, for you shall not go across yonder *Yarden*.

כז עֲלֵה רֹאשׁ הַפִּסְגָּה וְשָׂא עֵינֶיךָ יָמָּה וְצָפֹנָה וְתֵימָנָה וּמִזְרָחָה וּרְאֵה בְעֵינֶיךָ כִּי־לֹא תַעֲבֹר אֶת־הַיַּרְדֵּן הַזֶּה:

²⁸ Give *Yehoshua* his instructions, and imbue him with strength and courage, for he shall go across at the head of this people, and he shall allot to them the land that you may only see."

כח וְצַו אֶת־יְהוֹשֻׁעַ וְחַזְּקֵהוּ וְאַמְּצֵהוּ כִּי־הוּא יַעֲבֹר לִפְנֵי הָעָם הַזֶּה וְהוּא יַנְחִיל אוֹתָם אֶת־הָאָרֶץ אֲשֶׁר תִּרְאֶה:

²⁹ Meanwhile we stayed on in the valley near Beth-peor.

כט וַנֵּשֶׁב בַּגָּיְא מוּל בֵּית פְּעוֹר:

Scenic view of the Jezreel Valley

3:25 Let me, I pray, cross over and see the good land In this verse, *Moshe* demonstrates his pure love for the Land of Israel. Though *Hashem* already forbade him from setting foot in the Promised Land, *Moshe* pleads with God to change His mind. The words "Let me, I pray, cross over and see the good land on the other side of the *Yarden*" highlight the motivation behind *Moshe's* request. It is not arrogance nor a desire for power that leads to his request, as he did not ask to lead the people into *Eretz Yisrael*. He simply wants to see the land, to breathe its air, to experience its goodness. Though *Moshe* wanted desperately to enter *Eretz Yisrael*, he could not. A visit to the Land of Israel has never been as easy as it is today, and the love for the land espoused by *Moshe* inspires millions of tourists to visit Israel each year. Visitors to Israel must remember that by entering the land, they are experiencing a blessing that even *Moshe* was not able to achieve.

10

4 ¹ And now, O *Yisrael*, give heed to the laws and rules that I am instructing you to observe, so that you may live to enter and occupy the land that *Hashem*, the God of your fathers, is giving you.

ד א וְעַתָּה יִשְׂרָאֵל שְׁמַע אֶל־הַחֻקִּים וְאֶל־הַמִּשְׁפָּטִים אֲשֶׁר אָנֹכִי מְלַמֵּד אֶתְכֶם לַעֲשׂוֹת לְמַעַן תִּחְיוּ וּבָאתֶם וִירִשְׁתֶּם אֶת־הָאָרֶץ אֲשֶׁר יְהוָה אֱלֹהֵי אֲבֹתֵיכֶם נֹתֵן לָכֶם:

v'-a-TAH yis-ra-AYL sh'-MA el ha-khu-KEEM v'-el ha-mish-pa-TEEM
a-SHER a-no-KHEE m'-la-MAYD et-KHEM la-a-SOT l'-MA-an
tikh-YU u-VA-tem vee-rish-TEM et ha-A-retz a-SHER a-do-NAI
e-lo-HAY a-vo-tay-KHEM no-TAYN la-KHEM

² You shall not add anything to what I command you or take anything away from it, but keep the commandments of *Hashem* your God that I enjoin upon you.

ב לֹא תֹסִפוּ עַל־הַדָּבָר אֲשֶׁר אָנֹכִי מְצַוֶּה אֶתְכֶם וְלֹא תִגְרְעוּ מִמֶּנּוּ לִשְׁמֹר אֶת־מִצְוֹת יְהוָה אֱלֹהֵיכֶם אֲשֶׁר אָנֹכִי מְצַוֶּה אֶתְכֶם:

³ You saw with your own eyes what *Hashem* did in the matter of Baal-peor, that *Hashem* your God wiped out from among you every person who followed Baal-peor;

ג עֵינֵיכֶם הָרֹאֹת אֵת אֲשֶׁר־עָשָׂה יְהוָה בְּבַעַל פְּעוֹר כִּי כָל־הָאִישׁ אֲשֶׁר הָלַךְ אַחֲרֵי בַעַל־פְּעוֹר הִשְׁמִידוֹ יְהוָה אֱלֹהֶיךָ מִקִּרְבֶּךָ:

⁴ while you, who held fast to *Hashem* your God, are all alive today.

ד וְאַתֶּם הַדְּבֵקִים בַּיהוָה אֱלֹהֵיכֶם חַיִּים כֻּלְּכֶם הַיּוֹם:

⁵ See, I have imparted to you laws and rules, as *Hashem* my God has commanded me, for you to abide by in the land that you are about to enter and occupy.

ה רְאֵה לִמַּדְתִּי אֶתְכֶם חֻקִּים וּמִשְׁפָּטִים כַּאֲשֶׁר צִוַּנִי יְהוָה אֱלֹהָי לַעֲשׂוֹת כֵּן בְּקֶרֶב הָאָרֶץ אֲשֶׁר אַתֶּם בָּאִים שָׁמָּה לְרִשְׁתָּהּ:

⁶ Observe them faithfully, for that will be proof of your wisdom and discernment to other peoples, who on hearing of all these laws will say, "Surely, that great nation is a wise and discerning people."

ו וּשְׁמַרְתֶּם וַעֲשִׂיתֶם כִּי הִוא חָכְמַתְכֶם וּבִינַתְכֶם לְעֵינֵי הָעַמִּים אֲשֶׁר יִשְׁמְעוּן אֵת כָּל־הַחֻקִּים הָאֵלֶּה וְאָמְרוּ רַק עַם־חָכָם וְנָבוֹן הַגּוֹי הַגָּדוֹל הַזֶּה:

⁷ For what great nation is there that has a god so close at hand as is *Hashem* our God whenever we call upon Him?

ז כִּי מִי־גוֹי גָּדוֹל אֲשֶׁר־לוֹ אֱלֹהִים קְרֹבִים אֵלָיו כַּיהוָה אֱלֹהֵינוּ בְּכָל־קָרְאֵנוּ אֵלָיו:

⁸ Or what great nation has laws and rules as perfect as all this Teaching that I set before you this day?

ח וּמִי גּוֹי גָּדוֹל אֲשֶׁר־לוֹ חֻקִּים וּמִשְׁפָּטִים צַדִּיקִם כְּכֹל הַתּוֹרָה הַזֹּאת אֲשֶׁר אָנֹכִי נֹתֵן לִפְנֵיכֶם הַיּוֹם:

⁹ But take utmost care and watch yourselves scrupulously, so that you do not forget the things that you saw with your own eyes and so that they do not fade from your mind as long as you live. And make them known to your children and to your children's children:

ט רַק הִשָּׁמֶר לְךָ וּשְׁמֹר נַפְשְׁךָ מְאֹד פֶּן־תִּשְׁכַּח אֶת־הַדְּבָרִים אֲשֶׁר־רָאוּ עֵינֶיךָ וּפֶן־יָסוּרוּ מִלְּבָבְךָ כֹּל יְמֵי חַיֶּיךָ וְהוֹדַעְתָּם לְבָנֶיךָ וְלִבְנֵי בָנֶיךָ:

¹⁰ The day you stood before *Hashem* your God at Horeb, when *Hashem* said to Me, "Gather the people to Me that I may let them hear My words, in order that they may learn to revere Me as long as they live on earth, and may so teach their children."

י יוֹם אֲשֶׁר עָמַדְתָּ לִפְנֵי יְהוָה אֱלֹהֶיךָ בְּחֹרֵב בֶּאֱמֹר יְהוָה אֵלַי הַקְהֶל־לִי אֶת־הָעָם וְאַשְׁמִעֵם אֶת־דְּבָרָי אֲשֶׁר יִלְמְדוּן לְיִרְאָה אֹתִי כָּל־הַיָּמִים אֲשֶׁר הֵם חַיִּים עַל־הָאֲדָמָה וְאֶת־בְּנֵיהֶם יְלַמֵּדוּן:

11 You came forward and stood at the foot of the mountain. The mountain was ablaze with flames to the very skies, dark with densest clouds.

וַתִּקְרְבוּן וַתַּעַמְדוּן תַּחַת הָהָר וְהָהָר בֹּעֵר בָּאֵשׁ עַד־לֵב הַשָּׁמַיִם חֹשֶׁךְ עָנָן וַעֲרָפֶל: יא

12 *Hashem* spoke to you out of the fire; you heard the sound of words but perceived no shape – nothing but a voice.

וַיְדַבֵּר יְהֹוָה אֲלֵיכֶם מִתּוֹךְ הָאֵשׁ קוֹל דְּבָרִים אַתֶּם שֹׁמְעִים וּתְמוּנָה אֵינְכֶם רֹאִים זוּלָתִי קוֹל: יב

13 He declared to you the covenant that He commanded you to observe, the Ten Commandments; and He inscribed them on two tablets of stone.

וַיַּגֵּד לָכֶם אֶת־בְּרִיתוֹ אֲשֶׁר צִוָּה אֶתְכֶם לַעֲשׂוֹת עֲשֶׂרֶת הַדְּבָרִים וַיִּכְתְּבֵם עַל־שְׁנֵי לֻחוֹת אֲבָנִים: יג

14 At the same time *Hashem* commanded me to impart to you laws and rules for you to observe in the land that you are about to cross into and occupy.

וְאֹתִי צִוָּה יְהֹוָה בָּעֵת הַהִוא לְלַמֵּד אֶתְכֶם חֻקִּים וּמִשְׁפָּטִים לַעֲשֹׂתְכֶם אֹתָם בָּאָרֶץ אֲשֶׁר אַתֶּם עֹבְרִים שָׁמָּה לְרִשְׁתָּהּ: יד

15 For your own sake, therefore, be most careful – since you saw no shape when *Hashem* your God spoke to you at Horeb out of the fire

וְנִשְׁמַרְתֶּם מְאֹד לְנַפְשֹׁתֵיכֶם כִּי לֹא רְאִיתֶם כָּל־תְּמוּנָה בְּיוֹם דִּבֶּר יְהֹוָה אֲלֵיכֶם בְּחֹרֵב מִתּוֹךְ הָאֵשׁ: טו

16 not to act wickedly and make for yourselves a sculptured image in any likeness whatever: the form of a man or a woman,

פֶּן־תַּשְׁחִתוּן וַעֲשִׂיתֶם לָכֶם פֶּסֶל תְּמוּנַת כָּל־סָמֶל תַּבְנִית זָכָר אוֹ נְקֵבָה: טז

17 the form of any beast on earth, the form of any winged bird that flies in the sky,

תַּבְנִית כָּל־בְּהֵמָה אֲשֶׁר בָּאָרֶץ תַּבְנִית כָּל־צִפּוֹר כָּנָף אֲשֶׁר תָּעוּף בַּשָּׁמָיִם: יז

18 the form of anything that creeps on the ground, the form of any fish that is in the waters below the earth.

תַּבְנִית כָּל־רֹמֵשׂ בָּאֲדָמָה תַּבְנִית כָּל־דָּגָה אֲשֶׁר־בַּמַּיִם מִתַּחַת לָאָרֶץ: יח

19 And when you look up to the sky and behold the sun and the moon and the stars, the whole heavenly host, you must not be lured into bowing down to them or serving them. These *Hashem* your God allotted to other peoples everywhere under heaven;

וּפֶן־תִּשָּׂא עֵינֶיךָ הַשָּׁמַיְמָה וְרָאִיתָ אֶת־הַשֶּׁמֶשׁ וְאֶת־הַיָּרֵחַ וְאֶת־הַכּוֹכָבִים כֹּל צְבָא הַשָּׁמַיִם וְנִדַּחְתָּ וְהִשְׁתַּחֲוִיתָ לָהֶם וַעֲבַדְתָּם אֲשֶׁר חָלַק יְהֹוָה אֱלֹהֶיךָ אֹתָם לְכֹל הָעַמִּים תַּחַת כָּל־הַשָּׁמָיִם: יט

20 but you *Hashem* took and brought out of Egypt, that iron blast furnace, to be His very own people, as is now the case.

וְאֶתְכֶם לָקַח יְהֹוָה וַיּוֹצִא אֶתְכֶם מִכּוּר הַבַּרְזֶל מִמִּצְרָיִם לִהְיוֹת לוֹ לְעַם נַחֲלָה כַּיּוֹם הַזֶּה: כ

21 Now *Hashem* was angry with me on your account and swore that I should not cross the *Yarden* and enter the good land that *Hashem* your God is assigning you as a heritage.

וַיהֹוָה הִתְאַנַּף־בִּי עַל־דִּבְרֵיכֶם וַיִּשָּׁבַע לְבִלְתִּי עָבְרִי אֶת־הַיַּרְדֵּן וּלְבִלְתִּי־בֹא אֶל־הָאָרֶץ הַטּוֹבָה אֲשֶׁר יְהֹוָה אֱלֹהֶיךָ נֹתֵן לְךָ נַחֲלָה: כא

22 For I must die in this land; I shall not cross the *Yarden*. But you will cross and take possession of that good land.

כִּי אָנֹכִי מֵת בָּאָרֶץ הַזֹּאת אֵינֶנִּי עֹבֵר אֶת־הַיַּרְדֵּן וְאַתֶּם עֹבְרִים וִירִשְׁתֶּם אֶת־הָאָרֶץ הַטּוֹבָה הַזֹּאת: כב

23 Take care, then, not to forget the covenant that *Hashem* your God concluded with you, and not to make for yourselves a sculptured image in any likeness, against which *Hashem* your God has enjoined you.

כג הִשָּׁמְרוּ לָכֶם פֶּן־תִּשְׁכְּחוּ אֶת־בְּרִית יְהֹוָה אֱלֹהֵיכֶם אֲשֶׁר כָּרַת עִמָּכֶם וַעֲשִׂיתֶם לָכֶם פֶּסֶל תְּמוּנַת כֹּל אֲשֶׁר צִוְּךָ יְהֹוָה אֱלֹהֶיךָ:

24 For *Hashem* your God is a consuming fire, an impassioned God.

כד כִּי יְהֹוָה אֱלֹהֶיךָ אֵשׁ אֹכְלָה הוּא אֵל קַנָּא:

25 When you have begotten children and children's children and are long established in the land, should you act wickedly and make for yourselves a sculptured image in any likeness, causing *Hashem* your God displeasure and vexation,

כה כִּי־תוֹלִיד בָּנִים וּבְנֵי בָנִים וְנוֹשַׁנְתֶּם בָּאָרֶץ וְהִשְׁחַתֶּם וַעֲשִׂיתֶם פֶּסֶל תְּמוּנַת כֹּל וַעֲשִׂיתֶם הָרַע בְּעֵינֵי יְהֹוָה־אֱלֹהֶיךָ לְהַכְעִיסוֹ:

26 I call heaven and earth this day to witness against you that you shall soon perish from the land that you are crossing the *Yarden* to possess; you shall not long endure in it, but shall be utterly wiped out.

כו הַעִידֹתִי בָכֶם הַיּוֹם אֶת־הַשָּׁמַיִם וְאֶת־הָאָרֶץ כִּי־אָבֹד תֹּאבֵדוּן מַהֵר מֵעַל הָאָרֶץ אֲשֶׁר אַתֶּם עֹבְרִים אֶת־הַיַּרְדֵּן שָׁמָּה לְרִשְׁתָּהּ לֹא־תַאֲרִיכֻן יָמִים עָלֶיהָ כִּי הִשָּׁמֵד תִּשָּׁמֵדוּן:

27 *Hashem* will scatter you among the peoples, and only a scant few of you shall be left among the nations to which *Hashem* will drive you.

כז וְהֵפִיץ יְהֹוָה אֶתְכֶם בָּעַמִּים וְנִשְׁאַרְתֶּם מְתֵי מִסְפָּר בַּגּוֹיִם אֲשֶׁר יְנַהֵג יְהֹוָה אֶתְכֶם שָׁמָּה:

28 There you will serve man-made gods of wood and stone, that cannot see or hear or eat or smell.

כח וַעֲבַדְתֶּם־שָׁם אֱלֹהִים מַעֲשֵׂה יְדֵי אָדָם עֵץ וָאֶבֶן אֲשֶׁר לֹא־יִרְאוּן וְלֹא יִשְׁמְעוּן וְלֹא יֹאכְלוּן וְלֹא יְרִיחֻן:

29 But if you search there for *Hashem* your God, you will find Him, if only you seek Him with all your heart and soul

כט וּבִקַּשְׁתֶּם מִשָּׁם אֶת־יְהֹוָה אֱלֹהֶיךָ וּמָצָאתָ כִּי תִדְרְשֶׁנּוּ בְּכָל־לְבָבְךָ וּבְכָל־נַפְשֶׁךָ:

30 when you are in distress because all these things have befallen you and, in the end, return to *Hashem* your God and obey Him.

ל בַּצַּר לְךָ וּמְצָאוּךָ כֹּל הַדְּבָרִים הָאֵלֶּה בְּאַחֲרִית הַיָּמִים וְשַׁבְתָּ עַד־יְהֹוָה אֱלֹהֶיךָ וְשָׁמַעְתָּ בְּקֹלוֹ:

31 For *Hashem* your God is a compassionate *Hashem*: He will not fail you nor will He let you perish; He will not forget the covenant which He made on oath with your fathers.

לא כִּי אֵל רַחוּם יְהֹוָה אֱלֹהֶיךָ לֹא יַרְפְּךָ וְלֹא יַשְׁחִיתֶךָ וְלֹא יִשְׁכַּח אֶת־בְּרִית אֲבֹתֶיךָ אֲשֶׁר נִשְׁבַּע לָהֶם:

32 You have but to inquire about bygone ages that came before you, ever since *Hashem* created man on earth, from one end of heaven to the other: has anything as grand as this ever happened, or has its like ever been known?

לב כִּי שְׁאַל־נָא לְיָמִים רִאשֹׁנִים אֲשֶׁר־הָיוּ לְפָנֶיךָ לְמִן־הַיּוֹם אֲשֶׁר בָּרָא אֱלֹהִים אָדָם עַל־הָאָרֶץ וּלְמִקְצֵה הַשָּׁמַיִם וְעַד־קְצֵה הַשָּׁמָיִם הֲנִהְיָה כַּדָּבָר הַגָּדוֹל הַזֶּה אוֹ הֲנִשְׁמַע כָּמֹהוּ:

33 Has any people heard the voice of a god speaking out of a fire, as you have, and survived?

לג הֲשָׁמַע עָם קוֹל אֱלֹהִים מְדַבֵּר מִתּוֹךְ־הָאֵשׁ כַּאֲשֶׁר־שָׁמַעְתָּ אַתָּה וַיֶּחִי:

34 Or has any god ventured to go and take for himself one nation from the midst of another by prodigious acts, by signs and portents, by war, by a mighty and an outstretched arm and awesome power, as *Hashem* your God did for you in Egypt before your very eyes?

לד אוֹ הֲנִסָּה אֱלֹהִים לָבוֹא לָקַחַת לוֹ גוֹי מִקֶּרֶב גּוֹי בְּמַסֹּת בְּאֹתֹת וּבְמוֹפְתִים וּבְמִלְחָמָה וּבְיָד חֲזָקָה וּבִזְרוֹעַ נְטוּיָה וּבְמוֹרָאִים גְּדֹלִים כְּכֹל אֲשֶׁר־עָשָׂה לָכֶם יְהוָה אֱלֹהֵיכֶם בְּמִצְרַיִם לְעֵינֶיךָ:

35 It has been clearly demonstrated to you that *Hashem* alone is God; there is none beside Him.

לה אַתָּה הָרְאֵתָ לָדַעַת כִּי יְהוָה הוּא הָאֱלֹהִים אֵין עוֹד מִלְבַדּוֹ:

a-TAH ha-r'-ay-TA la-DA-at KEE a-do-NAI HU ha-e-lo-HEEM
AYN OD mi-l'-va-DO

36 From the heavens He let you hear His voice to discipline you; on earth He let you see His great fire; and from amidst that fire you heard His words.

לו מִן־הַשָּׁמַיִם הִשְׁמִיעֲךָ אֶת־קֹלוֹ לְיַסְּרֶךָּ וְעַל־הָאָרֶץ הֶרְאֲךָ אֶת־אִשּׁוֹ הַגְּדוֹלָה וּדְבָרָיו שָׁמַעְתָּ מִתּוֹךְ הָאֵשׁ:

37 And because He loved your fathers, He chose their heirs after them; He Himself, in His great might, led you out of Egypt,

לז וְתַחַת כִּי אָהַב אֶת־אֲבֹתֶיךָ וַיִּבְחַר בְּזַרְעוֹ אַחֲרָיו וַיּוֹצִאֲךָ בְּפָנָיו בְּכֹחוֹ הַגָּדֹל מִמִּצְרָיִם:

38 to drive from your path nations greater and more populous than you, to take you into their land and assign it to you as a heritage, as is still the case.

לח לְהוֹרִישׁ גּוֹיִם גְּדֹלִים וַעֲצֻמִים מִמְּךָ מִפָּנֶיךָ לַהֲבִיאֲךָ לָתֶת־לְךָ אֶת־אַרְצָם נַחֲלָה כַּיּוֹם הַזֶּה:

39 Know therefore this day and keep in mind that *Hashem* alone is God in heaven above and on earth below; there is no other.

לט וְיָדַעְתָּ הַיּוֹם וַהֲשֵׁבֹתָ אֶל־לְבָבֶךָ כִּי יְהוָה הוּא הָאֱלֹהִים בַּשָּׁמַיִם מִמַּעַל וְעַל־הָאָרֶץ מִתָּחַת אֵין עוֹד:

40 Observe His laws and commandments, which I enjoin upon you this day, that it may go well with you and your children after you, and that you may long remain in the land that *Hashem* your God is assigning to you for all time.

מ וְשָׁמַרְתָּ אֶת־חֻקָּיו וְאֶת־מִצְוֹתָיו אֲשֶׁר אָנֹכִי מְצַוְּךָ הַיּוֹם אֲשֶׁר יִיטַב לְךָ וּלְבָנֶיךָ אַחֲרֶיךָ וּלְמַעַן תַּאֲרִיךְ יָמִים עַל־הָאֲדָמָה אֲשֶׁר יְהוָה אֱלֹהֶיךָ נֹתֵן לְךָ כָּל־הַיָּמִים:

v'-sha-mar-TA et khu-KAV v'-et mitz-vo-TAV a-SHER a-no-KHEE
m'-tza-v'-KHA ha-YOM a-SHER yee-TAV l'-KHA ul-va-NE-kha
a-kha-RE-kha ul-MA-an ta-a-REEKH ya-MEEM al ha-a-da-MAH
a-SHER a-do-NAI e-lo-HE-kha no-TAYN l'-KHA kol ha-ya-MEEM

41 Then *Moshe* set aside three cities on the east side of the *Yarden*

מא אָז יַבְדִּיל מֹשֶׁה שָׁלֹשׁ עָרִים בְּעֵבֶר הַיַּרְדֵּן מִזְרְחָה שָׁמֶשׁ:

4:35 It has been clearly demonstrated to you that *Hashem* alone is God Our greatest ability as humans is our capacity to think and ponder. In this verse, we are told that we must recognize, or know about, the existence of the one true God. The Hebrew phrase in this verse for 'clearly demonstrated' is *har'eita lada'at*

Praying to God at sunset

(הראת לדעת). However, in Biblical Hebrew, *da'at* also refers to a deep, intimate connection, as in, "Now the man knew his wife *Chava*" (Genesis 4:1). It therefore follows that the verse actually means that as humans, we are required not just to know about *Hashem*, but also to forge a deep connection with Him, the Almighty Creator.

דעת

⁴² to which a manslayer could escape, one who unwittingly slew a fellow man without having been hostile to him in the past; he could flee to one of these cities and live:

מב לָנֻס שָׁמָּה רוֹצֵחַ אֲשֶׁר יִרְצַח אֶת־רֵעֵהוּ בִּבְלִי־דַעַת וְהוּא לֹא־שֹׂנֵא לוֹ מִתְּמֹל שִׁלְשֹׁם וְנָס אֶל־אַחַת מִן־הֶעָרִים הָאֵל וָחָי:

⁴³ Bezer, in the wilderness in the Tableland, belonging to the Reubenites; Ramoth, in *Gilad*, belonging to the Gadites; and Golan, in Bashan, belonging to the Manassites.

מג אֶת־בֶּצֶר בַּמִּדְבָּר בְּאֶרֶץ הַמִּישֹׁר לָרֶאוּבֵנִי וְאֶת־רָאמֹת בַּגִּלְעָד לַגָּדִי וְאֶת־גּוֹלָן בַּבָּשָׁן לַמְנַשִּׁי:

⁴⁴ This is the Teaching that *Moshe* set before the Israelites:

מד וְזֹאת הַתּוֹרָה אֲשֶׁר־שָׂם מֹשֶׁה לִפְנֵי בְּנֵי יִשְׂרָאֵל:

⁴⁵ these are the decrees, laws, and rules that *Moshe* addressed to the people of *Yisrael*, after they had left Egypt,

מה אֵלֶּה הָעֵדֹת וְהַחֻקִּים וְהַמִּשְׁפָּטִים אֲשֶׁר דִּבֶּר מֹשֶׁה אֶל־בְּנֵי יִשְׂרָאֵל בְּצֵאתָם מִמִּצְרָיִם:

⁴⁶ beyond the *Yarden*, in the valley at Beth-peor, in the land of King Sihon of the Amorites, who dwelt in Heshbon, whom *Moshe* and the Israelites defeated after they had left Egypt.

מו בְּעֵבֶר הַיַּרְדֵּן בַּגַּיְא מוּל בֵּית פְּעוֹר בְּאֶרֶץ סִיחֹן מֶלֶךְ הָאֱמֹרִי אֲשֶׁר יוֹשֵׁב בְּחֶשְׁבּוֹן אֲשֶׁר הִכָּה מֹשֶׁה וּבְנֵי יִשְׂרָאֵל בְּצֵאתָם מִמִּצְרָיִם:

⁴⁷ They had taken possession of his country and that of King Og of Bashan – the two kings of the Amorites – which were on the east side of the *Yarden*

מז וַיִּירְשׁוּ אֶת־אַרְצוֹ וְאֶת־אֶרֶץ עוֹג מֶלֶךְ־ הַבָּשָׁן שְׁנֵי מַלְכֵי הָאֱמֹרִי אֲשֶׁר בְּעֵבֶר הַיַּרְדֵּן מִזְרַח שָׁמֶשׁ:

⁴⁸ from Aroer on the banks of the wadiArnon, as far as Mount Sion, that is, *Chermon*;

מח מֵעֲרֹעֵר אֲשֶׁר עַל־שְׂפַת־נַחַל אַרְנֹן וְעַד־הַר שִׂיאֹן הוּא חֶרְמוֹן:

⁴⁹ also the whole Arabah on the east side of the *Yarden*, as far as the Sea of the Arabah, at the foot of the slopes of Pisgah.

מט וְכָל־הָעֲרָבָה עֵבֶר הַיַּרְדֵּן מִזְרָחָה וְעַד יָם הָעֲרָבָה תַּחַת אַשְׁדֹּת הַפִּסְגָּה:

5 ¹ *Moshe* summoned all the Israelites and said to them: Hear, O *Yisrael*, the laws and rules that I proclaim to you this day! Study them and observe them faithfully!

ה א וַיִּקְרָא מֹשֶׁה אֶל־כָּל־יִשְׂרָאֵל וַיֹּאמֶר אֲלֵהֶם שְׁמַע יִשְׂרָאֵל אֶת־הַחֻקִּים וְאֶת־ הַמִּשְׁפָּטִים אֲשֶׁר אָנֹכִי דֹּבֵר בְּאָזְנֵיכֶם הַיּוֹם וּלְמַדְתֶּם אֹתָם וּשְׁמַרְתֶּם לַעֲשֹׂתָם:

² *Hashem* our God made a covenant with us at Horeb.

ב יְהוָֹה אֱלֹהֵינוּ כָּרַת עִמָּנוּ בְּרִית בְּחֹרֵב:

³ It was not with our fathers that *Hashem* made this covenant, but with us, the living, every one of us who is here today.

ג לֹא אֶת־אֲבֹתֵינוּ כָּרַת יְהוָֹה אֶת־הַבְּרִית הַזֹּאת כִּי אִתָּנוּ אֲנַחְנוּ אֵלֶּה פֹה הַיּוֹם כֻּלָּנוּ חַיִּים:

⁴ Face to face *Hashem* spoke to you on the mountain out of the fire

ד פָּנִים בְּפָנִים דִּבֶּר יְהוָֹה עִמָּכֶם בָּהָר מִתּוֹךְ הָאֵשׁ:

⁵ I stood between *Hashem* and you at that time to convey *Hashem*'s words to you, for you were afraid of the fire and did not go up the mountain – saying:

ה אָנֹכִי עֹמֵד בֵּין־יְהוָֹה וּבֵינֵיכֶם בָּעֵת הַהִוא לְהַגִּיד לָכֶם אֶת־דְּבַר יְהוָֹה כִּי יְרֵאתֶם מִפְּנֵי הָאֵשׁ וְלֹא־עֲלִיתֶם בָּהָר לֵאמֹר:

6 I *Hashem* am your God who brought you out of the land of Egypt, the house of bondage:

ו אָנֹכִי יְהוָה אֱלֹהֶיךָ אֲשֶׁר הוֹצֵאתִיךָ מֵאֶרֶץ מִצְרַיִם מִבֵּית עֲבָדִים:

7 You shall have no other gods beside Me.

ז לֹא יִהְיֶה־לְךָ אֱלֹהִים אֲחֵרִים עַל־פָּנָי:

8 You shall not make for yourself a sculptured image, any likeness of what is in the heavens above, or on the earth below, or in the waters below the earth.

ח לֹא־תַעֲשֶׂה־לְךָ פֶסֶל כָּל־תְּמוּנָה אֲשֶׁר בַּשָּׁמַיִם מִמַּעַל וַאֲשֶׁר בָּאָרֶץ מִתַּחַת וַאֲשֶׁר בַּמַּיִם מִתַּחַת לָאָרֶץ:

9 You shall not bow down to them or serve them. For I *Hashem* your God am an impassioned God, visiting the guilt of the parents upon the children, upon the third and upon the fourth generations of those who reject Me,

ט לֹא־תִשְׁתַּחֲוֶה לָהֶם וְלֹא תָעָבְדֵם כִּי אָנֹכִי יְהוָה אֱלֹהֶיךָ אֵל קַנָּא פֹּקֵד עֲוֺן אָבֹת עַל־בָּנִים וְעַל־שִׁלֵּשִׁים וְעַל־רִבֵּעִים לְשֹׂנְאָי:

10 but showing kindness to the thousandth generation of those who love Me and keep My commandments.

י וְעֹשֶׂה חֶסֶד לַאֲלָפִים לְאֹהֲבַי וּלְשֹׁמְרֵי מצותו [מִצְוֺתָי]:

11 You shall not swear falsely by the name of *Hashem* your God; for *Hashem* will not clear one who swears falsely by His name.

יא לֹא תִשָּׂא אֶת־שֵׁם־יְהוָה אֱלֹהֶיךָ לַשָּׁוְא כִּי לֹא יְנַקֶּה יְהוָה אֵת אֲשֶׁר־יִשָּׂא אֶת־שְׁמוֹ לַשָּׁוְא:

12 Observe the *Shabbat* day and keep it holy, as *Hashem* your God has commanded you.

יב שָׁמוֹר אֶת־יוֹם הַשַּׁבָּת לְקַדְּשׁוֹ כַּאֲשֶׁר צִוְּךָ יְהוָה אֱלֹהֶיךָ:

13 Six days you shall labor and do all your work,

יג שֵׁשֶׁת יָמִים תַּעֲבֹד וְעָשִׂיתָ כָּל־מְלַאכְתֶּךָ:

14 but the seventh day is a *Shabbat* of *Hashem* your God; you shall not do any work – you, your son or your daughter, your male or female slave, your ox or your ass, or any of your cattle, or the stranger in your settlements, so that your male and female slave may rest as you do.

יד וְיוֹם הַשְּׁבִיעִי שַׁבָּת לַיהוָה אֱלֹהֶיךָ לֹא תַעֲשֶׂה כָל־מְלָאכָה אַתָּה וּבִנְךָ־וּבִתֶּךָ וְעַבְדְּךָ־וַאֲמָתֶךָ וְשׁוֹרְךָ וַחֲמֹרְךָ וְכָל־בְּהֶמְתֶּךָ וְגֵרְךָ אֲשֶׁר בִּשְׁעָרֶיךָ לְמַעַן יָנוּחַ עַבְדְּךָ וַאֲמָתְךָ כָּמוֹךָ:

15 Remember that you were a slave in the land of Egypt and *Hashem* your God freed you from there with a mighty hand and an outstretched arm; therefore *Hashem* your God has commanded you to observe the *Shabbat* day.

טו וְזָכַרְתָּ כִּי־עֶבֶד הָיִיתָ בְּאֶרֶץ מִצְרַיִם וַיֹּצִאֲךָ יְהוָה אֱלֹהֶיךָ מִשָּׁם בְּיָד חֲזָקָה וּבִזְרֹעַ נְטוּיָה עַל־כֵּן צִוְּךָ יְהוָה אֱלֹהֶיךָ לַעֲשׂוֹת אֶת־יוֹם הַשַּׁבָּת:

16 Honor your father and your mother, as *Hashem* your God has commanded you, that you may long endure, and that you may fare well, in the land that *Hashem* your God is assigning to you.

טז כַּבֵּד אֶת־אָבִיךָ וְאֶת־אִמֶּךָ כַּאֲשֶׁר צִוְּךָ יְהוָה אֱלֹהֶיךָ לְמַעַן יַאֲרִיכֻן יָמֶיךָ וּלְמַעַן יִיטַב לָךְ עַל הָאֲדָמָה אֲשֶׁר־יְהוָה אֱלֹהֶיךָ נֹתֵן לָךְ:

17 You shall not murder. You shall not commit adultery. You shall not steal. You shall not bear false witness against your neighbor.

יז לֹא תִרְצָח: וְלֹא תִּנְאָף: וְלֹא תִּגְנֹב: וְלֹא־תַעֲנֶה בְרֵעֲךָ עֵד שָׁוְא:

18 You shall not covet your neighbor's wife. You shall not crave your neighbor's house, or his field, or his male or female slave, or his ox, or his ass, or anything that is your neighbor's.

יח וְלֹא תַחְמֹד אֵשֶׁת רֵעֶךָ וְלֹא תִתְאַוֶּה בֵּית רֵעֶךָ שָׂדֵהוּ וְעַבְדּוֹ וַאֲמָתוֹ שׁוֹרוֹ וַחֲמֹרוֹ וְכֹל אֲשֶׁר לְרֵעֶךָ:

16

19 *Hashem* spoke those words – those and no more – to your whole congregation at the mountain, with a mighty voice out of the fire and the dense clouds. He inscribed them on two tablets of stone, which He gave to me.

יט אֶת־הַדְּבָרִים הָאֵלֶּה דִּבֶּר יְהוָה אֶל־כָּל־קְהַלְכֶם בָּהָר מִתּוֹךְ הָאֵשׁ הֶעָנָן וְהָעֲרָפֶל קוֹל גָּדוֹל וְלֹא יָסָף וַיִּכְתְּבֵם עַל־שְׁנֵי לֻחֹת אֲבָנִים וַיִּתְּנֵם אֵלָי:

20 When you heard the voice out of the darkness, while the mountain was ablaze with fire, you came up to me, all your tribal heads and elders,

כ וַיְהִי כְּשָׁמְעֲכֶם אֶת־הַקּוֹל מִתּוֹךְ הַחֹשֶׁךְ וְהָהָר בֹּעֵר בָּאֵשׁ וַתִּקְרְבוּן אֵלַי כָּל־רָאשֵׁי שִׁבְטֵיכֶם וְזִקְנֵיכֶם:

21 and said, "*Hashem* our God has just shown us His majestic Presence, and we have heard His voice out of the fire; we have seen this day that man may live though *Hashem* has spoken to him.

כא וַתֹּאמְרוּ הֵן הֶרְאָנוּ יְהוָה אֱלֹהֵינוּ אֶת־כְּבֹדוֹ וְאֶת־גָּדְלוֹ וְאֶת־קֹלוֹ שָׁמַעְנוּ מִתּוֹךְ הָאֵשׁ הַיּוֹם הַזֶּה רָאִינוּ כִּי־יְדַבֵּר אֱלֹהִים אֶת־הָאָדָם וָחָי:

22 Let us not die, then, for this fearsome fire will consume us; if we hear the voice of *Hashem* our God any longer, we shall die.

כב וְעַתָּה לָמָּה נָמוּת כִּי תֹאכְלֵנוּ הָאֵשׁ הַגְּדֹלָה הַזֹּאת אִם־יֹסְפִים אֲנַחְנוּ לִשְׁמֹעַ אֶת־קוֹל יְהוָה אֱלֹהֵינוּ עוֹד וָמָתְנוּ:

23 For what mortal ever heard the voice of the living *Hashem* speak out of the fire, as we did, and lived?

כג כִּי מִי כָל־בָּשָׂר אֲשֶׁר שָׁמַע קוֹל אֱלֹהִים חַיִּים מְדַבֵּר מִתּוֹךְ־הָאֵשׁ כָּמֹנוּ וַיֶּחִי:

24 You go closer and hear all that *Hashem* our God says, and then you tell us everything that *Hashem* our God tells you, and we will willingly do it."

כד קְרַב אַתָּה וּשֲׁמַע אֵת כָּל־אֲשֶׁר יֹאמַר יְהוָה אֱלֹהֵינוּ וְאַתְּ תְּדַבֵּר אֵלֵינוּ אֵת כָּל־אֲשֶׁר יְדַבֵּר יְהוָה אֱלֹהֵינוּ אֵלֶיךָ וְשָׁמַעְנוּ וְעָשִׂינוּ:

25 *Hashem* heard the plea that you made to me, and *Hashem* said to me, "I have heard the plea that this people made to you; they did well to speak thus.

כה וַיִּשְׁמַע יְהוָה אֶת־קוֹל דִּבְרֵיכֶם בְּדַבֶּרְכֶם אֵלָי וַיֹּאמֶר יְהוָה אֵלַי שָׁמַעְתִּי אֶת־קוֹל דִּבְרֵי הָעָם הַזֶּה אֲשֶׁר דִּבְּרוּ אֵלֶיךָ הֵיטִיבוּ כָּל־אֲשֶׁר דִּבֵּרוּ:

26 May they always be of such mind, to revere Me and follow all My commandments, that it may go well with them and with their children forever!

כו מִי־יִתֵּן וְהָיָה לְבָבָם זֶה לָהֶם לְיִרְאָה אֹתִי וְלִשְׁמֹר אֶת־כָּל־מִצְוֹתַי כָּל־הַיָּמִים לְמַעַן יִיטַב לָהֶם וְלִבְנֵיהֶם לְעֹלָם:

27 Go, say to them, 'Return to your tents.'

כז לֵךְ אֱמֹר לָהֶם שׁוּבוּ לָכֶם לְאָהֳלֵיכֶם:

28 But you remain here with Me, and I will give you the whole Instruction – the laws and the rules – that you shall impart to them, for them to observe in the land that I am giving them to possess."

כח וְאַתָּה פֹּה עֲמֹד עִמָּדִי וַאֲדַבְּרָה אֵלֶיךָ אֵת כָּל־הַמִּצְוָה וְהַחֻקִּים וְהַמִּשְׁפָּטִים אֲשֶׁר תְּלַמְּדֵם וְעָשׂוּ בָאָרֶץ אֲשֶׁר אָנֹכִי נֹתֵן לָהֶם לְרִשְׁתָּהּ:

v'-a-TAH POH a-MOD i-ma-DEE va-a-da-b'-RA ay-LE-kha AYT kol
ha-mitz-VAH v'-ha-khu-KEEM v'-ha-mish-pa-TEEM a-SHER t'-la-m'-DAYM
v'-a-SU va-A-retz a-SHER a-no-KHEE no-TAYN la-HEM l'-rish-TAH

5:28 For them to observe in the land that I am giving them to possess Some of the commandments are unique to the Land of Israel, while others apply everywhere. However, according to the Sages, even those commandments that can be performed anywhere in the world carry greater weight when performed in *Eretz Yisrael*. Not only is the land itself special, but every good deed done there takes on added meaning and value.

A vineyard in Gush Etzion, Israel

Deuteronomy

Deuteronomy

29 Be careful, then, to do as *Hashem* your God has commanded you. Do not turn aside to the right or to the left:

כט וּשְׁמַרְתֶּם לַעֲשׂוֹת כַּאֲשֶׁר צִוָּה יְהֹוָה אֱלֹהֵיכֶם אֶתְכֶם לֹא תָסֻרוּ יָמִין וּשְׂמֹאל:

30 follow only the path that *Hashem* your God has enjoined upon you, so that you may thrive and that it may go well with you, and that you may long endure in the land you are to possess.

ל בְּכָל־הַדֶּרֶךְ אֲשֶׁר צִוָּה יְהֹוָה אֱלֹהֵיכֶם אֶתְכֶם תֵּלֵכוּ לְמַעַן תִּחְיוּן וְטוֹב לָכֶם וְהַאֲרַכְתֶּם יָמִים בָּאָרֶץ אֲשֶׁר תִּירָשׁוּן:

6 ¹ And this is the Instruction – the laws and the rules – that *Hashem* your God has commanded [me] to impart to you, to be observed in the land that you are about to cross into and occupy,

א וְזֹאת הַמִּצְוָה הַחֻקִּים וְהַמִּשְׁפָּטִים אֲשֶׁר צִוָּה יְהֹוָה אֱלֹהֵיכֶם לְלַמֵּד אֶתְכֶם לַעֲשׂוֹת בָּאָרֶץ אֲשֶׁר אַתֶּם עֹבְרִים שָׁמָּה לְרִשְׁתָּהּ:

² so that you, your children, and your children's children may revere *Hashem* your God and follow, as long as you live, all His laws and commandments that I enjoin upon you, to the end that you may long endure.

ב לְמַעַן תִּירָא אֶת־יְהֹוָה אֱלֹהֶיךָ לִשְׁמֹר אֶת־כָּל־חֻקֹּתָיו וּמִצְוֹתָיו אֲשֶׁר אָנֹכִי מְצַוֶּךָ אַתָּה וּבִנְךָ וּבֶן־בִּנְךָ כֹּל יְמֵי חַיֶּיךָ וּלְמַעַן יַאֲרִכֻן יָמֶיךָ:

³ Obey, O *Yisrael*, willingly and faithfully, that it may go well with you and that you may increase greatly [in] a land flowing with milk and honey, as *Hashem*, the God of your fathers, spoke to you.

ג וְשָׁמַעְתָּ יִשְׂרָאֵל וְשָׁמַרְתָּ לַעֲשׂוֹת אֲשֶׁר יִיטַב לְךָ וַאֲשֶׁר תִּרְבּוּן מְאֹד כַּאֲשֶׁר דִּבֶּר יְהֹוָה אֱלֹהֵי אֲבֹתֶיךָ לָךְ אֶרֶץ זָבַת חָלָב וּדְבָשׁ:

⁴ Hear, O *Yisrael*! *Hashem* is our God, *Hashem* alone.

ד שְׁמַע יִשְׂרָאֵל יְהֹוָה אֱלֹהֵינוּ יְהֹוָה אֶחָד:

sh'-MA yis-ra-AYL a-do-NAI e-lo-HAY-nu a-do-NAI e-KHAD

⁵ You shall love *Hashem* your God with all your heart and with all your soul and with all your might.

ה וְאָהַבְתָּ אֵת יְהֹוָה אֱלֹהֶיךָ בְּכָל־לְבָבְךָ וּבְכָל־נַפְשְׁךָ וּבְכָל־מְאֹדֶךָ:

⁶ Take to heart these instructions with which I charge you this day.

ו וְהָיוּ הַדְּבָרִים הָאֵלֶּה אֲשֶׁר אָנֹכִי מְצַוְּךָ הַיּוֹם עַל־לְבָבֶךָ:

v'-ha-YU ha-d'-va-REEM ha-AY-leh a-SHER a-no-KHEE m'-tza-v'-KHA ha-YOM al l'-va-VE-kha

6:4 *Hashem* is our God, *Hashem* alone The single most important belief in Judaism is the belief in monotheism, the oneness of God. This key principle is attested to in this fundamental verse, known as the *Shema*, which is recited twice each day by Jews. In the unique system of *gematriya*, in which every Hebrew letter is assigned a numerical value, the word echad (אחד), which means 'one' and is translated here as 'alone,' adds up to 13: א equals 1, ח equals 8, and ד equals 4. Interestingly, 13 is also the numerical value of the word *ahava* (אהבה), 'love,' as א equals 1, ה equals 5, ב equals 2, and ה equals 5. The hidden message of this *gematriya* is that the greatest love a person can feel is the love of the one and only God, whose very essence is love.

Reading from the *Torah* at the Western Wall

6:6 These instructions with which I charge you this day *Rashi*, the great *Torah* commentator, asks why *Moshe* says that he is commanding the people the laws of the *Torah* "this day," since the *Torah* had actually been given thirty-eight years earlier. He explains that this expression indicates that we must always look at the teachings of the Bible as if they are new and exciting, as if they were given today, and not as outdated or relics of the past. New lessons of growth and inspiration relevant to our contemporary lives can always be found in the *Torah*, if we merely look for them.

אחד

7 Impress them upon your children. Recite them when you stay at home and when you are away, when you lie down and when you get up.

ז וְשִׁנַּנְתָּ֣ם לְבָנֶ֔יךָ וְדִבַּרְתָּ֖ בָּ֑ם בְּשִׁבְתְּךָ֤ בְּבֵיתֶ֨ךָ֙ וּבְלֶכְתְּךָ֣ בַדֶּ֔רֶךְ וּֽבְשָׁכְבְּךָ֖ וּבְקוּמֶֽךָ:

8 Bind them as a sign on your hand and let them serve as a symbol on your forehead;

ח וּקְשַׁרְתָּ֥ם לְא֖וֹת עַל־יָדֶ֑ךָ וְהָי֥וּ לְטֹטָפֹ֖ת בֵּ֥ין עֵינֶֽיךָ:

9 inscribe them on the doorposts of your house and on your gates.

ט וּכְתַבְתָּ֛ם עַל־מְזֻז֥וֹת בֵּיתֶ֖ךָ וּבִשְׁעָרֶֽיךָ:

10 When *Hashem* your God brings you into the land that He swore to your fathers, *Avraham, Yitzchak,* and *Yaakov,* to assign to you – great and flourishing cities that you did not build,

י וְהָיָ֞ה כִּ֥י יְבִֽיאֲךָ֣ ׀ יְהֹוָ֣ה אֱלֹהֶ֗יךָ אֶל־הָאָ֜רֶץ אֲשֶׁ֨ר נִשְׁבַּ֧ע לַֽאֲבֹתֶ֛יךָ לְאַבְרָהָ֛ם לְיִצְחָ֥ק וּֽלְיַֽעֲקֹ֖ב לָ֣תֶת לָ֑ךְ עָרִ֛ים גְּדֹלֹ֥ת וְטֹבֹ֖ת אֲשֶׁ֥ר לֹֽא־בָנִֽיתָ:

11 houses full of all good things that you did not fill, hewn cisterns that you did not hew, vineyards and olive groves that you did not plant – and you eat your fill,

יא וּבָתִּ֜ים מְלֵאִ֣ים כָּל־טוּב֮ אֲשֶׁ֣ר לֹֽא־מִלֵּ֒אתָ֒ וּבֹרֹ֤ת חֲצוּבִים֙ אֲשֶׁ֣ר לֹֽא־חָצַ֔בְתָּ כְּרָמִ֥ים וְזֵיתִ֖ים אֲשֶׁ֣ר לֹֽא־נָטָ֑עְתָּ וְאָֽכַלְתָּ֖ וְשָׂבָֽעְתָּ:

12 take heed that you do not forget *Hashem* who freed you from the land of Egypt, the house of bondage.

יב הִשָּׁ֣מֶר לְךָ֔ פֶּן־תִּשְׁכַּ֖ח אֶת־יְהֹוָ֑ה אֲשֶׁ֧ר הֽוֹצִיאֲךָ֛ מֵאֶ֥רֶץ מִצְרַ֖יִם מִבֵּ֥ית עֲבָדִֽים:

13 Revere only *Hashem* your God and worship Him alone, and swear only by His name.

יג אֶת־יְהֹוָ֧ה אֱלֹהֶ֛יךָ תִּירָ֖א וְאֹת֣וֹ תַֽעֲבֹ֑ד וּבִשְׁמ֖וֹ תִּשָּׁבֵֽעַ:

14 Do not follow other gods, any gods of the peoples about you

יד לֹ֣א תֵֽלְכ֔וּן אַֽחֲרֵ֖י אֱלֹהִ֣ים אֲחֵרִ֑ים מֵֽאֱלֹהֵי֙ הָֽעַמִּ֔ים אֲשֶׁ֖ר סְבִיבֽוֹתֵיכֶֽם:

15 for *Hashem* your God in your midst is an impassioned God – lest the anger of *Hashem* your God blaze forth against you and He wipe you off the face of the earth.

טו כִּ֣י אֵ֥ל קַנָּ֛א יְהֹוָ֥ה אֱלֹהֶ֖יךָ בְּקִרְבֶּ֑ךָ פֶּן־יֶֽ֠חֱרֶ֠ה אַף־יְהֹוָ֤ה אֱלֹהֶ֨יךָ֙ בָּ֔ךְ וְהִשְׁמִ֣ידְךָ֔ מֵעַ֖ל פְּנֵ֥י הָֽאֲדָמָֽה:

16 Do not try *Hashem* your God, as you did at Massah.

טז לֹ֣א תְנַסּ֔וּ אֶת־יְהֹוָ֖ה אֱלֹֽהֵיכֶ֑ם כַּֽאֲשֶׁ֥ר נִסִּיתֶ֖ם בַּמַּסָּֽה:

17 Be sure to keep the commandments, decrees, and laws that *Hashem* your God has enjoined upon you.

יז שָׁמ֣וֹר תִּשְׁמְר֔וּן אֶת־מִצְוֺ֖ת יְהֹוָ֣ה אֱלֹֽהֵיכֶ֑ם וְעֵֽדֹתָ֖יו וְחֻקָּ֥יו אֲשֶׁ֥ר צִוָּֽךְ:

18 Do what is right and good in the sight of *Hashem,* that it may go well with you and that you may be able to possess the good land that *Hashem* your God promised on oath to your fathers,

יח וְעָשִׂ֛יתָ הַיָּשָׁ֥ר וְהַטּ֖וֹב בְּעֵינֵ֣י יְהֹוָ֑ה לְמַ֨עַן֙ יִ֣יטַב לָ֔ךְ וּבָ֗אתָ וְיָֽרַשְׁתָּ֙ אֶת־הָאָ֣רֶץ הַטֹּבָ֔ה אֲשֶׁר־נִשְׁבַּ֥ע יְהֹוָ֖ה לַֽאֲבֹתֶֽיךָ:

19 and that all your enemies may be driven out before you, as *Hashem* has spoken.

יט לַֽהֲדֹ֥ף אֶת־כָּל־אֹֽיְבֶ֖יךָ מִפָּנֶ֑יךָ כַּֽאֲשֶׁ֖ר דִּבֶּ֥ר יְהֹוָֽה:

20 When, in time to come, your children ask you, "What mean the decrees, laws, and rules that *Hashem* our God has enjoined upon you?"

כ כִּֽי־יִשְׁאָֽלְךָ֥ בִנְךָ֛ מָחָ֖ר לֵאמֹ֑ר מָ֣ה הָֽעֵדֹ֗ת וְהַֽחֻקִּים֙ וְהַמִּשְׁפָּטִ֔ים אֲשֶׁ֥ר צִוָּ֛ה יְהֹוָ֥ה אֱלֹהֵ֖ינוּ אֶתְכֶֽם:

21 you shall say to your children, "We were slaves to Pharaoh in Egypt and *Hashem* freed us from Egypt with a mighty hand.

כא וְאָֽמַרְתָּ֣ לְבִנְךָ֔ עֲבָדִ֥ים הָיִ֛ינוּ לְפַרְעֹ֖ה בְּמִצְרָ֑יִם וַיֹּֽצִיאֵ֧נוּ יְהֹוָ֛ה מִמִּצְרַ֖יִם בְּיָ֥ד חֲזָקָֽה:

22 *Hashem* wrought before our eyes marvelous and destructive signs and portents in Egypt, against Pharaoh and all his household;

כב וַיִּתֵּן יְהֹוָה אוֹתֹת וּמֹפְתִים גְּדֹלִים וְרָעִים בְּמִצְרַיִם בְּפַרְעֹה וּבְכָל־בֵּיתוֹ לְעֵינֵינוּ:

23 and us He freed from there, that He might take us and give us the land that He had promised on oath to our fathers.

כג וְאוֹתָנוּ הוֹצִיא מִשָּׁם לְמַעַן הָבִיא אֹתָנוּ לָתֶת לָנוּ אֶת־הָאָרֶץ אֲשֶׁר נִשְׁבַּע לַאֲבֹתֵינוּ:

v'-o-TA-nu ho-TZEE mi-SHAM l'-MA-an ha-VEE o-TA-nu LA-tet
LA-nu et ha-A-retz a-SHER nish-BA la-a-vo-TAY-nu

24 Then *Hashem* commanded us to observe all these laws, to revere *Hashem* our God, for our lasting good and for our survival, as is now the case.

כד וַיְצַוֵּנוּ יְהֹוָה לַעֲשׂוֹת אֶת־כָּל־הַחֻקִּים הָאֵלֶּה לְיִרְאָה אֶת־יְהֹוָה אֱלֹהֵינוּ לְטוֹב לָנוּ כָּל־הַיָּמִים לְחַיֹּתֵנוּ כְּהַיּוֹם הַזֶּה:

25 It will be therefore to our merit before *Hashem* our God to observe faithfully this whole Instruction, as He has commanded us."

כה וּצְדָקָה תִּהְיֶה־לָּנוּ כִּי־נִשְׁמֹר לַעֲשׂוֹת אֶת־כָּל־הַמִּצְוָה הַזֹּאת לִפְנֵי יְהֹוָה אֱלֹהֵינוּ כַּאֲשֶׁר צִוָּנוּ:

7 1 When *Hashem* your God brings you to the land that you are about to enter and possess, and He dislodges many nations before you – the Hittites, Girgashites, Amorites, Canaanites, Perizzites, Hivites, and Jebusites, seven nations much larger than you

ז א כִּי יְבִיאֲךָ יְהֹוָה אֱלֹהֶיךָ אֶל־הָאָרֶץ אֲשֶׁר־אַתָּה בָא־שָׁמָּה לְרִשְׁתָּהּ וְנָשַׁל גּוֹיִם־רַבִּים מִפָּנֶיךָ הַחִתִּי וְהַגִּרְגָּשִׁי וְהָאֱמֹרִי וְהַכְּנַעֲנִי וְהַפְּרִזִּי וְהַחִוִּי וְהַיְבוּסִי שִׁבְעָה גוֹיִם רַבִּים וַעֲצוּמִים מִמֶּךָּ:

2 and *Hashem* your God delivers them to you and you defeat them, you must doom them to destruction: grant them no terms and give them no quarter.

ב וּנְתָנָם יְהֹוָה אֱלֹהֶיךָ לְפָנֶיךָ וְהִכִּיתָם הַחֲרֵם תַּחֲרִים אֹתָם לֹא־תִכְרֹת לָהֶם בְּרִית וְלֹא תְחָנֵּם:

3 You shall not intermarry with them: do not give your daughters to their sons or take their daughters for your sons.

ג וְלֹא תִתְחַתֵּן בָּם בִּתְּךָ לֹא־תִתֵּן לִבְנוֹ וּבִתּוֹ לֹא־תִקַּח לִבְנֶךָ:

4 For they will turn your children away from Me to worship other gods, and *Hashem*'s anger will blaze forth against you and He will promptly wipe you out.

ד כִּי־יָסִיר אֶת־בִּנְךָ מֵאַחֲרַי וְעָבְדוּ אֱלֹהִים אֲחֵרִים וְחָרָה אַף־יְהֹוָה בָּכֶם וְהִשְׁמִידְךָ מַהֵר:

6:23 And us He freed from there Israel's first Prime Minister, David Ben Gurion, summed up this verse in a speech he gave to the Peel Commission in 1936. "Three-hundred years ago, there came to the New World a boat, and its name was the Mayflower. The Mayflower's landing on Plymouth Rock was one of the great historical events in the history of England and in the history of America. But I would like to ask any Englishman sitting here on the commission, what date did the Mayflower leave port? How many people were on the boat? Who were their leaders? What kind of food did they eat on the boat? More than three-thousand three-hundred years ago, long before the Mayflower, our people left Egypt, and every Jew in the world, wherever he is, knows what day they left. And he knows what food they ate. And we still eat that food with every anniversary. And we know who our leader was. And we sit down and tell the story to our children and grandchildren, in order to guarantee that it will never be forgotten. And we say our two slogans: 'Now we may be enslaved, but next year, we'll be a free people.' ... Now we are in the prison of the Soviet Union. Now, we're in Germany where Hitler is destroying us. Now we're scattered throughout the world, but next year, we'll be in Jerusalem. There'll come a day that we'll come home to Zion, to the Land of Israel. That is the nature of the Jewish people."

Prime Minister
David Ben Gurion
(1886–1973)

5 Instead, this is what you shall do to them: you shall tear down their altars, smash their pillars, cut down their sacred posts, and consign their images to the fire.

6 For you are a people consecrated to *Hashem* your God: of all the peoples on earth *Hashem* your God chose you to be His treasured people.

7 It is not because you are the most numerous of peoples that *Hashem* set His heart on you and chose you – indeed, you are the smallest of peoples;

8 but it was because *Hashem* favored you and kept the oath He made to your fathers that *Hashem* freed you with a mighty hand and rescued you from the house of bondage, from the power of Pharaoh king of Egypt.

9 Know, therefore, that only *Hashem* your God is *Hashem*, the steadfast *Hashem* who keeps His covenant faithfully to the thousandth generation of those who love Him and keep His commandments,

10 but who instantly requites with destruction those who reject Him – never slow with those who reject Him, but requiting them instantly.

11 Therefore, observe faithfully the Instruction – the laws and the rules – with which I charge you today.

12 And if you do obey these rules and observe them carefully, *Hashem* your God will maintain faithfully for you the covenant that He made on oath with your fathers:

ה כִּי־אִם־כֹּה תַעֲשׂוּ לָהֶם מִזְבְּחֹתֵיהֶם תִּתֹּצוּ וּמַצֵּבֹתָם תְּשַׁבֵּרוּ וַאֲשֵׁירֵהֶם תְּגַדֵּעוּן וּפְסִילֵיהֶם תִּשְׂרְפוּן בָּאֵשׁ:

ו כִּי עַם קָדוֹשׁ אַתָּה לַיהוָה אֱלֹהֶיךָ בְּךָ בָּחַר יְהוָה אֱלֹהֶיךָ לִהְיוֹת לוֹ לְעַם סְגֻלָּה מִכֹּל הָעַמִּים אֲשֶׁר עַל־פְּנֵי הָאֲדָמָה:

ז לֹא מֵרֻבְּכֶם מִכָּל־הָעַמִּים חָשַׁק יְהוָה בָּכֶם וַיִּבְחַר בָּכֶם כִּי־אַתֶּם הַמְעַט מִכָּל־הָעַמִּים:

ח כִּי מֵאַהֲבַת יְהוָה אֶתְכֶם וּמִשָּׁמְרוֹ אֶת־הַשְּׁבֻעָה אֲשֶׁר נִשְׁבַּע לַאֲבֹתֵיכֶם הוֹצִיא יְהוָה אֶתְכֶם בְּיָד חֲזָקָה וַיִּפְדְּךָ מִבֵּית עֲבָדִים מִיַּד פַּרְעֹה מֶלֶךְ־מִצְרָיִם:

ט וְיָדַעְתָּ כִּי־יְהוָה אֱלֹהֶיךָ הוּא הָאֱלֹהִים הָאֵל הַנֶּאֱמָן שֹׁמֵר הַבְּרִית וְהַחֶסֶד לְאֹהֲבָיו וּלְשֹׁמְרֵי מצותו [מִצְוֹתָיו] לְאֶלֶף דּוֹר:

י וּמְשַׁלֵּם לְשֹׂנְאָיו אֶל־פָּנָיו לְהַאֲבִידוֹ לֹא יְאַחֵר לְשֹׂנְאוֹ אֶל־פָּנָיו יְשַׁלֶּם־לוֹ:

יא וְשָׁמַרְתָּ אֶת־הַמִּצְוָה וְאֶת־הַחֻקִּים וְאֶת־הַמִּשְׁפָּטִים אֲשֶׁר אָנֹכִי מְצַוְּךָ הַיּוֹם לַעֲשׂוֹתָם:

יב וְהָיָה עֵקֶב תִּשְׁמְעוּן אֵת הַמִּשְׁפָּטִים הָאֵלֶּה וּשְׁמַרְתֶּם וַעֲשִׂיתֶם אֹתָם וְשָׁמַר יְהוָה אֱלֹהֶיךָ לְךָ אֶת־הַבְּרִית וְאֶת־הַחֶסֶד אֲשֶׁר נִשְׁבַּע לַאֲבֹתֶיךָ:

v'-ha-YAH AY-kev tish-m'-UN AYT ha-mish-pa-TEEM ha-AY-leh
ush-mar-TEM va-a-see-TEM o-TAM v'-sha-MAR a-do-NAI e-lo-HE-kha
l'-KHA et ha-b'-REET v'-et ha-KHE-sed a-SHER nish-BA la-a-vo-TE-kha

עקב

7:12 And if you do obey these rules In this verse, *Hashem* promises that if we listen to His commandments, He will bless us and multiply us, and grant us success in the Land of Israel. The Hebrew word for 'and if you do,' *eikev* (עקב), also means 'heel.' *Rashi* quotes the Sages who teach that the use of the word *eikev* hints to the fact that we must keep all the commandments equally, even the ones that seem unimportant, which people tend to figuratively step on with their heels. If we are careful to follow all the commandments of *Hashem*, even the seemingly insignificant ones, then

A flourishing field in the Galilee

we will certainly be rewarded with great blessings in the Promised Land.

13 He will favor you and bless you and multiply you; He will bless the issue of your womb and the produce of your soil, your new grain and wine and oil, the calving of your herd and the lambing of your flock, in the land that He swore to your fathers to assign to you.

14 You shall be blessed above all other peoples: there shall be no sterile male or female among you or among your livestock.

15 *Hashem* will ward off from you all sickness; He will not bring upon you any of the dreadful diseases of Egypt, about which you know, but will inflict them upon all your enemies.

16 You shall destroy all the peoples that *Hashem* your God delivers to you, showing them no pity. And you shall not worship their gods, for that would be a snare to you.

17 Should you say to yourselves, "These nations are more numerous than we; how can we dispossess them?"

18 You need have no fear of them. You have but to bear in mind what *Hashem* your God did to Pharaoh and all the Egyptians:

19 the wondrous acts that you saw with your own eyes, the signs and the portents, the mighty hand, and the outstretched arm by which *Hashem* your God liberated you. Thus will *Hashem* your God do to all the peoples you now fear.

20 *Hashem* your God will also send a plague against them, until those who are left in hiding perish before you.

21 Do not stand in dread of them, for *Hashem* your God is in your midst, a great and awesome God.

22 *Hashem* your God will dislodge those peoples before you little by little; you will not be able to put an end to them at once, else the wild beasts would multiply to your hurt.

יג וַאֲהֵבְךָ וּבֵרַכְךָ וְהִרְבֶּךָ וּבֵרַךְ פְּרִי־בִטְנְךָ וּפְרִי־אַדְמָתֶךָ דְּגָנְךָ וְתִירֹשְׁךָ וְיִצְהָרֶךָ שְׁגַר־אֲלָפֶיךָ וְעַשְׁתְּרֹת צֹאנֶךָ עַל הָאֲדָמָה אֲשֶׁר־נִשְׁבַּע לַאֲבֹתֶיךָ לָתֶת לָךְ:

יד בָּרוּךְ תִּהְיֶה מִכָּל־הָעַמִּים לֹא־יִהְיֶה בְךָ עָקָר וַעֲקָרָה וּבִבְהֶמְתֶּךָ:

טו וְהֵסִיר יְהוָֹה מִמְּךָ כָּל־חֹלִי וְכָל־מַדְוֵי מִצְרַיִם הָרָעִים אֲשֶׁר יָדַעְתָּ לֹא יְשִׂימָם בָּךְ וּנְתָנָם בְּכָל־שֹׂנְאֶיךָ:

טז וְאָכַלְתָּ אֶת־כָּל־הָעַמִּים אֲשֶׁר יְהוָֹה אֱלֹהֶיךָ נֹתֵן לָךְ לֹא־תָחֹס עֵינְךָ עֲלֵיהֶם וְלֹא תַעֲבֹד אֶת־אֱלֹהֵיהֶם כִּי־מוֹקֵשׁ הוּא לָךְ:

יז כִּי תֹאמַר בִּלְבָבְךָ רַבִּים הַגּוֹיִם הָאֵלֶּה מִמֶּנִּי אֵיכָה אוּכַל לְהוֹרִישָׁם:

יח לֹא תִירָא מֵהֶם זָכֹר תִּזְכֹּר אֵת אֲשֶׁר־עָשָׂה יְהוָֹה אֱלֹהֶיךָ לְפַרְעֹה וּלְכָל־מִצְרָיִם:

יט הַמַּסֹּת הַגְּדֹלֹת אֲשֶׁר־רָאוּ עֵינֶיךָ וְהָאֹתֹת וְהַמֹּפְתִים וְהַיָּד הַחֲזָקָה וְהַזְּרֹעַ הַנְּטוּיָה אֲשֶׁר הוֹצִאֲךָ יְהוָֹה אֱלֹהֶיךָ כֵּן־יַעֲשֶׂה יְהוָֹה אֱלֹהֶיךָ לְכָל־הָעַמִּים אֲשֶׁר־אַתָּה יָרֵא מִפְּנֵיהֶם:

כ וְגַם אֶת־הַצִּרְעָה יְשַׁלַּח יְהוָֹה אֱלֹהֶיךָ בָּם עַד־אֲבֹד הַנִּשְׁאָרִים וְהַנִּסְתָּרִים מִפָּנֶיךָ:

כא לֹא תַעֲרֹץ מִפְּנֵיהֶם כִּי־יְהוָֹה אֱלֹהֶיךָ בְּקִרְבֶּךָ אֵל גָּדוֹל וְנוֹרָא:

כב וְנָשַׁל יְהוָֹה אֱלֹהֶיךָ אֶת־הַגּוֹיִם הָאֵל מִפָּנֶיךָ מְעַט מְעָט לֹא תוּכַל כַּלֹּתָם מַהֵר פֶּן־תִּרְבֶּה עָלֶיךָ חַיַּת הַשָּׂדֶה:

*v'-na-SHAL a-do-NAI e-lo-HE-kha et ha-go-YIM ha-AYL
mi-pa-NE-kha m'-AT m'-AT LO tu-KHAL ka-lo-TAM
ma-HAYR pen tir-BEH a-LE-kha kha-YAT ha-sa-DEH*

7:22 ***Hashem*** **your God will dislodge those peoples before you little by little** In response to the concern that the People of Israel will not be able to drive the nations of Canaan out of their land, *Hashem* reassures them with a surprising promise: "*Hashem* your God will dislodge those peoples before you little by little." Would it not be

²³ *Hashem* your God will deliver them up to you, throwing them into utter panic until they are wiped out.

כג וּנְתָנָם יְהוָה אֱלֹהֶיךָ לְפָנֶיךָ וְהָמָם מְהוּמָה גְדֹלָה עַד הִשָּׁמְדָם:

²⁴ He will deliver their kings into your hand, and you shall obliterate their name from under the heavens; no man shall stand up to you, until you have wiped them out.

כד וְנָתַן מַלְכֵיהֶם בְּיָדֶךָ וְהַאֲבַדְתָּ אֶת־שְׁמָם מִתַּחַת הַשָּׁמָיִם לֹא־יִתְיַצֵּב אִישׁ בְּפָנֶיךָ עַד הִשְׁמִדְךָ אֹתָם:

²⁵ You shall consign the images of their gods to the fire; you shall not covet the silver and gold on them and keep it for yourselves, lest you be ensnared thereby; for that is abhorrent to *Hashem* your God.

כה פְּסִילֵי אֱלֹהֵיהֶם תִּשְׂרְפוּן בָּאֵשׁ לֹא־תַחְמֹד כֶּסֶף וְזָהָב עֲלֵיהֶם וְלָקַחְתָּ לָךְ פֶּן תִּוָּקֵשׁ בּוֹ כִּי תוֹעֲבַת יְהוָה אֱלֹהֶיךָ הוּא:

²⁶ You must not bring an abhorrent thing into your house, or you will be proscribed like it; you must reject it as abominable and abhorrent, for it is proscribed.

כו וְלֹא־תָבִיא תוֹעֵבָה אֶל־בֵּיתֶךָ וְהָיִיתָ חֵרֶם כָּמֹהוּ שַׁקֵּץ תְּשַׁקְּצֶנּוּ וְתַעֵב תְּתַעֲבֶנּוּ כִּי־חֵרֶם הוּא:

8 ¹ You shall faithfully observe all the Instruction that I enjoin upon you today, that you may thrive and increase and be able to possess the land that *Hashem* promised on oath to your fathers.

ח א כָּל־הַמִּצְוָה אֲשֶׁר אָנֹכִי מְצַוְּךָ הַיּוֹם תִּשְׁמְרוּן לַעֲשׂוֹת לְמַעַן תִּחְיוּן וּרְבִיתֶם וּבָאתֶם וִירִשְׁתֶּם אֶת־הָאָרֶץ אֲשֶׁר־נִשְׁבַּע יְהוָה לַאֲבֹתֵיכֶם:

*kol ha-mitz-VAH a-SHER a-no-KHEE m'-tza-v'-KHA ha-YOM
tish-m'-RUN la-a-SOT l'-MA-an tikh-YUN ur-vee-TEM u-va-TEM
vee-rish-TEM et ha-A-retz a-sher nish-BA a-do-NAI la-a-vo-tay-KHEM*

² Remember the long way that *Hashem* your God has made you travel in the wilderness these past forty years, that He might test you by hardships to learn what was in your hearts: whether you would keep His commandments or not.

ב וְזָכַרְתָּ אֶת־כָּל־הַדֶּרֶךְ אֲשֶׁר הֹלִיכְךָ יְהוָה אֱלֹהֶיךָ זֶה אַרְבָּעִים שָׁנָה בַּמִּדְבָּר לְמַעַן עַנֹּתְךָ לְנַסֹּתְךָ לָדַעַת אֶת־אֲשֶׁר בִּלְבָבְךָ הֲתִשְׁמֹר מִצְוֹתוֹ [מִצְוֹתָיו] אִם־לֹא:

חי more comforting to know that the period of conquest would be quick, as opposed to long and drawn out? How is this promise of a, protracted military campaign of comfort to the people? The end of the verse provides the answer. If all of the people of *Canaan* would have fled at one time, large portions of land would have been left

The Negev desert

unpopulated, allowing for dangerous, wild beasts to enter and roam the land. In order to prevent this from happening, the Israelites were told that they would capture the land in stages. The modern era has also seen the remarkable return of Jewish people to their land, and it has again happened in stages, "little by little."

א **8:1 That you may thrive** The *Kli Yakar* notes that in Hebrew this verse starts in the singular, "all the Instruction that I enjoin upon you today," but finishes in the plural, "that you may thrive and increase and be able to possess the land that *Hashem* promised on oath to your fathers." He suggests that this is because the positive actions of even a single person can benefit the entire world. An individual following one commandment can bring merit to many, and ensure that they live and thrive. Furthermore, the words in this verse, as in so many others throughout the Bible, directly connect the blessing of life to living in the Land of Israel. It is in every person's power not only to enable others to live, but to "thrive and increase and be able to possess the land that *Hashem* promised on oath to your fathers."

³ He subjected you to the hardship of hunger and then gave you manna to eat, which neither you nor your fathers had ever known, in order to teach you that man does not live on bread alone, but that man may live on anything that *Hashem* decrees.

ג וַיְעַנְּךָ וַיַּרְעִבֶךָ וַיַּאֲכִלְךָ אֶת־הַמָּן אֲשֶׁר לֹא־יָדַעְתָּ וְלֹא יָדְעוּן אֲבֹתֶיךָ לְמַעַן הוֹדִיעֲךָ כִּי לֹא עַל־הַלֶּחֶם לְבַדּוֹ יִחְיֶה הָאָדָם כִּי עַל־כָּל־מוֹצָא פִי־יהוה יִחְיֶה הָאָדָם:

⁴ The clothes upon you did not wear out, nor did your feet swell these forty years.

ד שִׂמְלָתְךָ לֹא בָלְתָה מֵעָלֶיךָ וְרַגְלְךָ לֹא בָצֵקָה זֶה אַרְבָּעִים שָׁנָה:

⁵ Bear in mind that *Hashem* your God disciplines you just as a man disciplines his son.

ה וְיָדַעְתָּ עִם־לְבָבֶךָ כִּי כַּאֲשֶׁר יְיַסֵּר אִישׁ אֶת־בְּנוֹ יהוה אֱלֹהֶיךָ מְיַסְּרֶךָּ:

⁶ Therefore keep the commandments of *Hashem* your God: walk in His ways and revere Him.

ו וְשָׁמַרְתָּ אֶת־מִצְוֹת יהוה אֱלֹהֶיךָ לָלֶכֶת בִּדְרָכָיו וּלְיִרְאָה אֹתוֹ:

⁷ For *Hashem* your God is bringing you into a good land, a land with streams and springs and fountains issuing from plain and hill;

ז כִּי יהוה אֱלֹהֶיךָ מְבִיאֲךָ אֶל־אֶרֶץ טוֹבָה אֶרֶץ נַחֲלֵי מָיִם עֲיָנֹת וּתְהֹמֹת יֹצְאִים בַּבִּקְעָה וּבָהָר:

KEE a-do-NAI e-lo-HE-kha m'-vee-a-KHA el E-retz to-VAH E-retz NA-kha-lay
MA-yim a-ya-NOT ut-ho-MOT yo-tz'-EEM ba-bik-AH u-va-HAR

⁸ a land of wheat and barley, of vines, figs, and pomegranates, a land of olive trees and honey;

ח אֶרֶץ חִטָּה וּשְׂעֹרָה וְגֶפֶן וּתְאֵנָה וְרִמּוֹן אֶרֶץ־זֵית שֶׁמֶן וּדְבָשׁ:

E-retz khi-TAH us-o-RAH v'-GE-fen ut-ay-NAH
v'-ree-MON e-retz ZAYT SHE-men ud-VASH

⁹ a land where you may eat food without stint, where you will lack nothing; a land whose rocks are iron and from whose hills you can mine copper.

ט אֶרֶץ אֲשֶׁר לֹא בְמִסְכֵּנֻת תֹּאכַל־בָּהּ לֶחֶם לֹא־תֶחְסַר כֹּל בָּהּ אֶרֶץ אֲשֶׁר אֲבָנֶיהָ בַרְזֶל וּמֵהֲרָרֶיהָ תַּחְצֹב נְחֹשֶׁת:

E-retz a-SHER LO v'-mis-kay-NUT to-khal BA LE-khem lo tekh-SAR KOL BA
E-retz a-SHER a-va-NE-ha var-ZEL u-may-ha-ra-RE-ha takh-TZOV n'-KHO-shet

¹⁰ When you have eaten your fill, give thanks to *Hashem* your God for the good land which He has given you.

י וְאָכַלְתָּ וְשָׂבָעְתָּ וּבֵרַכְתָּ אֶת־יהוה אֱלֹהֶיךָ עַל־הָאָרֶץ הַטֹּבָה אֲשֶׁר נָתַן־לָךְ:

¹¹ Take care lest you forget *Hashem* your God and fail to keep His commandments, His rules, and His laws, which I enjoin upon you today.

יא הִשָּׁמֶר לְךָ פֶּן־תִּשְׁכַּח אֶת־יהוה אֱלֹהֶיךָ לְבִלְתִּי שְׁמֹר מִצְוֹתָיו וּמִשְׁפָּטָיו וְחֻקֹּתָיו אֲשֶׁר אָנֹכִי מְצַוְּךָ הַיּוֹם:

¹² When you have eaten your fill, and have built fine houses to live in,

יב פֶּן־תֹּאכַל וְשָׂבָעְתָּ וּבָתִּים טוֹבִים תִּבְנֶה וְיָשָׁבְתָּ:

¹³ and your herds and flocks have multiplied, and your silver and gold have increased, and everything you own has prospered,

יג וּבְקָרְךָ וְצֹאנְךָ יִרְבְּיֻן וְכֶסֶף וְזָהָב יִרְבֶּה־לָּךְ וְכֹל אֲשֶׁר־לְךָ יִרְבֶּה:

8:8 A land of wheat and barley, of vines, figs, and pomegranates The *Torah* names seven species as the special agricultural products of *Eretz Yisrael*. Even today, these seven crops can be seen growing all over Israel. In particular, the pomegranate has always been a symbol of beauty. Its unique shape was a favorite design element, appearing on the priestly garments and the pillars at the entrance to the *Beit Hamikdash* in *Yerushalayim*.

The seven species

24

Deuteronomy

14 beware lest* your heart grow haughty and you forget *Hashem* your God – who freed you from the land of Egypt, the house of bondage;

יד וְרָם לְבָבֶךָ וְשָׁכַחְתָּ אֶת־יְהוָה אֱלֹהֶיךָ הַמּוֹצִיאֲךָ מֵאֶרֶץ מִצְרַיִם מִבֵּית עֲבָדִים:

15 who led you through the great and terrible wilderness with its seraph serpents and scorpions, a parched land with no water in it, who brought forth water for you from the flinty rock;

טו הַמּוֹלִיכֲךָ בַּמִּדְבָּר הַגָּדֹל וְהַנּוֹרָא נָחָשׁ שָׂרָף וְעַקְרָב וְצִמָּאוֹן אֲשֶׁר אֵין־מָיִם הַמּוֹצִיא לְךָ מַיִם מִצּוּר הַחַלָּמִישׁ:

16 who fed you in the wilderness with manna, which your fathers had never known, in order to test you by hardships only to benefit you in the end

טז הַמַּאֲכִלְךָ מָן בַּמִּדְבָּר אֲשֶׁר לֹא־יָדְעוּן אֲבֹתֶיךָ לְמַעַן עַנֹּתְךָ וּלְמַעַן נַסֹּתֶךָ לְהֵיטִבְךָ בְּאַחֲרִיתֶךָ:

17 and you say to yourselves, "My own power and the might of my own hand have won this wealth for me."

יז וְאָמַרְתָּ בִּלְבָבֶךָ כֹּחִי וְעֹצֶם יָדִי עָשָׂה לִי אֶת־הַחַיִל הַזֶּה:

18 Remember that it is *Hashem* your God who gives you the power to get wealth, in fulfillment of the covenant that He made on oath with your fathers, as is still the case.

יח וְזָכַרְתָּ אֶת־יְהוָה אֱלֹהֶיךָ כִּי הוּא הַנֹּתֵן לְךָ כֹּחַ לַעֲשׂוֹת חָיִל לְמַעַן הָקִים אֶת־בְּרִיתוֹ אֲשֶׁר־נִשְׁבַּע לַאֲבֹתֶיךָ כַּיּוֹם הַזֶּה:

19 If you do forget *Hashem* your God and follow other gods to serve them or bow down to them, I warn you this day that you shall certainly perish;

יט וְהָיָה אִם־שָׁכֹחַ תִּשְׁכַּח אֶת־יְהוָה אֱלֹהֶיךָ וְהָלַכְתָּ אַחֲרֵי אֱלֹהִים אֲחֵרִים וַעֲבַדְתָּם וְהִשְׁתַּחֲוִיתָ לָהֶם הַעִדֹתִי בָכֶם הַיּוֹם כִּי אָבֹד תֹּאבֵדוּן:

20 like the nations that *Hashem* will cause to perish before you, so shall you perish – because you did not heed *Hashem* your God.

כ כַּגּוֹיִם אֲשֶׁר יְהוָה מַאֲבִיד מִפְּנֵיכֶם כֵּן תֹּאבֵדוּן עֵקֶב לֹא תִשְׁמְעוּן בְּקוֹל יְהוָה אֱלֹהֵיכֶם:

9 1 Hear, O *Yisrael*! You are about to cross the *Yarden* to go in and dispossess nations greater and more populous than you: great cities with walls sky-high;

ט א שְׁמַע יִשְׂרָאֵל אַתָּה עֹבֵר הַיּוֹם אֶת־הַיַּרְדֵּן לָבֹא לָרֶשֶׁת גּוֹיִם גְּדֹלִים וַעֲצֻמִים מִמֶּךָּ עָרִים גְּדֹלֹת וּבְצֻרֹת בַּשָּׁמָיִם:

*sh'-MA yis-ra-AYL a-TAH o-VAYR ha-YOM et ha-yar-DAYN
la-VO la-RE-shet go-YIM g'-do-LEEM va-a-tzu-MEEM mi-ME-ka
a-REEM g'-do-LOT uv-tzu-ROT ba-sha-MA-yim*

---

* Heb. "pen" (beware lest) moved down from v. 12 for clarity

The Jordan River

עבר

9:1 Hear, O *Yisrael*! You are about to cross the *Yarden* The word for 'Hebrew', *Ivrit* (עברית), comes from the root *avar* (עבר), 'to cross over', which appears in this verse. *Moshe* tells the people that they are about to cross into the land on the other side of the Jordan. Similarly, our forefather *Avraham* was called *Ha'Ivri* (Genesis 14:13) because he came from the other side of the river, and because his monotheistic views were on the "other side" compared to those of the rest of the world. *Avraham*'s heirs still carry the responsibility of being the world's moral compass, reminding others not to necessarily conform to popular norms and mores, but to do only what is right. Accordingly, the State of Israel has adopted this responsibility as its mission, to do what is right among the international community of nations even when it is not popular. Indeed, Israel comes under great scrutiny by the nations of the world. It is often viewed as being on the "other side," as a result of its historic mission to live by the principles of the Bible.

2 a people great and tall, the Anakites, of whom you have knowledge; for you have heard it said, "Who can stand up to the children of Anak?"

ב עַם־גָּדוֹל וָרָם בְּנֵי עֲנָקִים אֲשֶׁר אַתָּה יָדַעְתָּ וְאַתָּה שָׁמַעְתָּ מִי יִתְיַצֵּב לִפְנֵי בְּנֵי עֲנָק:

3 Know then this day that none other than *Hashem* your God is crossing at your head, a devouring fire; it is He who will wipe them out. He will subdue them before you, that you may quickly dispossess and destroy them, as *Hashem* promised you.

ג וְיָדַעְתָּ הַיּוֹם כִּי יְהֹוָה אֱלֹהֶיךָ הוּא־הָעֹבֵר לְפָנֶיךָ אֵשׁ אֹכְלָה הוּא יַשְׁמִידֵם וְהוּא יַכְנִיעֵם לְפָנֶיךָ וְהוֹרַשְׁתָּם וְהַאֲבַדְתָּם מַהֵר כַּאֲשֶׁר דִּבֶּר יְהֹוָה לָךְ:

4 And when *Hashem* your God has thrust them from your path, say not to yourselves, "*Hashem* has enabled us to possess this land because of our virtues"; it is rather because of the wickedness of those nations that *Hashem* is dispossessing them before you.

ד אַל־תֹּאמַר בִּלְבָבְךָ בַּהֲדֹף יְהֹוָה אֱלֹהֶיךָ אֹתָם מִלְּפָנֶיךָ לֵאמֹר בְּצִדְקָתִי הֱבִיאַנִי יְהֹוָה לָרֶשֶׁת אֶת־הָאָרֶץ הַזֹּאת וּבְרִשְׁעַת הַגּוֹיִם הָאֵלֶּה יְהֹוָה מוֹרִישָׁם מִפָּנֶיךָ:

5 It is not because of your virtues and your rectitude that you will be able to possess their country; but it is because of their wickedness that *Hashem* your God is dispossessing those nations before you, and in order to fulfill the oath that *Hashem* made to your fathers, *Avraham, Yitzchak,* and *Yaakov.*

ה לֹא בְצִדְקָתְךָ וּבְיֹשֶׁר לְבָבְךָ אַתָּה בָא לָרֶשֶׁת אֶת־אַרְצָם כִּי בְּרִשְׁעַת הַגּוֹיִם הָאֵלֶּה יְהֹוָה אֱלֹהֶיךָ מוֹרִישָׁם מִפָּנֶיךָ וּלְמַעַן הָקִים אֶת־הַדָּבָר אֲשֶׁר נִשְׁבַּע יְהֹוָה לַאֲבֹתֶיךָ לְאַבְרָהָם לְיִצְחָק וּלְיַעֲקֹב:

6 Know, then, that it is not for any virtue of yours that *Hashem* your God is giving you this good land to possess; for you are a stiffnecked people.

ו וְיָדַעְתָּ כִּי לֹא בְצִדְקָתְךָ יְהֹוָה אֱלֹהֶיךָ נֹתֵן לְךָ אֶת־הָאָרֶץ הַטּוֹבָה הַזֹּאת לְרִשְׁתָּהּ כִּי עַם־קְשֵׁה־עֹרֶף אָתָּה:

7 Remember, never forget, how you provoked *Hashem* your God to anger in the wilderness: from the day that you left the land of Egypt until you reached this place, you have continued defiant toward *Hashem.*

ז זְכֹר אַל־תִּשְׁכַּח אֵת אֲשֶׁר־הִקְצַפְתָּ אֶת־יְהֹוָה אֱלֹהֶיךָ בַּמִּדְבָּר לְמִן־הַיּוֹם אֲשֶׁר־יָצָאתָ מֵאֶרֶץ מִצְרַיִם עַד־בֹּאֲכֶם עַד־הַמָּקוֹם הַזֶּה מַמְרִים הֱיִיתֶם עִם־יְהֹוָה:

8 At Horeb you so provoked *Hashem* that *Hashem* was angry enough with you to have destroyed you.

ח וּבְחֹרֵב הִקְצַפְתֶּם אֶת־יְהֹוָה וַיִּתְאַנַּף יְהֹוָה בָּכֶם לְהַשְׁמִיד אֶתְכֶם:

9 I had ascended the mountain to receive the tablets of stone, the Tablets of the Covenant that *Hashem* had made with you, and I stayed on the mountain forty days and forty nights, eating no bread and drinking no water.

ט בַּעֲלֹתִי הָהָרָה לָקַחַת לוּחֹת הָאֲבָנִים לוּחֹת הַבְּרִית אֲשֶׁר־כָּרַת יְהֹוָה עִמָּכֶם וָאֵשֵׁב בָּהָר אַרְבָּעִים יוֹם וְאַרְבָּעִים לַיְלָה לֶחֶם לֹא אָכַלְתִּי וּמַיִם לֹא שָׁתִיתִי:

10 And *Hashem* gave me the two tablets of stone inscribed by the finger of *Hashem,* with the exact words that *Hashem* had addressed to you on the mountain out of the fire on the day of the Assembly.

י וַיִּתֵּן יְהֹוָה אֵלַי אֶת־שְׁנֵי לוּחֹת הָאֲבָנִים כְּתֻבִים בְּאֶצְבַּע אֱלֹהִים וַעֲלֵיהֶם כְּכָל־הַדְּבָרִים אֲשֶׁר דִּבֶּר יְהֹוָה עִמָּכֶם בָּהָר מִתּוֹךְ הָאֵשׁ בְּיוֹם הַקָּהָל:

11 At the end of those forty days and forty nights, *Hashem* gave me the two tablets of stone, the Tablets of the Covenant.

יא וַיְהִי מִקֵּץ אַרְבָּעִים יוֹם וְאַרְבָּעִים לָיְלָה נָתַן יְהֹוָה אֵלַי אֶת־שְׁנֵי לֻחֹת הָאֲבָנִים לֻחֹת הַבְּרִית:

12 And *Hashem* said to me, "Hurry, go down from here at once, for the people whom you brought out of Egypt have acted wickedly; they have been quick to stray from the path that I enjoined upon them; they have made themselves a molten image."

13 *Hashem* further said to me, "I see that this is a stiffnecked people.

14 Let Me alone and I will destroy them and blot out their name from under heaven, and I will make you a nation far more numerous than they."

15 I started down the mountain, a mountain ablaze with fire, the two Tablets of the Covenant in my two hands.

16 I saw how you had sinned against *Hashem* your God: you had made yourselves a molten calf; you had been quick to stray from the path that *Hashem* had enjoined upon you.

17 Thereupon I gripped the two tablets and flung them away with both my hands, smashing them before your eyes.

18 I threw myself down before *Hashem* – eating no bread and drinking no water forty days and forty nights, as before – because of the great wrong you had committed, doing what displeased *Hashem* and vexing Him.

19 For I was in dread of *Hashem*'s fierce anger against you, which moved Him to wipe you out. And that time, too, *Hashem* gave heed to me.

20 Moreover, *Hashem* was angry enough with *Aharon* to have destroyed him; so I also interceded for *Aharon* at that time.

21 As for that sinful thing you had made, the calf, I took it and put it to the fire; I broke it to bits and ground it thoroughly until it was fine as dust, and I threw its dust into the brook that comes down from the mountain.

22 Again you provoked *Hashem* at Taberah, and at Massah, and at Kibroth-hattaavah.

23 And when *Hashem* sent you on from Kadesh-barnea, saying, "Go up and take possession of the land that I am giving you," you flouted the command of *Hashem* your God; you did not put your trust in Him and did not obey Him.

יב וַיֹּ֨אמֶר יְהֹוָ֜ה אֵלַ֗י ק֣וּם רֵ֤ד מַהֵר֙ מִזֶּ֔ה כִּ֤י שִׁחֵת֙ עַמְּךָ֔ אֲשֶׁ֥ר הוֹצֵ֖אתָ מִמִּצְרָ֑יִם סָ֣רוּ מַהֵ֗ר מִן־הַדֶּ֨רֶךְ֙ אֲשֶׁ֣ר צִוִּיתִ֔ם עָשׂ֥וּ לָהֶ֖ם מַסֵּכָֽה׃

יג וַיֹּ֥אמֶר יְהֹוָ֖ה אֵלַ֣י לֵאמֹ֑ר רָאִ֨יתִי֙ אֶת־הָעָ֣ם הַזֶּ֔ה וְהִנֵּ֥ה עַם־קְשֵׁה־עֹ֖רֶף הֽוּא׃

יד הֶ֤רֶף מִמֶּ֨נִּי֙ וְאַשְׁמִידֵ֔ם וְאֶמְחֶ֣ה אֶת־שְׁמָ֔ם מִתַּ֖חַת הַשָּׁמָ֑יִם וְאֶֽעֱשֶׂה֙ אֽוֹתְךָ֔ לְגֽוֹי־עָצ֥וּם וָרָ֖ב מִמֶּֽנּוּ׃

טו וָאֵ֗פֶן וָֽאֵרֵד֙ מִן־הָהָ֔ר וְהָהָ֖ר בֹּעֵ֣ר בָּאֵ֑שׁ וּשְׁנֵי֙ לֻחֹ֣ת הַבְּרִ֔ית עַ֖ל שְׁתֵּ֥י יָדָֽי׃

טז וָאֵ֗רֶא וְהִנֵּ֤ה חֲטָאתֶם֙ לַֽיהֹוָ֣ה אֱלֹֽהֵיכֶ֔ם עֲשִׂיתֶ֣ם לָכֶ֔ם עֵ֖גֶל מַסֵּכָ֑ה סַרְתֶּ֣ם מַהֵ֔ר מִן־הַדֶּ֕רֶךְ אֲשֶׁר־צִוָּ֥ה יְהֹוָ֖ה אֶתְכֶֽם׃

יז וָֽאֶתְפֹּ֗שׂ בִּשְׁנֵ֣י הַלֻּחֹ֔ת וָֽאַשְׁלִכֵ֔ם מֵעַ֖ל שְׁתֵּ֣י יָדָ֑י וָֽאֲשַׁבְּרֵ֖ם לְעֵֽינֵיכֶֽם׃

יח וָֽאֶתְנַפַּל֩ לִפְנֵ֨י יְהֹוָ֜ה כָּרִֽאשֹׁנָ֗ה אַרְבָּעִ֥ים יוֹם֙ וְאַרְבָּעִ֣ים לַ֔יְלָה לֶ֚חֶם לֹ֣א אָכַ֔לְתִּי וּמַ֖יִם לֹ֣א שָׁתִ֑יתִי עַ֤ל כָּל־חַטַּאתְכֶם֙ אֲשֶׁ֣ר חֲטָאתֶ֔ם לַעֲשׂ֥וֹת הָרַ֛ע בְּעֵינֵ֥י יְהֹוָ֖ה לְהַכְעִיסֽוֹ׃

יט כִּ֣י יָגֹ֗רְתִּי מִפְּנֵ֤י הָאַף֙ וְהַ֣חֵמָ֔ה אֲשֶׁ֨ר קָצַ֧ף יְהֹוָ֛ה עֲלֵיכֶ֖ם לְהַשְׁמִ֣יד אֶתְכֶ֑ם וַיִּשְׁמַ֤ע יְהֹוָה֙ אֵלַ֔י גַּ֖ם בַּפַּ֥עַם הַהִֽוא׃

כ וּֽבְאַהֲרֹ֗ן הִתְאַנַּ֧ף יְהֹוָ֛ה מְאֹ֖ד לְהַשְׁמִיד֑וֹ וָֽאֶתְפַּלֵּ֛ל גַּם־בְּעַ֥ד אַהֲרֹ֖ן בָּעֵ֥ת הַהִֽוא׃

כא וְֽאֶת־חַטַּאתְכֶ֞ם אֲשֶׁר־עֲשִׂיתֶ֣ם אֶת־הָעֵ֗גֶל לָקַ֘חְתִּי֮ וָאֶשְׂרֹ֣ף אֹת֣וֹ ׀ בָּאֵשׁ֒ וָֽאֶכֹּ֨ת אֹת֤וֹ טָחוֹן֙ הֵיטֵ֔ב עַ֥ד אֲשֶׁר־דַּ֖ק לְעָפָ֑ר וָֽאַשְׁלִךְ֙ אֶת־עֲפָר֔וֹ אֶל־הַנַּ֖חַל הַיֹּרֵ֥ד מִן־הָהָֽר׃

כב וּבְתַבְעֵרָה֙ וּבְמַסָּ֔ה וּבְקִבְרֹ֖ת הַֽתַּאֲוָ֑ה מַקְצִפִ֥ים הֱיִיתֶ֖ם אֶת־יְהֹוָֽה׃

כג וּבִשְׁלֹ֨חַ יְהֹוָ֜ה אֶתְכֶ֗ם מִקָּדֵ֤שׁ בַּרְנֵ֨עַ֙ לֵאמֹ֔ר עֲל וּ֙ וּרְשׁ֣וּ אֶת־הָאָ֔רֶץ אֲשֶׁ֥ר נָתַ֖תִּי לָכֶ֑ם וַתַּמְר֗וּ אֶת־פִּ֤י יְהֹוָה֙ אֱלֹ֣הֵיכֶ֔ם וְלֹ֤א הֶֽאֱמַנְתֶּם֙ ל֔וֹ וְלֹ֥א שְׁמַעְתֶּ֖ם בְּקֹלֽוֹ׃

²⁴ As long as I have known you, you have been defiant toward *Hashem*.

כד מַמְרִים הֱיִיתֶם עִם־יְהֹוָה מִיּוֹם דַּעְתִּי אֶתְכֶם:

²⁵ When I lay prostrate before *Hashem* those forty days and forty nights, because *Hashem* was determined to destroy you,

כה וָאֶתְנַפַּל לִפְנֵי יְהֹוָה אֵת אַרְבָּעִים הַיּוֹם וְאֶת־אַרְבָּעִים הַלַּיְלָה אֲשֶׁר הִתְנַפָּלְתִּי כִּי־אָמַר יְהֹוָה לְהַשְׁמִיד אֶתְכֶם:

²⁶ I prayed to *Hashem* and said, "O *Hashem*, do not annihilate Your very own people, whom You redeemed in Your majesty and whom You freed from Egypt with a mighty hand.

כו וָאֶתְפַּלֵּל אֶל־יְהֹוָה וָאֹמַר אֲדֹנָי יֱהֹוִה אַל־תַּשְׁחֵת עַמְּךָ וְנַחֲלָתְךָ אֲשֶׁר פָּדִיתָ בְּגׇדְלֶךָ אֲשֶׁר־הוֹצֵאתָ מִמִּצְרַיִם בְּיָד חֲזָקָה:

²⁷ Give thought to Your servants, *Avraham, Yitzchak,* and *Yaakov,* and pay no heed to the stubbornness of this people, its wickedness, and its sinfulness.

כז זְכֹר לַעֲבָדֶיךָ לְאַבְרָהָם לְיִצְחָק וּלְיַעֲקֹב אַל־תֵּפֶן אֶל־קְשִׁי הָעָם הַזֶּה וְאֶל־רִשְׁעוֹ וְאֶל־חַטָּאתוֹ:

²⁸ Else the country from which You freed us will say, 'It was because *Hashem* was powerless to bring them into the land that He had promised them, and because He rejected them, that He brought them out to have them die in the wilderness.'

כח פֶּן־יֹאמְרוּ הָאָרֶץ אֲשֶׁר הוֹצֵאתָנוּ מִשָּׁם מִבְּלִי יְכֹלֶת יְהֹוָה לַהֲבִיאָם אֶל־הָאָרֶץ אֲשֶׁר־דִּבֶּר לָהֶם וּמִשִּׂנְאָתוֹ אוֹתָם הוֹצִיאָם לַהֲמִתָם בַּמִּדְבָּר:

²⁹ Yet they are Your very own people, whom You freed with Your great might and Your outstretched arm."

כט וְהֵם עַמְּךָ וְנַחֲלָתֶךָ אֲשֶׁר הוֹצֵאתָ בְּכֹחֲךָ הַגָּדֹל וּבִזְרֹעֲךָ הַנְּטוּיָה:

10 ¹ Thereupon *Hashem* said to me, "Carve out two tablets of stone like the first, and come up to Me on the mountain; and make an ark of wood.

א בָּעֵת הַהִוא אָמַר יְהֹוָה אֵלַי פְּסׇל־לְךָ שְׁנֵי־לוּחֹת אֲבָנִים כָּרִאשֹׁנִים וַעֲלֵה אֵלַי הָהָרָה וְעָשִׂיתָ לְּךָ אֲרוֹן עֵץ:

² I will inscribe on the tablets the commandments that were on the first tablets that you smashed, and you shall deposit them in the ark."

ב וְאֶכְתֹּב עַל־הַלֻּחֹת אֶת־הַדְּבָרִים אֲשֶׁר הָיוּ עַל־הַלֻּחֹת הָרִאשֹׁנִים אֲשֶׁר שִׁבַּרְתָּ וְשַׂמְתָּם בָּאָרוֹן:

³ I made an ark of acacia wood and carved out two tablets of stone like the first; I took the two tablets with me and went up the mountain.

ג וָאַעַשׂ אֲרוֹן עֲצֵי שִׁטִּים וָאֶפְסֹל שְׁנֵי־לֻחֹת אֲבָנִים כָּרִאשֹׁנִים וָאַעַל הָהָרָה וּשְׁנֵי הַלֻּחֹת בְּיָדִי:

⁴ *Hashem* inscribed on the tablets the same text as on the first, the Ten Commandments that He addressed to you on the mountain out of the fire on the day of the Assembly; and *Hashem* gave them to me.

ד וַיִּכְתֹּב עַל־הַלֻּחֹת כַּמִּכְתָּב הָרִאשׁוֹן אֵת עֲשֶׂרֶת הַדְּבָרִים אֲשֶׁר דִּבֶּר יְהֹוָה אֲלֵיכֶם בָּהָר מִתּוֹךְ הָאֵשׁ בְּיוֹם הַקָּהָל וַיִּתְּנֵם יְהֹוָה אֵלָי:

⁵ Then I left and went down from the mountain, and I deposited the tablets in the ark that I had made, where they still are, as *Hashem* had commanded me.

ה וָאֵפֶן וָאֵרֵד מִן־הָהָר וָאָשִׂם אֶת־הַלֻּחֹת בָּאָרוֹן אֲשֶׁר עָשִׂיתִי וַיִּהְיוּ שָׁם כַּאֲשֶׁר צִוַּנִי יְהֹוָה:

⁶ From Beeroth-bene-jaakan the Israelites marched to Moserah. *Aharon* died there and was buried there; and his son *Elazar* became *Kohen* in his stead.

ו וּבְנֵי יִשְׂרָאֵל נָסְעוּ מִבְּאֵרֹת בְּנֵי־יַעֲקָן מוֹסֵרָה שָׁם מֵת אַהֲרֹן וַיִּקָּבֵר שָׁם וַיְכַהֵן אֶלְעָזָר בְּנוֹ תַּחְתָּיו:

⁷ From there they marched to Gudgod, and from Gudgod to Jotbath, a region of running brooks.

ז מִשָּׁם נָסְעוּ הַגֻּדְגֹּדָה וּמִן־הַגֻּדְגֹּדָה יׇטְבָתָה אֶרֶץ נַחֲלֵי מָיִם:

Deuteronomy

8 At that time *Hashem* set apart the tribe of *Levi* to carry the *Aron* Brit *Hashem*, to stand in attendance upon *Hashem*, and to bless in His name, as is still the case.

ח בָּעֵת הַהִוא הִבְדִּיל יְהֹוָה אֶת־שֵׁבֶט הַלֵּוִי לָשֵׂאת אֶת־אֲרוֹן בְּרִית־יְהֹוָה לַעֲמֹד לִפְנֵי יְהֹוָה לְשָׁרְתוֹ וּלְבָרֵךְ בִּשְׁמוֹ עַד הַיּוֹם הַזֶּה:

9 That is why the *Leviim* have received no hereditary portion along with their kinsmen: *Hashem* is their portion, as *Hashem* your God spoke concerning them.

ט עַל־כֵּן לֹא־הָיָה לְלֵוִי חֵלֶק וְנַחֲלָה עִם־ אֶחָיו יְהֹוָה הוּא נַחֲלָתוֹ כַּאֲשֶׁר דִּבֶּר יְהֹוָה אֱלֹהֶיךָ לוֹ:

10 I had stayed on the mountain, as I did the first time, forty days and forty nights; and *Hashem* heeded me once again: *Hashem* agreed not to destroy you.

י וְאָנֹכִי עָמַדְתִּי בָהָר כַּיָּמִים הָרִאשֹׁנִים אַרְבָּעִים יוֹם וְאַרְבָּעִים לָיְלָה וַיִּשְׁמַע יְהֹוָה אֵלַי גַּם בַּפַּעַם הַהִוא לֹא־אָבָה יְהֹוָה הַשְׁחִיתֶךָ:

11 And *Hashem* said to me, "Up, resume the march at the head of the people, that they may go in and possess the land that I swore to their fathers to give them."

יא וַיֹּאמֶר יְהֹוָה אֵלַי קוּם לֵךְ לְמַסַּע לִפְנֵי הָעָם וְיָבֹאוּ וְיִרְשׁוּ אֶת־הָאָרֶץ אֲשֶׁר־ נִשְׁבַּעְתִּי לַאֲבֹתָם לָתֵת לָהֶם:

12 And now, O *Yisrael*, what does *Hashem* your God demand of you? Only this: to revere *Hashem* your God, to walk only in His paths, to love Him, and to serve *Hashem* your God with all your heart and soul,

יב וְעַתָּה יִשְׂרָאֵל מָה יְהֹוָה אֱלֹהֶיךָ שֹׁאֵל מֵעִמָּךְ כִּי אִם־לְיִרְאָה אֶת־יְהֹוָה אֱלֹהֶיךָ לָלֶכֶת בְּכָל־דְּרָכָיו וּלְאַהֲבָה אֹתוֹ וְלַעֲבֹד אֶת־יְהֹוָה אֱלֹהֶיךָ בְּכָל־לְבָבְךָ וּבְכָל־ נַפְשֶׁךָ:

13 keeping *Hashem*'s commandments and laws, which I enjoin upon you today, for your good.

יג לִשְׁמֹר אֶת־מִצְוֹת יְהֹוָה וְאֶת־חֻקֹּתָיו אֲשֶׁר אָנֹכִי מְצַוְּךָ הַיּוֹם לְטוֹב לָךְ:

14 Mark, the heavens to their uttermost reaches belong to *Hashem* your God, the earth and all that is on it!

יד הֵן לַיהֹוָה אֱלֹהֶיךָ הַשָּׁמַיִם וּשְׁמֵי הַשָּׁמָיִם הָאָרֶץ וְכָל־אֲשֶׁר־בָּהּ:

15 Yet it was to your fathers that *Hashem* was drawn in His love for them, so that He chose you, their lineal descendants, from among all peoples – as is now the case.

טו רַק בַּאֲבֹתֶיךָ חָשַׁק יְהֹוָה לְאַהֲבָה אוֹתָם וַיִּבְחַר בְּזַרְעָם אַחֲרֵיהֶם בָּכֶם מִכָּל־ הָעַמִּים כַּיּוֹם הַזֶּה:

16 Cut away, therefore, the thickening about your hearts and stiffen your necks no more.

טז וּמַלְתֶּם אֵת עָרְלַת לְבַבְכֶם וְעָרְפְּכֶם לֹא תַקְשׁוּ עוֹד:

17 For *Hashem* your God is God supreme and Lord supreme, the great, the mighty, and the awesome *Hashem*, who shows no favor and takes no bribe,

יז כִּי יְהֹוָה אֱלֹהֵיכֶם הוּא אֱלֹהֵי הָאֱלֹהִים וַאֲדֹנֵי הָאֲדֹנִים הָאֵל הַגָּדֹל הַגִּבֹּר וְהַנּוֹרָא אֲשֶׁר לֹא־יִשָּׂא פָנִים וְלֹא יִקַּח שֹׁחַד:

18 but upholds the cause of the fatherless and the widow, and bef riends the stranger, providing him with food and clothing.

יח עֹשֶׂה מִשְׁפַּט יָתוֹם וְאַלְמָנָה וְאֹהֵב גֵּר לָתֶת לוֹ לֶחֶם וְשִׂמְלָה:

19 You too must befriend the stranger, for you were strangers in the land of Egypt.

יט וַאֲהַבְתֶּם אֶת־הַגֵּר כִּי־גֵרִים הֱיִיתֶם בְּאֶרֶץ מִצְרָיִם:

va-a-hav-TEM et ha-GAYR kee gay-REEM he-yee-TEM b'-E-retz mitz-RA-yim

20 You must revere *Hashem* your God: only Him shall you worship, to Him shall you hold fast, and by His name shall you swear.

כ אֶת־יְהֹוָה אֱלֹהֶיךָ תִּירָא אֹתוֹ תַעֲבֹד וּבוֹ תִדְבָּק וּבִשְׁמוֹ תִּשָּׁבֵעַ:

21 He is your glory and He is your God, who wrought for you those marvelous, awesome deeds that you saw with your own eyes.

כא הוּא תְהִלָּתְךָ וְהוּא אֱלֹהֶיךָ אֲשֶׁר־עָשָׂה אִתְּךָ אֶת־הַגְּדֹלֹת וְאֶת־הַנּוֹרָאֹת הָאֵלֶּה אֲשֶׁר רָאוּ עֵינֶיךָ:

22 Your ancestors went down to Egypt seventy persons in all; and now *Hashem* your God has made you as numerous as the stars of heaven.

כב בְּשִׁבְעִים נֶפֶשׁ יָרְדוּ אֲבֹתֶיךָ מִצְרָיְמָה וְעַתָּה שָׂמְךָ יְהֹוָה אֱלֹהֶיךָ כְּכוֹכְבֵי הַשָּׁמַיִם לָרֹב:

11 1 Love, therefore, *Hashem* your God, and always keep His charge, His laws, His rules, and His commandments.

יא א וְאָהַבְתָּ אֵת יְהֹוָה אֱלֹהֶיךָ וְשָׁמַרְתָּ מִשְׁמַרְתּוֹ וְחֻקֹּתָיו וּמִשְׁפָּטָיו וּמִצְוֺתָיו כָּל־הַיָּמִים:

2 Take thought this day that it was not your children, who neither experienced nor witnessed the lesson of *Hashem* your God – His majesty, His mighty hand, His outstretched arm;

ב וִידַעְתֶּם הַיּוֹם כִּי לֹא אֶת־בְּנֵיכֶם אֲשֶׁר לֹא־יָדְעוּ וַאֲשֶׁר לֹא־רָאוּ אֶת־מוּסַר יְהֹוָה אֱלֹהֵיכֶם אֶת־גָּדְלוֹ אֶת־יָדוֹ הַחֲזָקָה וּזְרֹעוֹ הַנְּטוּיָה:

3 the signs and the deeds that He performed in Egypt against Pharaoh king of Egypt and all his land;

ג וְאֶת־אֹתֹתָיו וְאֶת־מַעֲשָׂיו אֲשֶׁר עָשָׂה בְּתוֹךְ מִצְרָיִם לְפַרְעֹה מֶלֶךְ־מִצְרַיִם וּלְכָל־אַרְצוֹ:

4 what He did to Egypt's army, its horses and chariots; how *Hashem* rolled back upon them the waters of the Sea of Reeds when they were pursuing you, thus destroying them once and for all;

ד וַאֲשֶׁר עָשָׂה לְחֵיל מִצְרַיִם לְסוּסָיו וּלְרִכְבּוֹ אֲשֶׁר הֵצִיף אֶת־מֵי יַם־סוּף עַל־פְּנֵיהֶם בְּרָדְפָם אַחֲרֵיכֶם וַיְאַבְּדֵם יְהֹוָה עַד הַיּוֹם הַזֶּה:

5 what He did for you in the wilderness before you arrived in this place;

ה וַאֲשֶׁר עָשָׂה לָכֶם בַּמִּדְבָּר עַד־בֹּאֲכֶם עַד־הַמָּקוֹם הַזֶּה:

6 and what He did to *Datan* and *Aviram*, sons of *Eliav* son of *Reuven*, when the earth opened her mouth and swallowed them, along with their households, their tents, and every living thing in their train, from amidst all *Yisrael* –

ו וַאֲשֶׁר עָשָׂה לְדָתָן וְלַאֲבִירָם בְּנֵי אֱלִיאָב בֶּן־רְאוּבֵן אֲשֶׁר פָּצְתָה הָאָרֶץ אֶת־פִּיהָ וַתִּבְלָעֵם וְאֶת־בָּתֵּיהֶם וְאֶת־אָהֳלֵיהֶם וְאֵת כָּל־הַיְקוּם אֲשֶׁר בְּרַגְלֵיהֶם בְּקֶרֶב כָּל־יִשְׂרָאֵל:

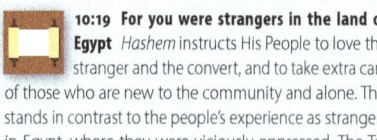

10:19 For you were strangers in the land of Egypt *Hashem* instructs His People to love the stranger and the convert, and to take extra care of those who are new to the community and alone. This stands in contrast to the people's experience as strangers in Egypt, where they were viciously oppressed. The Talmud (*Bava Metzia* 59b) points out that this commandment is repeated no less than thirty-six times throughout the Bible, to emphasize that as the People of Israel prepare to enter the Land of Israel, where they will be the masters and no longer the strangers, they are warned not to forget what is was like to be outsiders. They must do whatever they can to ease the struggles of strangers in their land.

Israel365 sends *Tu B'shvat* packages to lone soldiers in Israel

7 but that it was you who saw with your own eyes all the marvelous deeds that *Hashem* performed.

ז כִּי עֵינֵיכֶם הָרֹאֹת אֶת־כָּל־מַעֲשֵׂה יְהוָֹה הַגָּדֹל אֲשֶׁר עָשָׂה:

8 Keep, therefore, all the Instruction that I enjoin upon you today, so that you may have the strength to enter and take possession of the land that you are about to cross into and possess,

ח וּשְׁמַרְתֶּם אֶת־כָּל־הַמִּצְוָה אֲשֶׁר אָנֹכִי מְצַוְּךָ הַיּוֹם לְמַעַן תֶּחֶזְקוּ וּבָאתֶם וִירִשְׁתֶּם אֶת־הָאָרֶץ אֲשֶׁר אַתֶּם עֹבְרִים שָׁמָּה לְרִשְׁתָּהּ:

9 and that you may long endure upon the soil that *Hashem* swore to your fathers to assign to them and to their heirs, a land flowing with milk and honey.

ט וּלְמַעַן תַּאֲרִיכוּ יָמִים עַל־הָאֲדָמָה אֲשֶׁר נִשְׁבַּע יְהוָֹה לַאֲבֹתֵיכֶם לָתֵת לָהֶם וּלְזַרְעָם אֶרֶץ זָבַת חָלָב וּדְבָשׁ:

10 For the land that you are about to enter and possess is not like the land of Egypt from which you have come. There the grain you sowed had to be watered by your own labors, like a vegetable garden;

י כִּי הָאָרֶץ אֲשֶׁר אַתָּה בָא־שָׁמָּה לְרִשְׁתָּהּ לֹא כְאֶרֶץ מִצְרַיִם הִוא אֲשֶׁר יְצָאתֶם מִשָּׁם אֲשֶׁר תִּזְרַע אֶת־זַרְעֲךָ וְהִשְׁקִיתָ בְרַגְלְךָ כְּגַן הַיָּרָק:

11 but the land you are about to cross into and possess, a land of hills and valleys, soaks up its water from the rains of heaven.

יא וְהָאָרֶץ אֲשֶׁר אַתֶּם עֹבְרִים שָׁמָּה לְרִשְׁתָּהּ אֶרֶץ הָרִים וּבְקָעֹת לִמְטַר הַשָּׁמַיִם תִּשְׁתֶּה־מָּיִם:

12 It is a land which *Hashem* your God looks after, on which *Hashem* your God always keeps His eye, from year's beginning to year's end.

יב אֶרֶץ אֲשֶׁר־יְהוָֹה אֱלֹהֶיךָ דֹּרֵשׁ אֹתָהּ תָּמִיד עֵינֵי יְהוָֹה אֱלֹהֶיךָ בָּהּ מֵרֵשִׁית הַשָּׁנָה וְעַד אַחֲרִית שָׁנָה:

E-retz a-sher a-do-NAI e-lo-HE-kha do-RAYSH o-TAH
ta-MEED ay-NAY a-do-NAI e-lo-HE-kha BA may-ray-SHEET
ha-sha-NAH v'-AD a-kha-REET sha-NAH

13 If, then, you obey the commandments that I enjoin upon you this day, loving *Hashem* your God and serving Him with all your heart and soul,

יג וְהָיָה אִם־שָׁמֹעַ תִּשְׁמְעוּ אֶל־מִצְוֹתַי אֲשֶׁר אָנֹכִי מְצַוֶּה אֶתְכֶם הַיּוֹם לְאַהֲבָה אֶת־יְהוָֹה אֱלֹהֵיכֶם וּלְעָבְדוֹ בְּכָל־לְבַבְכֶם וּבְכָל־נַפְשְׁכֶם:

14 I will grant the rain for your land in season, the early rain and the late. You shall gather in your new grain and wine and oil

יד וְנָתַתִּי מְטַר־אַרְצְכֶם בְּעִתּוֹ יוֹרֶה וּמַלְקוֹשׁ וְאָסַפְתָּ דְגָנֶךָ וְתִירֹשְׁךָ וְיִצְהָרֶךָ:

15 I will also provide grass in the fields for your cattle – and thus you shall eat your fill.

טו וְנָתַתִּי עֵשֶׂב בְּשָׂדְךָ לִבְהֶמְתֶּךָ וְאָכַלְתָּ וְשָׂבָעְתָּ:

16 Take care not to be lured away to serve other gods and bow to them.

טז הִשָּׁמְרוּ לָכֶם פֶּן יִפְתֶּה לְבַבְכֶם וְסַרְתֶּם וַעֲבַדְתֶּם אֱלֹהִים אֲחֵרִים וְהִשְׁתַּחֲוִיתֶם לָהֶם:

Nimrod's Fortress in Northern Israel

 11:12 From year's beginning to year's end This is the only time the Bible tells us how *Hashem* "spends His time." From the beginning of the year until the end, it says, the Creator of the universe focuses "His eyes" and attention on Israel. If we combine this idea with that mentioned in verse 22 instructing us to walk in *Hashem's* ways and hold fast to Him, we must likewise keep our eyes focused on *Eretz Yisrael* "from year's beginning to year's end." This verse inspired Rabbi Tuly Weisz to start "Israel365," which enables hundreds of thousands of people all over the world to connect with Israel each and every day of the year.

31

17 For *Hashem*'s anger will flare up against you, and He will shut up the skies so that there will be no rain and the ground will not yield its produce; and you will soon perish from the good land that *Hashem* is assigning to you.

יז וְחָרָה אַף־יְהֹוָה בָּכֶם וְעָצַר אֶת־הַשָּׁמַיִם וְלֹא־יִהְיֶה מָטָר וְהָאֲדָמָה לֹא תִתֵּן אֶת־יְבוּלָהּ וַאֲבַדְתֶּם מְהֵרָה מֵעַל הָאָרֶץ הַטֹּבָה אֲשֶׁר יְהֹוָה נֹתֵן לָכֶם:

18 Therefore impress these My words upon your very heart: bind them as a sign on your hand and let them serve as a symbol on your forehead,

יח וְשַׂמְתֶּם אֶת־דְּבָרַי אֵלֶּה עַל־לְבַבְכֶם וְעַל־נַפְשְׁכֶם וּקְשַׁרְתֶּם אֹתָם לְאוֹת עַל־יֶדְכֶם וְהָיוּ לְטוֹטָפֹת בֵּין עֵינֵיכֶם:

19 and teach them to your children – reciting them when you stay at home and when you are away, when you lie down and when you get up;

יט וְלִמַּדְתֶּם אֹתָם אֶת־בְּנֵיכֶם לְדַבֵּר בָּם בְּשִׁבְתְּךָ בְּבֵיתֶךָ וּבְלֶכְתְּךָ בַדֶּרֶךְ וּבְשָׁכְבְּךָ וּבְקוּמֶךָ:

20 and inscribe them on the doorposts of your house and on your gates

כ וּכְתַבְתָּם עַל־מְזוּזוֹת בֵּיתֶךָ וּבִשְׁעָרֶיךָ:

21 to the end that you and your children may endure, in the land that *Hashem* swore to your fathers to assign to them, as long as there is a heaven over the earth.

כא לְמַעַן יִרְבּוּ יְמֵיכֶם וִימֵי בְנֵיכֶם עַל הָאֲדָמָה אֲשֶׁר נִשְׁבַּע יְהֹוָה לַאֲבֹתֵיכֶם לָתֵת לָהֶם כִּימֵי הַשָּׁמַיִם עַל־הָאָרֶץ:

22 If, then, you faithfully keep all this Instruction that I command you, loving *Hashem* your God, walking in all His ways, and holding fast to Him,

כב כִּי אִם־שָׁמֹר תִּשְׁמְרוּן אֶת־כָּל־הַמִּצְוָה הַזֹּאת אֲשֶׁר אָנֹכִי מְצַוֶּה אֶתְכֶם לַעֲשֹׂתָהּ לְאַהֲבָה אֶת־יְהֹוָה אֱלֹהֵיכֶם לָלֶכֶת בְּכָל־דְּרָכָיו וּלְדָבְקָה־בוֹ:

23 *Hashem* will dislodge before you all these nations: you will dispossess nations greater and more numerous than you.

כג וְהוֹרִישׁ יְהֹוָה אֶת־כָּל־הַגּוֹיִם הָאֵלֶּה מִלִּפְנֵיכֶם וִירִשְׁתֶּם גּוֹיִם גְּדֹלִים וַעֲצֻמִים מִכֶּם:

24 Every spot on which your foot treads shall be yours; your territory shall extend from the wilderness to the Lebanon and from the River – the Euphrates – to the Western Sea.

כד כָּל־הַמָּקוֹם אֲשֶׁר תִּדְרֹךְ כַּף־רַגְלְכֶם בּוֹ לָכֶם יִהְיֶה מִן־הַמִּדְבָּר וְהַלְּבָנוֹן מִן־הַנָּהָר נְהַר־פְּרָת וְעַד הַיָּם הָאַחֲרוֹן יִהְיֶה גְּבֻלְכֶם:

25 No man shall stand up to you: *Hashem* your God will put the dread and the fear of you over the whole land in which you set foot, as He promised you.

כה לֹא־יִתְיַצֵּב אִישׁ בִּפְנֵיכֶם פַּחְדְּכֶם וּמוֹרַאֲכֶם יִתֵּן יְהֹוָה אֱלֹהֵיכֶם עַל־פְּנֵי כָל־הָאָרֶץ אֲשֶׁר תִּדְרְכוּ־בָהּ כַּאֲשֶׁר דִּבֶּר לָכֶם:

26 See, this day I set before you blessing and curse:

כו רְאֵה אָנֹכִי נֹתֵן לִפְנֵיכֶם הַיּוֹם בְּרָכָה וּקְלָלָה:

27 blessing, if you obey the commandments of *Hashem* your God that I enjoin upon you this day;

כז אֶת־הַבְּרָכָה אֲשֶׁר תִּשְׁמְעוּ אֶל־מִצְוֹת יְהֹוָה אֱלֹהֵיכֶם אֲשֶׁר אָנֹכִי מְצַוֶּה אֶתְכֶם הַיּוֹם:

28 and curse, if you do not obey the commandments of *Hashem* your God, but turn away from the path that I enjoin upon you this day and follow other gods, whom you have not experienced.

כח וְהַקְּלָלָה אִם־לֹא תִשְׁמְעוּ אֶל־מִצְוֹת יְהֹוָה אֱלֹהֵיכֶם וְסַרְתֶּם מִן־הַדֶּרֶךְ אֲשֶׁר אָנֹכִי מְצַוֶּה אֶתְכֶם הַיּוֹם לָלֶכֶת אַחֲרֵי אֱלֹהִים אֲחֵרִים אֲשֶׁר לֹא־יְדַעְתֶּם:

Deuteronomy

29 When *Hashem* your God brings you into the land that you are about to enter and possess, you shall pronounce the blessing at *Har Gerizim* and the curse at *Har Eival.*

כט וְהָיָה כִּי יְבִיאֲךָ יְהוָה אֱלֹהֶיךָ אֶל־הָאָרֶץ אֲשֶׁר־אַתָּה בָא־שָׁמָּה לְרִשְׁתָּהּ וְנָתַתָּה אֶת־הַבְּרָכָה עַל־הַר גְּרִזִים וְאֶת־ הַקְּלָלָה עַל־הַר עֵיבָל:

*v'-ha-YA KEE y'-vee-a-KHA a-do-NAI e-lo-HE-kha el ha-A-retz
a-sher a-TA va SHA-ma l'-rish-TA v'-na-ta-TA et ha-b'-ra-KHAH
al HAR g'-ri-ZEEM v'-et ha-k'-la-LAH al HAR ay-VAL*

30 Both are on the other side of the *Yarden*, beyond the west road that is in the land of the Canaanites who dwell in the Arabah – near *Gilgal*, by the terebinths of Moreh.

ל הֲלֹא־הֵמָּה בְּעֵבֶר הַיַּרְדֵּן אַחֲרֵי דֶּרֶךְ מְבוֹא הַשֶּׁמֶשׁ בְּאֶרֶץ הַכְּנַעֲנִי הַיֹּשֵׁב בָּעֲרָבָה מוּל הַגִּלְגָּל אֵצֶל אֵלוֹנֵי מֹרֶה:

31 For you are about to cross the *Yarden* to enter and possess the land that *Hashem* your God is assigning to you. When you have occupied it and are settled in it,

לא כִּי אַתֶּם עֹבְרִים אֶת־הַיַּרְדֵּן לָבֹא לָרֶשֶׁת אֶת־הָאָרֶץ אֲשֶׁר־יְהוָה אֱלֹהֵיכֶם נֹתֵן לָכֶם וִירִשְׁתֶּם אֹתָהּ וִישַׁבְתֶּם־בָּהּ:

32 take care to observe all the laws and rules that I have set before you this day.

לב וּשְׁמַרְתֶּם לַעֲשׂוֹת אֵת כָּל־הַחֻקִּים וְאֶת־הַמִּשְׁפָּטִים אֲשֶׁר אָנֹכִי נֹתֵן לִפְנֵיכֶם הַיּוֹם:

12 **1** These are the laws and rules that you must carefully observe in the land that *Hashem*, God of your fathers, is giving you to possess, as long as you live on earth.

יב א אֵלֶּה הַחֻקִּים וְהַמִּשְׁפָּטִים אֲשֶׁר תִּשְׁמְרוּן לַעֲשׂוֹת בָּאָרֶץ אֲשֶׁר נָתַן יְהוָה אֱלֹהֵי אֲבֹתֶיךָ לְךָ לְרִשְׁתָּהּ כָּל־הַיָּמִים אֲשֶׁר־אַתֶּם חַיִּים עַל־הָאֲדָמָה:

2 You must destroy all the sites at which the nations you are to dispossess worshiped their gods, whether on lofty mountains and on hills or under any luxuriant tree.

ב אַבֵּד תְּאַבְּדוּן אֶת־כָּל־הַמְּקֹמוֹת אֲשֶׁר עָבְדוּ־שָׁם הַגּוֹיִם אֲשֶׁר אַתֶּם יֹרְשִׁים אֹתָם אֶת־אֱלֹהֵיהֶם עַל־הֶהָרִים הָרָמִים וְעַל־הַגְּבָעוֹת וְתַחַת כָּל־עֵץ רַעֲנָן:

3 Tear down their altars, smash their pillars, put their sacred posts to the fire, and cut down the images of their gods, obliterating their name from that site.

ג וְנִתַּצְתֶּם אֶת־מִזְבְּחֹתָם וְשִׁבַּרְתֶּם אֶת־ מַצֵּבֹתָם וַאֲשֵׁרֵיהֶם תִּשְׂרְפוּן בָּאֵשׁ וּפְסִילֵי אֱלֹהֵיהֶם תְּגַדֵּעוּן וְאִבַּדְתֶּם אֶת־שְׁמָם מִן־הַמָּקוֹם הַהוּא:

4 Do not worship *Hashem* your God in like manner,

ד לֹא־תַעֲשׂוּן כֵּן לַיהוָה אֱלֹהֵיכֶם:

5 but look only to the site that *Hashem* your God will choose amidst all your tribes as His habitation, to establish His name there. There you are to go,

ה כִּי אִם־אֶל־הַמָּקוֹם אֲשֶׁר־יִבְחַר יְהוָה אֱלֹהֵיכֶם מִכָּל־שִׁבְטֵיכֶם לָשׂוּם אֶת־ שְׁמוֹ שָׁם לְשִׁכְנוֹ תִדְרְשׁוּ וּבָאתָ שָׁמָּה:

*KEE im el ha-ma-KOM a-sher yiv-KHAR a-do-NAI
e-lo-hay-KHEM mi-kol shiv-tay-KHEM la-SUM et sh'-MO
SHAM l'-shikh-NO tid-r'-SHU u-VA-ta SHA-ma*

שכינה

12:5 To establish His name there The Hebrew word for 'to establish His name' is *l'shichno* (לשכנו). The root of this word, *shachen* (ש-כ-נ), means 'to dwell', and is also the root of the word *shechina* (שכינה), used to refer to *Hashem*'s presence. The use of this word to refer to His presence alludes to our close, personal, relationship with the Almighty, as the name indicates that He dwells among us. Additionally, this verse reminds us that the place on earth where *Hashem*'s presence is perceived more than any other is the Temple Mount in *Yerushalayim*, the place where he chose "to establish His name."

The Temple Mount and Western Wall

6 and there you are to bring your burnt offerings and other sacrifices, your tithes and contributions, your votive and freewill offerings, and the firstlings of your herds and flocks.

ו וַהֲבֵאתֶם שָׁמָּה עֹלֹתֵיכֶם וְזִבְחֵיכֶם וְאֵת מַעְשְׂרֹתֵיכֶם וְאֵת תְּרוּמַת יֶדְכֶם וְנִדְרֵיכֶם וְנִדְבֹתֵיכֶם וּבְכֹרֹת בְּקַרְכֶם וְצֹאנְכֶם:

7 Together with your households, you shall feast there before *Hashem* your God, happy in all the undertakings in which *Hashem* your God has blessed you.

ז וַאֲכַלְתֶּם־שָׁם לִפְנֵי יְהֹוָה אֱלֹהֵיכֶם וּשְׂמַחְתֶּם בְּכֹל מִשְׁלַח יֶדְכֶם אַתֶּם וּבָתֵּיכֶם אֲשֶׁר בֵּרַכְךָ יְהֹוָה אֱלֹהֶיךָ:

8 You shall not act at all as we now act here, every man as he pleases,

ח לֹא תַעֲשׂוּן כְּכֹל אֲשֶׁר אֲנַחְנוּ עֹשִׂים פֹּה הַיּוֹם אִישׁ כָּל־הַיָּשָׁר בְּעֵינָיו:

9 because you have not yet come to the allotted haven that *Hashem* your God is giving you.

ט כִּי לֹא־בָאתֶם עַד־עָתָּה אֶל־הַמְּנוּחָה וְאֶל־הַנַּחֲלָה אֲשֶׁר־יְהֹוָה אֱלֹהֶיךָ נֹתֵן לָךְ:

10 When you cross the *Yarden* and settle in the land that *Hashem* your God is allotting to you, and He grants you safety from all your enemies around you and you live in security,

י וַעֲבַרְתֶּם אֶת־הַיַּרְדֵּן וִישַׁבְתֶּם בָּאָרֶץ אֲשֶׁר־יְהֹוָה אֱלֹהֵיכֶם מַנְחִיל אֶתְכֶם וְהֵנִיחַ לָכֶם מִכָּל־אֹיְבֵיכֶם מִסָּבִיב וִישַׁבְתֶּם־בֶּטַח:

*va-a-var-TEM et ha-yar-DAYN vee-shav-TEM ba-A-retz a-sher a-do-NAI
e-lo-hay-KHEM man-KHEEL et-KHEM v'-hay-NEE-akh la-KHEM
mi-kol o-y'-vay-KHEM mi-sa-VEEV vee-shav-tem BE-takh*

11 then you must bring everything that I command you to the site where *Hashem* your God will choose to establish His name: your burnt offerings and other sacrifices, your tithes and contributions, and all the choice votive offerings that you vow to *Hashem*.

יא וְהָיָה הַמָּקוֹם אֲשֶׁר־יִבְחַר יְהֹוָה אֱלֹהֵיכֶם בּוֹ לְשַׁכֵּן שְׁמוֹ שָׁם שָׁמָּה תָבִיאוּ אֵת כָּל־אֲשֶׁר אָנֹכִי מְצַוֶּה אֶתְכֶם עוֹלֹתֵיכֶם וְזִבְחֵיכֶם מַעְשְׂרֹתֵיכֶם וּתְרוּמַת יֶדְכֶם וְכֹל מִבְחַר נִדְרֵיכֶם אֲשֶׁר תִּדְּרוּ לַיהֹוָה:

12 And you shall rejoice before *Hashem* your God with your sons and daughters and with your male and female slaves, along with the Levite in your settlements, for he has no territorial allotment among you.

יב וּשְׂמַחְתֶּם לִפְנֵי יְהֹוָה אֱלֹהֵיכֶם אַתֶּם וּבְנֵיכֶם וּבְנֹתֵיכֶם וְעַבְדֵיכֶם וְאַמְהֹתֵיכֶם וְהַלֵּוִי אֲשֶׁר בְּשַׁעֲרֵיכֶם כִּי אֵין לוֹ חֵלֶק וְנַחֲלָה אִתְּכֶם:

13 Take care not to sacrifice your burnt offerings in any place you like,

יג הִשָּׁמֶר לְךָ פֶּן־תַּעֲלֶה עֹלֹתֶיךָ בְּכָל־מָקוֹם אֲשֶׁר תִּרְאֶה:

IDF soldier praying at the Western Wall

12:10 He grants you safety from all your enemies around you *Moshe* promises the Children of Israel peace and security in the Land of Israel. Indeed, after conquering and dividing the land under the leadership of *Yehoshua*, the Children of Israel did dwell peacefully in the land, as the verse says "*Hashem* had given Israel rest from all the enemies around them" (Joshua 23:1). However, this peace was short-lived; it did not take long after the death of *Yehoshua* for enemy nations to begin harassing them in their land. Throughout history, there have been periods of relative quiet in the land, but none have lasted very long. We pray for the complete fulfillment of this verse, when we will be blessed with everlasting safety and security in *Eretz Yisrael*.

14 but only in the place that *Hashem* will choose in one of your tribal territories. There you shall sacrifice your burnt offerings and there you shall observe all that I enjoin upon you.

יד כִּי אִם־בַּמָּקוֹם אֲשֶׁר־יִבְחַר יְהֹוָה בְּאַחַד שְׁבָטֶיךָ שָׁם תַּעֲלֶה עֹלֹתֶיךָ וְשָׁם תַּעֲשֶׂה כֹּל אֲשֶׁר אָנֹכִי מְצַוֶּךָּ:

15 But whenever you desire, you may slaughter and eat meat in any of your settlements, according to the blessing that *Hashem* your God has granted you. The unclean and the clean alike may partake of it, as of the gazelle and the deer.

טו רַק בְּכָל־אַוַּת נַפְשְׁךָ תִּזְבַּח וְאָכַלְתָּ בָשָׂר כְּבִרְכַּת יְהֹוָה אֱלֹהֶיךָ אֲשֶׁר נָתַן־לְךָ בְּכָל־שְׁעָרֶיךָ הַטָּמֵא וְהַטָּהוֹר יֹאכְלֶנּוּ כַּצְּבִי וְכָאַיָּל:

16 But you must not partake of the blood; you shall pour it out on the ground like water.

טז רַק הַדָּם לֹא תֹאכֵלוּ עַל־הָאָרֶץ תִּשְׁפְּכֶנּוּ כַּמָּיִם:

17 You may not partake in your settlements of the tithes of your new grain or wine or oil, or of the firstlings of your herds and flocks, or of any of the votive offerings that you vow, or of your freewill offerings, or of your contributions.

יז לֹא־תוּכַל לֶאֱכֹל בִּשְׁעָרֶיךָ מַעְשַׂר דְּגָנְךָ וְתִירֹשְׁךָ וְיִצְהָרֶךָ וּבְכֹרֹת בְּקָרְךָ וְצֹאנֶךָ וְכָל־נְדָרֶיךָ אֲשֶׁר תִּדֹּר וְנִדְבֹתֶיךָ וּתְרוּמַת יָדֶךָ:

18 These you must consume before *Hashem* your God in the place that *Hashem* your God will choose – you and your sons and your daughters, your male and female slaves, and the Levite in your settlements – happy before *Hashem* your God in all your undertakings.

יח כִּי אִם־לִפְנֵי יְהֹוָה אֱלֹהֶיךָ תֹּאכְלֶנּוּ בַּמָּקוֹם אֲשֶׁר יִבְחַר יְהֹוָה אֱלֹהֶיךָ בּוֹ אַתָּה וּבִנְךָ וּבִתֶּךָ וְעַבְדְּךָ וַאֲמָתֶךָ וְהַלֵּוִי אֲשֶׁר בִּשְׁעָרֶיךָ וְשָׂמַחְתָּ לִפְנֵי יְהֹוָה אֱלֹהֶיךָ בְּכֹל מִשְׁלַח יָדֶךָ:

19 Be sure not to neglect the Levite as long as you live in your land.

יט הִשָּׁמֶר לְךָ פֶּן־תַּעֲזֹב אֶת־הַלֵּוִי כָּל־יָמֶיךָ עַל־אַדְמָתֶךָ:

20 When *Hashem* enlarges your territory, as He has promised you, and you say, "I shall eat some meat," for you have the urge to eat meat, you may eat meat whenever you wish.

כ כִּי־יַרְחִיב יְהֹוָה אֱלֹהֶיךָ אֶת־גְּבֻלְךָ כַּאֲשֶׁר דִּבֶּר־לָךְ וְאָמַרְתָּ אֹכְלָה בָשָׂר כִּי־תְאַוֶּה נַפְשְׁךָ לֶאֱכֹל בָּשָׂר בְּכָל־אַוַּת נַפְשְׁךָ תֹּאכַל בָּשָׂר:

21 If the place where *Hashem* has chosen to establish His name is too far from you, you may slaughter any of the cattle or sheep that *Hashem* gives you, as I have instructed you; and you may eat to your heart's content in your settlements.

כא כִּי־יִרְחַק מִמְּךָ הַמָּקוֹם אֲשֶׁר יִבְחַר יְהֹוָה אֱלֹהֶיךָ לָשׂוּם שְׁמוֹ שָׁם וְזָבַחְתָּ מִבְּקָרְךָ וּמִצֹּאנְךָ אֲשֶׁר נָתַן יְהֹוָה לְךָ כַּאֲשֶׁר צִוִּיתִךָ וְאָכַלְתָּ בִּשְׁעָרֶיךָ בְּכֹל אַוַּת נַפְשֶׁךָ:

22 Eat it, however, as the gazelle and the deer are eaten: the unclean may eat it together with the clean.

כב אַךְ כַּאֲשֶׁר יֵאָכֵל אֶת־הַצְּבִי וְאֶת־הָאַיָּל כֵּן תֹּאכְלֶנּוּ הַטָּמֵא וְהַטָּהוֹר יַחְדָּו יֹאכְלֶנּוּ:

23 But make sure that you do not partake of the blood; for the blood is the life, and you must not consume the life with the flesh.

כג רַק חֲזַק לְבִלְתִּי אֲכֹל הַדָּם כִּי הַדָּם הוּא הַנָּפֶשׁ וְלֹא־תֹאכַל הַנֶּפֶשׁ עִם־הַבָּשָׂר:

24 You must not partake of it; you must pour it out on the ground like water:

כד לֹא תֹּאכְלֶנּוּ עַל־הָאָרֶץ תִּשְׁפְּכֶנּוּ כַּמָּיִם:

25 you must not partake of it, in order that it may go well with you and with your descendants to come, for you will be doing what is right in the sight of *Hashem*.

כה לֹא תֹּאכְלֶנּוּ לְמַעַן יִיטַב לְךָ וּלְבָנֶיךָ אַחֲרֶיךָ כִּי־תַעֲשֶׂה הַיָּשָׁר בְּעֵינֵי יְהֹוָה:

26 But such sacred and votive donations as you may have shall be taken by you to the site that *Hashem* will choose.

כו רַק קׇדָשֶׁיךָ אֲשֶׁר־יִהְיוּ לְךָ וּנְדָרֶיךָ תִּשָּׂא וּבָאתָ אֶל־הַמָּקוֹם אֲשֶׁר־יִבְחַר יְהֹוָה:

27 You shall offer your burnt offerings, both the flesh and the blood, on the *Mizbayach* of *Hashem* your God; and of your other sacrifices, the blood shall be poured out on the *Mizbayach* of *Hashem* your God, and you shall eat the flesh.

כז וְעָשִׂיתָ עֹלֹתֶיךָ הַבָּשָׂר וְהַדָּם עַל־מִזְבַּח יְהֹוָה אֱלֹהֶיךָ וְדַם־זְבָחֶיךָ יִשָּׁפֵךְ עַל־ מִזְבַּח יְהֹוָה אֱלֹהֶיךָ וְהַבָּשָׂר תֹּאכֵל:

28 Be careful to heed all these commandments that I enjoin upon you; thus it will go well with you and with your descendants after you forever, for you will be doing what is good and right in the sight of *Hashem* your God.

כח שְׁמֹר וְשָׁמַעְתָּ אֵת כׇּל־הַדְּבָרִים הָאֵלֶּה אֲשֶׁר אָנֹכִי מְצַוֶּךָּ לְמַעַן יִיטַב לְךָ וּלְבָנֶיךָ אַחֲרֶיךָ עַד־עוֹלָם כִּי תַעֲשֶׂה הַטּוֹב וְהַיָּשָׁר בְּעֵינֵי יְהֹוָה אֱלֹהֶיךָ:

29 When *Hashem* your God has cut down before you the nations that you are about to enter and dispossess, and you have dispossessed them and settled in their land,

כט כִּי־יַכְרִית יְהֹוָה אֱלֹהֶיךָ אֶת־הַגּוֹיִם אֲשֶׁר אַתָּה בָא־שָׁמָּה לָרֶשֶׁת אוֹתָם מִפָּנֶיךָ וְיָרַשְׁתָּ אֹתָם וְיָשַׁבְתָּ בְּאַרְצָם:

30 beware of being lured into their ways after they have been wiped out before you! Do not inquire about their gods, saying, "How did those nations worship their gods? I too will follow those practices."

ל הִשָּׁמֶר לְךָ פֶּן־תִּנָּקֵשׁ אַחֲרֵיהֶם אַחֲרֵי הִשָּׁמְדָם מִפָּנֶיךָ וּפֶן־תִּדְרֹשׁ לֵאלֹהֵיהֶם לֵאמֹר אֵיכָה יַעַבְדוּ הַגּוֹיִם הָאֵלֶּה אֶת־ אֱלֹהֵיהֶם וְאֶעֱשֶׂה־כֵּן גַּם־אָנִי:

31 You shall not act thus toward *Hashem* your God, for they perform for their gods every abhorrent act that *Hashem* detests; they even offer up their sons and daughters in fire to their gods.

לא לֹא־תַעֲשֶׂה כֵן לַיהֹוָה אֱלֹהֶיךָ כִּי כׇל־תּוֹעֲבַת יְהֹוָה אֲשֶׁר שָׂנֵא עָשׂוּ לֵאלֹהֵיהֶם כִּי גַם אֶת־בְּנֵיהֶם וְאֶת־ בְּנֹתֵיהֶם יִשְׂרְפוּ בָאֵשׁ לֵאלֹהֵיהֶם:

13 1 Be careful to observe only that which I enjoin upon you: neither add to it nor take away from it.

יג א אֵת כׇּל־הַדָּבָר אֲשֶׁר אָנֹכִי מְצַוֶּה אֶתְכֶם אֹתוֹ תִשְׁמְרוּ לַעֲשׂוֹת לֹא־תֹסֵף עָלָיו וְלֹא תִגְרַע מִמֶּנּוּ:

2 If there appears among you a prophet or a dream-diviner and he gives you a sign or a portent,

ב כִּי־יָקוּם בְּקִרְבְּךָ נָבִיא אוֹ חֹלֵם חֲלוֹם וְנָתַן אֵלֶיךָ אוֹת אוֹ מוֹפֵת:

3 saying, "Let us follow and worship another god" – whom you have not experienced – even if the sign or portent that he named to you comes true,

ג וּבָא הָאוֹת וְהַמּוֹפֵת אֲשֶׁר־דִּבֶּר אֵלֶיךָ לֵאמֹר נֵלְכָה אַחֲרֵי אֱלֹהִים אֲחֵרִים אֲשֶׁר לֹא־יְדַעְתָּם וְנׇעׇבְדֵם:

4 do not heed the words of that prophet or that dream-diviner. For *Hashem* your God is testing you to see whether you really love *Hashem* your God with all your heart and soul.

ד לֹא תִשְׁמַע אֶל־דִּבְרֵי הַנָּבִיא הַהוּא אוֹ אֶל־חוֹלֵם הַחֲלוֹם הַהוּא כִּי מְנַסֶּה יְהֹוָה אֱלֹהֵיכֶם אֶתְכֶם לָדַעַת הֲיִשְׁכֶם אֹהֲבִים אֶת־יְהֹוָה אֱלֹהֵיכֶם בְּכׇל־לְבַבְכֶם וּבְכׇל־ נַפְשְׁכֶם:

5 Follow none but *Hashem* your God, and revere none but Him; observe His commandments alone, and heed only His orders; worship none but Him, and hold fast to Him.

ה אַחֲרֵי יְהֹוָה אֱלֹהֵיכֶם תֵּלֵכוּ וְאֹתוֹ
תִירָאוּ וְאֶת־מִצְוֺתָיו תִּשְׁמֹרוּ וּבְקֹלוֹ
תִשְׁמָעוּ וְאֹתוֹ תַעֲבֹדוּ וּבוֹ תִדְבָּקוּן:

a-kha-RAY a-do-NAI e-lo-hay-KHEM tay-LAY-khu
v'-o-TO tee-RA-u v'-et mitz-vo-TAV tish-MO-ru uv-ko-LO
tish-MA-u v'-o-TO ta-a-VO-du u-VO tid-ba-KUN

6 As for that prophet or dream-diviner, he shall be put to death; for he urged disloyalty to *Hashem* your God – who freed you from the land of Egypt and who redeemed you from the house of bondage – to make you stray from the path that *Hashem* your God commanded you to follow. Thus you will sweep out evil from your midst.

ו וְהַנָּבִיא הַהוּא אוֹ חֹלֵם הַחֲלוֹם הַהוּא
יוּמָת כִּי דִבֶּר־סָרָה עַל־יְהֹוָה אֱלֹהֵיכֶם
הַמּוֹצִיא אֶתְכֶם מֵאֶרֶץ מִצְרַיִם וְהַפֹּדְךָ
מִבֵּית עֲבָדִים לְהַדִּיחֲךָ מִן־הַדֶּרֶךְ אֲשֶׁר
צִוְּךָ יְהֹוָה אֱלֹהֶיךָ לָלֶכֶת בָּהּ וּבִעַרְתָּ
הָרָע מִקִּרְבֶּךָ:

7 If your brother, your own mother's son, or your son or daughter, or the wife of your bosom, or your closest friend entices you in secret, saying, "Come let us worship other gods" – whom neither you nor your fathers have experienced

ז כִּי יְסִיתְךָ אָחִיךָ בֶן־אִמֶּךָ אוֹ־בִנְךָ אוֹ־
בִתְּךָ אוֹ אֵשֶׁת חֵיקֶךָ אוֹ רֵעֲךָ אֲשֶׁר
כְּנַפְשְׁךָ בַּסֵּתֶר לֵאמֹר נֵלְכָה וְנַעַבְדָה
אֱלֹהִים אֲחֵרִים אֲשֶׁר לֹא יָדַעְתָּ אַתָּה
וַאֲבֹתֶיךָ:

8 from among the gods of the peoples around you, either near to you or distant, anywhere from one end of the earth to the other:

ח מֵאֱלֹהֵי הָעַמִּים אֲשֶׁר סְבִיבֹתֵיכֶם
הַקְּרֹבִים אֵלֶיךָ אוֹ הָרְחֹקִים מִמֶּךָּ
מִקְצֵה הָאָרֶץ וְעַד־קְצֵה הָאָרֶץ:

9 do not assent or give heed to him. Show him no pity or compassion, and do not shield him;

ט לֹא־תֹאבֶה לוֹ וְלֹא תִשְׁמַע אֵלָיו וְלֹא־
תָחוֹס עֵינְךָ עָלָיו וְלֹא־תַחְמֹל וְלֹא־
תְכַסֶּה עָלָיו:

10 but take his life. Let your hand be the first against him to put him to death, and the hand of the rest of the people thereafter.

י כִּי הָרֹג תַּהַרְגֶנּוּ יָדְךָ תִּהְיֶה־בּוֹ
בָרִאשׁוֹנָה לַהֲמִיתוֹ וְיַד כָּל־הָעָם
בָּאַחֲרֹנָה:

11 Stone him to death, for he sought to make you stray from *Hashem* your God, who brought you out of the land of Egypt, out of the house of bondage.

יא וּסְקַלְתּוֹ בָאֲבָנִים וָמֵת כִּי בִקֵּשׁ
לְהַדִּיחֲךָ מֵעַל יְהֹוָה אֱלֹהֶיךָ הַמּוֹצִיאֲךָ
מֵאֶרֶץ מִצְרַיִם מִבֵּית עֲבָדִים:

12 Thus all *Yisrael* will hear and be afraid, and such evil things will not be done again in your midst.

יב וְכָל־יִשְׂרָאֵל יִשְׁמְעוּ וְיִרָאוּן וְלֹא־יוֹסִפוּ
לַעֲשׂוֹת כַּדָּבָר הָרָע הַזֶּה בְּקִרְבֶּךָ:

13:5 And hold fast to Him This verse concludes with the directive to cleave to *Hashem*. Since it is impossible to literally "hold fast" to a being that has no physical form, the Sages explain (*Sotah* 14a) that this commandment means we are required to emulate His ways. Just as *Hashem* performs kind deeds, buries the dead (Deuteronomy 33:6) and visits the sick (Genesis 18:1), so too must we be kind to others and take care of their needs. Contemporary Israel fulfills this mandate, and emulates God's compassion. It is often the first country to respond to natural disasters, providing medical aid and other assistance around the world. For example, when a devastating earthquake struck Haiti in 2010, the IDF was amongst the first responders on the scene. One woman who gave birth in an Israeli field hospital was so grateful to the Israeli medical team that she named her baby 'Israel.'

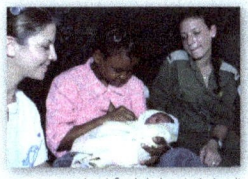

Israel, first baby born in the Israeli field hospital in Haiti

13 If you hear it said, of one of the towns that *Hashem* your God is giving you to dwell in,

יג כִּי־תִשְׁמַע בְּאַחַת עָרֶיךָ אֲשֶׁר יְהוָה אֱלֹהֶיךָ נֹתֵן לְךָ לָשֶׁבֶת שָׁם לֵאמֹר:

14 that some scoundrels from among you have gone and subverted the inhabitants of their town, saying, "Come let us worship other gods" – whom you have not experienced

יד יָצְאוּ אֲנָשִׁים בְּנֵי־בְלִיַּעַל מִקִּרְבֶּךָ וַיַּדִּיחוּ אֶת־יֹשְׁבֵי עִירָם לֵאמֹר נֵלְכָה וְנַעַבְדָה אֱלֹהִים אֲחֵרִים אֲשֶׁר לֹא־יְדַעְתֶּם:

15 you shall investigate and inquire and interrogate thoroughly. If it is true, the fact is established – that abhorrent thing was perpetrated in your midst

טו וְדָרַשְׁתָּ וְחָקַרְתָּ וְשָׁאַלְתָּ הֵיטֵב וְהִנֵּה אֱמֶת נָכוֹן הַדָּבָר נֶעֶשְׂתָה הַתּוֹעֵבָה הַזֹּאת בְּקִרְבֶּךָ:

16 put the inhabitants of that town to the sword and put its cattle to the sword. Doom it and all that is in it to destruction:

טז הַכֵּה תַכֶּה אֶת־יֹשְׁבֵי הָעִיר הַהִוא [הַהִיא] לְפִי־חָרֶב הַחֲרֵם אֹתָהּ וְאֶת־כָּל־אֲשֶׁר־בָּהּ וְאֶת־בְּהֶמְתָּהּ לְפִי־חָרֶב:

17 gather all its spoil into the open square, and burn the town and all its spoil as a holocaust to *Hashem* your God. And it shall remain an everlasting ruin, never to be rebuilt.

יז וְאֶת־כָּל־שְׁלָלָהּ תִּקְבֹּץ אֶל־תּוֹךְ רְחֹבָהּ וְשָׂרַפְתָּ בָאֵשׁ אֶת־הָעִיר וְאֶת־כָּל־שְׁלָלָהּ כָּלִיל לַיהוָה אֱלֹהֶיךָ וְהָיְתָה תֵּל עוֹלָם לֹא תִבָּנֶה עוֹד:

18 Let nothing that has been doomed stick to your hand, in order that *Hashem* may turn from His blazing anger and show you compassion, and in His compassion increase you as He promised your fathers on oath

יח וְלֹא־יִדְבַּק בְּיָדְךָ מְאוּמָה מִן־הַחֵרֶם לְמַעַן יָשׁוּב יְהוָה מֵחֲרוֹן אַפּוֹ וְנָתַן־לְךָ רַחֲמִים וְרִחַמְךָ וְהִרְבֶּךָ כַּאֲשֶׁר נִשְׁבַּע לַאֲבֹתֶיךָ:

19 for you will be heeding *Hashem* your God, obeying all His commandments that I enjoin upon you this day, doing what is right in the sight of *Hashem* your God.

יט כִּי תִשְׁמַע בְּקוֹל יְהוָה אֱלֹהֶיךָ לִשְׁמֹר אֶת־כָּל־מִצְוֹתָיו אֲשֶׁר אָנֹכִי מְצַוְּךָ הַיּוֹם לַעֲשׂוֹת הַיָּשָׁר בְּעֵינֵי יְהוָה אֱלֹהֶיךָ:

14

1 You are children of *Hashem* your God. You shall not gash yourselves or shave the front of your heads because of the dead.

יד א בָּנִים אַתֶּם לַיהוָה אֱלֹהֵיכֶם לֹא תִתְגֹּדְדוּ וְלֹא־תָשִׂימוּ קָרְחָה בֵּין עֵינֵיכֶם לָמֵת:

*ba-NEEM a-TEM la-do-NAI e-lo-hay-KHEM LO tit-go-d'DU v'-lo
ta-SEE-mu kor-KHAH BAYN ay-nay-KHEM la-MAYT*

2 For you are a people consecrated to *Hashem* your God: *Hashem* your God chose you from among all other peoples on earth to be His treasured people.

ב כִּי עַם קָדוֹשׁ אַתָּה לַיהוָה אֱלֹהֶיךָ וּבְךָ בָּחַר יְהוָה לִהְיוֹת לוֹ לְעַם סְגֻלָּה מִכֹּל הָעַמִּים אֲשֶׁר עַל־פְּנֵי הָאֲדָמָה:

3 You shall not eat anything abhorrent.

ג לֹא תֹאכַל כָּל־תּוֹעֵבָה:

14:1 You are children of *Hashem* your God These words explain why the Nation of Israel is sometimes held to a higher standard. Since they are the children of *Hashem*, they cannot express their mourning by hurting themselves and they may eat only certain foods, as the chapter goes on to describe. This is not meant to imply that they are the only children of *Hashem*, but rather that their special status reflects the fact that they were chosen by God to be His ambassadors and to set an example for the rest of His creations. As such, *Hashem* chose the Land of Israel as the place from which the Israelites are to serve as "a light unto the nations."

Sunset over *Yerushalayim*

Deuteronomy

4 These are the animals that you may eat: the ox, the sheep, and the goat;

ד זֹאת הַבְּהֵמָה אֲשֶׁר תֹּאכֵלוּ שׁוֹר שֵׂה כְשָׂבִים וְשֵׂה עִזִּים:

5 the deer, the gazelle, the roebuck, the wild goat, the ibex, the antelope, the mountain sheep,

ה אַיָּל וּצְבִי וְיַחְמוּר וְאַקּוֹ וְדִישֹׁן וּתְאוֹ וָזָמֶר:

6 and any other animal that has true hoofs which are cleft in two and brings up the cud – such you may eat.

ו וְכָל־בְּהֵמָה מַפְרֶסֶת פַּרְסָה וְשֹׁסַעַת שֶׁסַע שְׁתֵּי פְרָסוֹת מַעֲלַת גֵּרָה בַּבְּהֵמָה אֹתָהּ תֹּאכֵלוּ:

7 But the following, which do bring up the cud or have true hoofs which are cleft through, you may not eat: the camel, the hare, and the daman – for although they bring up the cud, they have no true hoofs – they are unclean for you;

ז אַךְ אֶת־זֶה לֹא תֹאכְלוּ מִמַּעֲלֵי הַגֵּרָה וּמִמַּפְרִיסֵי הַפַּרְסָה הַשְּׁסוּעָה אֶת־ הַגָּמָל וְאֶת־הָאַרְנֶבֶת וְאֶת־הַשָּׁפָן כִּי־ מַעֲלֵה גֵרָה הֵמָּה וּפַרְסָה לֹא הִפְרִיסוּ טְמֵאִים הֵם לָכֶם:

8 also the swine – for although it has true hoofs, it does not bring up the cud – is unclean for you. You shall not eat of their flesh or touch their carcasses.

ח וְאֶת־הַחֲזִיר כִּי־מַפְרִיס פַּרְסָה הוּא וְלֹא גֵרָה טָמֵא הוּא לָכֶם מִבְּשָׂרָם לֹא תֹאכֵלוּ וּבְנִבְלָתָם לֹא תִגָּעוּ:

9 These you may eat of all that live in water: you may eat anything that has fins and scales.

ט אֶת־זֶה תֹּאכְלוּ מִכֹּל אֲשֶׁר בַּמָּיִם כֹּל אֲשֶׁר־לוֹ סְנַפִּיר וְקַשְׂקֶשֶׂת תֹּאכֵלוּ:

10 But you may not eat anything that has no fins and scales: it is unclean for you.

י וְכֹל אֲשֶׁר אֵין־לוֹ סְנַפִּיר וְקַשְׂקֶשֶׂת לֹא תֹאכֵלוּ טָמֵא הוּא לָכֶם:

11 You may eat any clean bird.

יא כָּל־צִפּוֹר טְהֹרָה תֹּאכֵלוּ:

12 The following you may not eat: the eagle, the vulture, and the black vulture;

יב וְזֶה אֲשֶׁר לֹא־תֹאכְלוּ מֵהֶם הַנֶּשֶׁר וְהַפֶּרֶס וְהָעָזְנִיָּה:

13 the kite, the falcon, and the buzzard of any variety;

יג וְהָרָאָה וְאֶת־הָאַיָּה וְהַדַּיָּה לְמִינָהּ:

14 every variety of raven;

יד וְאֵת כָּל־עֹרֵב לְמִינוֹ:

15 the ostrich, the nighthawk, the sea gull, and the hawk of any variety;

טו וְאֵת בַּת הַיַּעֲנָה וְאֶת־הַתַּחְמָס וְאֶת־ הַשָּׁחַף וְאֶת־הַנֵּץ לְמִינֵהוּ:

16 the little owl, the great owl, and the white owl;

טז אֶת־הַכּוֹס וְאֶת־הַיַּנְשׁוּף וְהַתִּנְשָׁמֶת:

17 the pelican, the bustard, and the cormorant;

יז וְהַקָּאָת וְאֶת־הָרָחָמָה וְאֶת־הַשָּׁלָךְ:

18 the stork, any variety of heron, the hoopoe, and the bat.

יח וְהַחֲסִידָה וְהָאֲנָפָה לְמִינָהּ וְהַדּוּכִיפַת וְהָעֲטַלֵּף:

19 All winged swarming things are unclean for you: they may not be eaten.

יט וְכֹל שֶׁרֶץ הָעוֹף טָמֵא הוּא לָכֶם לֹא יֵאָכֵלוּ:

20 You may eat only clean winged creatures.

כ כָּל־עוֹף טָהוֹר תֹּאכֵלוּ:

21 You shall not eat anything that has died a natural death; give it to the stranger in your community to eat, or you may sell it to a foreigner. For you are a people consecrated to *Hashem* your God. You shall not boil a kid in its mother's milk.

כא לֹא תֹאכְלוּ כָל־נְבֵלָה לַגֵּר אֲשֶׁר־ בִּשְׁעָרֶיךָ תִּתְּנֶנָּה וַאֲכָלָהּ אוֹ מָכֹר לְנָכְרִי כִּי עַם קָדוֹשׁ אַתָּה לַיהוָה אֱלֹהֶיךָ לֹא־ תְבַשֵּׁל גְּדִי בַּחֲלֵב אִמּוֹ:

22 You shall set aside every year a tenth part of all the yield of your sowing that is brought from the field.

כב עַשֵּׂר תְּעַשֵּׂר אֵת כָּל־תְּבוּאַת זַרְעֶךָ הַיֹּצֵא הַשָּׂדֶה שָׁנָה שָׁנָה:

23 You shall consume the tithes of your new grain and wine and oil, and the firstlings of your herds and flocks, in the presence of *Hashem* your God, in the place where He will choose to establish His name, so that you may learn to revere *Hashem* your God forever.

כג וְאָכַלְתָּ לִפְנֵי יהוה אֱלֹהֶיךָ בַּמָּקוֹם אֲשֶׁר־יִבְחַר לְשַׁכֵּן שְׁמוֹ שָׁם מַעְשַׂר דְּגָנְךָ תִּירֹשְׁךָ וְיִצְהָרֶךָ וּבְכֹרֹת בְּקָרְךָ וְצֹאנֶךָ לְמַעַן תִּלְמַד לְיִרְאָה אֶת־יהוה אֱלֹהֶיךָ כָּל־הַיָּמִים:

24 Should the distance be too great for you, should you be unable to transport them, because the place where *Hashem* your God has chosen to establish His name is far from you and because *Hashem* your God has blessed you,

כד וְכִי־יִרְבֶּה מִמְּךָ הַדֶּרֶךְ כִּי לֹא תוּכַל שְׂאֵתוֹ כִּי־יִרְחַק מִמְּךָ הַמָּקוֹם אֲשֶׁר יִבְחַר יהוה אֱלֹהֶיךָ לָשׂוּם שְׁמוֹ שָׁם כִּי יְבָרֶכְךָ יהוה אֱלֹהֶיךָ:

25 you may convert them into money. Wrap up the money and take it with you to the place that *Hashem* your God has chosen,

כה וְנָתַתָּה בַּכָּסֶף וְצַרְתָּ הַכֶּסֶף בְּיָדְךָ וְהָלַכְתָּ אֶל־הַמָּקוֹם אֲשֶׁר יִבְחַר יהוה אֱלֹהֶיךָ בּוֹ:

26 and spend the money on anything you want – cattle, sheep, wine, or other intoxicant, or anything you may desire. And you shall feast there, in the presence of *Hashem* your God, and rejoice with your household.

כו וְנָתַתָּה הַכֶּסֶף בְּכֹל אֲשֶׁר־תְּאַוֶּה נַפְשְׁךָ בַּבָּקָר וּבַצֹּאן וּבַיַּיִן וּבַשֵּׁכָר וּבְכֹל אֲשֶׁר תִּשְׁאָלְךָ נַפְשֶׁךָ וְאָכַלְתָּ שָּׁם לִפְנֵי יהוה אֱלֹהֶיךָ וְשָׂמַחְתָּ אַתָּה וּבֵיתֶךָ:

27 But do not neglect the Levite in your community, for he has no hereditary portion as you have.

כז וְהַלֵּוִי אֲשֶׁר־בִּשְׁעָרֶיךָ לֹא תַעַזְבֶנּוּ כִּי אֵין לוֹ חֵלֶק וְנַחֲלָה עִמָּךְ:

28 Every third year you shall bring out the full tithe of your yield of that year, but leave it within your settlements.

כח מִקְצֵה שָׁלֹשׁ שָׁנִים תּוֹצִיא אֶת־כָּל־ מַעְשַׂר תְּבוּאָתְךָ בַּשָּׁנָה הַהִוא וְהִנַּחְתָּ בִּשְׁעָרֶיךָ:

29 Then the Levite, who has no hereditary portion as you have, and the stranger, the fatherless, and the widow in your settlements shall come and eat their fill, so that *Hashem* your God may bless you in all the enterprises you undertake.

כט וּבָא הַלֵּוִי כִּי אֵין־לוֹ חֵלֶק וְנַחֲלָה עִמָּךְ וְהַגֵּר וְהַיָּתוֹם וְהָאַלְמָנָה אֲשֶׁר בִּשְׁעָרֶיךָ וְאָכְלוּ וְשָׂבֵעוּ לְמַעַן יְבָרֶכְךָ יהוה אֱלֹהֶיךָ בְּכָל־מַעֲשֵׂה יָדְךָ אֲשֶׁר תַּעֲשֶׂה:

15 ¹ Every seventh year you shall practice remission of debts.

טו א מִקֵּץ שֶׁבַע־שָׁנִים תַּעֲשֶׂה שְׁמִטָּה:

2 This shall be the nature of the remission: every creditor shall remit the due that he claims from his fellow; he shall not dun his fellow or kinsman, for the remission proclaimed is of *Hashem*.

ב וְזֶה דְּבַר הַשְּׁמִטָּה שָׁמוֹט כָּל־בַּעַל מַשֵּׁה יָדוֹ אֲשֶׁר יַשֶּׁה בְּרֵעֵהוּ לֹא־יִגֹּשׂ אֶת־רֵעֵהוּ וְאֶת־אָחִיו כִּי־קָרָא שְׁמִטָּה לַיהוה:

³ You may dun the foreigner; but you must remit whatever is due you from your kinsmen.

ג אֶת־הַנׇּכְרִי תִּגֹּשׂ וַאֲשֶׁר יִהְיֶה לְךָ אֶת־אָחִיךָ תַּשְׁמֵט יָדֶךָ:

⁴ There shall be no needy among you – since *Hashem* your God will bless you in the land that *Hashem* your God is giving you as a hereditary portion

ד אֶפֶס כִּי לֹא יִהְיֶה־בְּךָ אֶבְיוֹן כִּי־בָרֵךְ יְבָרֶכְךָ יְהֹוָה בָּאָרֶץ אֲשֶׁר יְהֹוָה אֱלֹהֶיךָ נֹתֵן־לְךָ נַחֲלָה לְרִשְׁתָּהּ:

E-fes KEE LO yih-yeh b'-KHA ev-YON kee va-RAYKH y'-va-re-kh'-kha a-do-NAI
ba-A-retz a-SHER a-do-NAI e-lo-HE-kha no-tayn l'-KHA na-kha-LAH l'-rish-TAH

⁵ if only you heed *Hashem* your God and take care to keep all this Instruction that I enjoin upon you this day.

ה רַק אִם־שָׁמוֹעַ תִּשְׁמַע בְּקוֹל יְהֹוָה אֱלֹהֶיךָ לִשְׁמֹר לַעֲשׂוֹת אֶת־כׇּל־הַמִּצְוָה הַזֹּאת אֲשֶׁר אָנֹכִי מְצַוְּךָ הַיּוֹם:

⁶ For *Hashem* your God will bless you as He has promised you: you will extend loans to many nations, but require none yourself; you will dominate many nations, but they will not dominate you.

ו כִּי־יְהֹוָה אֱלֹהֶיךָ בֵּרַכְךָ כַּאֲשֶׁר דִּבֶּר־לָךְ וְהַעֲבַטְתָּ גּוֹיִם רַבִּים וְאַתָּה לֹא תַעֲבֹט וּמָשַׁלְתָּ בְּגוֹיִם רַבִּים וּבְךָ לֹא יִמְשֹׁלוּ:

⁷ If, however, there is a needy person among you, one of your kinsmen in any of your settlements in the land that *Hashem* your God is giving you, do not harden your heart and shut your hand against your needy kinsman.

ז כִּי־יִהְיֶה בְךָ אֶבְיוֹן מֵאַחַד אַחֶיךָ בְּאַחַד שְׁעָרֶיךָ בְּאַרְצְךָ אֲשֶׁר־יְהֹוָה אֱלֹהֶיךָ נֹתֵן לָךְ לֹא תְאַמֵּץ אֶת־לְבָבְךָ וְלֹא תִקְפֹּץ אֶת־יָדְךָ מֵאָחִיךָ הָאֶבְיוֹן:

⁸ Rather, you must open your hand and lend him sufficient for whatever he needs.

ח כִּי־פָתֹחַ תִּפְתַּח אֶת־יָדְךָ לוֹ וְהַעֲבֵט תַּעֲבִיטֶנּוּ דֵּי מַחְסֹרוֹ אֲשֶׁר יֶחְסַר לוֹ:

⁹ Beware lest you harbor the base thought, "The seventh year, the year of remission, is approaching," so that you are mean to your needy kinsman and give him nothing. He will cry out to *Hashem* against you, and you will incur guilt.

ט הִשָּׁמֶר לְךָ פֶּן־יִהְיֶה דָבָר עִם־לְבָבְךָ בְלִיַּעַל לֵאמֹר קָרְבָה שְׁנַת־הַשֶּׁבַע שְׁנַת הַשְּׁמִטָּה וְרָעָה עֵינְךָ בְּאָחִיךָ הָאֶבְיוֹן וְלֹא תִתֵּן לוֹ וְקָרָא עָלֶיךָ אֶל־יְהֹוָה וְהָיָה בְךָ חֵטְא:

¹⁰ Give to him readily and have no regrets when you do so, for in return *Hashem* your God will bless you in all your efforts and in all your undertakings.

י נָתוֹן תִּתֵּן לוֹ וְלֹא־יֵרַע לְבָבְךָ בְּתִתְּךָ לוֹ כִּי בִּגְלַל הַדָּבָר הַזֶּה יְבָרֶכְךָ יְהֹוָה אֱלֹהֶיךָ בְּכׇל־מַעֲשֶׂךָ וּבְכֹל מִשְׁלַח יָדֶךָ:

ברכה

15:4 *Hashem* **your God will bless you in the land that** *Hashem* **your God is giving you** The Hebrew word for 'blessing,' *beracha* (ברכה), is very similar to the word for 'pool of water,' *bereicha* (בריכה). Water refreshes, nourishes and purifies. In fact, immersing in the special pool of water known as a *mikveh* (מקוה), 'ritual bath,' is the final stage of purification for those who have become ritually impure. Similarly, when we bless something, we raise it spiritually. The Bible repeatedly refers to the Land of Israel as a blessing, teaching us that Israel is the source of abundant blessings, both material and spiritual, for the entire world.

David Waterfall at the *Ein Gedi* nature reserve

Deuteronomy

11 For there will never cease to be needy ones in your land, which is why I command you: open your hand to the poor and needy kinsman in your land.

יא כִּי לֹא־יֶחְדַּל אֶבְיוֹן מִקֶּרֶב הָאָרֶץ עַל־ כֵּן אָנֹכִי מְצַוְּךָ לֵאמֹר פָּתֹחַ תִּפְתַּח אֶת־יָדְךָ לְאָחִיךָ לַעֲנִיֶּךָ וּלְאֶבְיֹנְךָ בְּאַרְצֶךָ:

KEE lo yekh-DAL ev-YON mi-KE-rev ha-A-retz al KAYN a-no-KHEE m'-tza-v'-KHA lay-MOR pa-TO-akh tif-TAKH at ya-d'-KHA l'-a-KHEE-kha la-a-nee-YE-kha ul-ev-yo-n'-KHA b'-ar-TZE-kha

12 If a fellow Hebrew, man or woman, is sold to you, he shall serve you six years, and in the seventh year you shall set him free.

יב כִּי־יִמָּכֵר לְךָ אָחִיךָ הָעִבְרִי אוֹ הָעִבְרִיָּה וַעֲבָדְךָ שֵׁשׁ שָׁנִים וּבַשָּׁנָה הַשְּׁבִיעִת תְּשַׁלְּחֶנּוּ חָפְשִׁי מֵעִמָּךְ:

13 When you set him free, do not let him go empty-handed:

יג וְכִי־תְשַׁלְּחֶנּוּ חָפְשִׁי מֵעִמָּךְ לֹא תְשַׁלְּחֶנּוּ רֵיקָם:

14 Furnish him out of the flock, threshing floor, and vat, with which *Hashem* your God has blessed you.

יד הַעֲנֵיק תַּעֲנִיק לוֹ מִצֹּאנְךָ וּמִגָּרְנְךָ וּמִיִּקְבֶךָ אֲשֶׁר בֵּרַכְךָ יְהוָה אֱלֹהֶיךָ תִּתֶּן־לוֹ:

15 Bear in mind that you were slaves in the land of Egypt and *Hashem* your God redeemed you; therefore I enjoin this commandment upon you today.

טו וְזָכַרְתָּ כִּי עֶבֶד הָיִיתָ בְּאֶרֶץ מִצְרַיִם וַיִּפְדְּךָ יְהוָה אֱלֹהֶיךָ עַל־כֵּן אָנֹכִי מְצַוְּךָ אֶת־הַדָּבָר הַזֶּה הַיּוֹם:

16 But should he say to you, "I do not want to leave you" – for he loves you and your household and is happy with you

טז וְהָיָה כִּי־יֹאמַר אֵלֶיךָ לֹא אֵצֵא מֵעִמָּךְ כִּי אֲהֵבְךָ וְאֶת־בֵּיתֶךָ כִּי־טוֹב לוֹ עִמָּךְ:

17 you shall take an awl and put it through his ear into the door, and he shall become your slave in perpetuity. Do the same with your female slave.

יז וְלָקַחְתָּ אֶת־הַמַּרְצֵעַ וְנָתַתָּה בְאָזְנוֹ וּבַדֶּלֶת וְהָיָה לְךָ עֶבֶד עוֹלָם וְאַף לַאֲמָתְךָ תַּעֲשֶׂה־כֵּן:

18 When you do set him free, do not feel aggrieved; for in the six years he has given you double the service of a hired man. Moreover, *Hashem* your God will bless you in all you do.

יח לֹא־יִקְשֶׁה בְעֵינֶךָ בְּשַׁלֵּחֲךָ אֹתוֹ חָפְשִׁי מֵעִמָּךְ כִּי מִשְׁנֶה שְׂכַר שָׂכִיר עֲבָדְךָ שֵׁשׁ שָׁנִים וּבֵרַכְךָ יְהוָה אֱלֹהֶיךָ בְּכֹל אֲשֶׁר תַּעֲשֶׂה:

19 You shall consecrate to *Hashem* your God all male firstlings that are born in your herd and in your flock: you must not work your firstling ox or shear your firstling sheep.

יט כָּל־הַבְּכוֹר אֲשֶׁר יִוָּלֵד בִּבְקָרְךָ וּבְצֹאנְךָ הַזָּכָר תַּקְדִּישׁ לַיהוָה אֱלֹהֶיךָ לֹא תַעֲבֹד בִּבְכֹר שׁוֹרֶךָ וְלֹא תָגֹז בְּכוֹר צֹאנֶךָ:

Freshly baked *challah* bread at a bakery in Arad

15:11 Open your hand to the poor and needy kinsman Strangely, the word *lechem* (לחם), 'bread,' is the root of the word *milchama* (מלחמה), which means 'war.' According to Rabbi Benjamin Blech in his book *The Secrets of Hebrew Words*, people usually do not go to war because they are wicked, but rather because they are deprived of basic necessities, such as bread. If we take care of those who are needy and provide for those who are hungry, we will be one step closer to bringing peace to the world. This is one of the reasons why the State of Israel allows for an enormous amount of supplies to cross over into Gaza each day, supplying the people living in Gaza with goods such as food, medical devices and construction materials. The Hamas-controlled area remains extremely hostile towards Israel, nevertheless, Israel hopes that the daily deliveries of bread and other supplies will lead to peace.

מלחמה

Deuteronomy

20 You and your household shall eat it annually before *Hashem* your God in the place that *Hashem* will choose.

כ לִפְנֵי יְהֹוָה אֱלֹהֶיךָ תֹאכְלֶנּוּ שָׁנָה בְשָׁנָה בַּמָּקוֹם אֲשֶׁר־יִבְחַר יְהֹוָה אַתָּה וּבֵיתֶךָ׃

21 But if it has a defect, lameness or blindness, any serious defect, you shall not sacrifice it to *Hashem* your God.

כא וְכִי־יִהְיֶה בוֹ מוּם פִּסֵּחַ אוֹ עִוֵּר כֹּל מוּם רָע לֹא תִזְבָּחֶנּוּ לַיהֹוָה אֱלֹהֶיךָ׃

22 Eat it in your settlements, the unclean among you no less than the clean, just like the gazelle and the deer.

כב בִּשְׁעָרֶיךָ תֹּאכְלֶנּוּ הַטָּמֵא וְהַטָּהוֹר יַחְדָּו כַּצְּבִי וְכָאַיָּל׃

23 Only you must not partake of its blood; you shall pour it out on the ground like water.

כג רַק אֶת־דָּמוֹ לֹא תֹאכֵל עַל־הָאָרֶץ תִּשְׁפְּכֶנּוּ כַּמָּיִם׃

16 ¹ Observe the month of Abib and offer a *Pesach* sacrifice to *Hashem* your God, for it was in the month of Abib, at night, that *Hashem* your God freed you from Egypt.

טז א שָׁמוֹר אֶת־חֹדֶשׁ הָאָבִיב וְעָשִׂיתָ פֶּסַח לַיהֹוָה אֱלֹהֶיךָ כִּי בְּחֹדֶשׁ הָאָבִיב הוֹצִיאֲךָ יְהֹוָה אֱלֹהֶיךָ מִמִּצְרַיִם לָיְלָה׃

² You shall slaughter the *Pesach* sacrifice for *Hashem* your God, from the flock and the herd, in the place where *Hashem* will choose to establish His name.

ב וְזָבַחְתָּ פֶּסַח לַיהֹוָה אֱלֹהֶיךָ צֹאן וּבָקָר בַּמָּקוֹם אֲשֶׁר־יִבְחַר יְהֹוָה לְשַׁכֵּן שְׁמוֹ שָׁם׃

³ You shall not eat anything leavened with it; for seven days thereafter you shall eat unleavened bread, bread of distress – for you departed from the land of Egypt hurriedly – so that you may remember the day of your departure from the land of Egypt as long as you live.

ג לֹא־תֹאכַל עָלָיו חָמֵץ שִׁבְעַת יָמִים תֹּאכַל־עָלָיו מַצּוֹת לֶחֶם עֹנִי כִּי בְחִפָּזוֹן יָצָאתָ מֵאֶרֶץ מִצְרַיִם לְמַעַן תִּזְכֹּר אֶת־ יוֹם צֵאתְךָ מֵאֶרֶץ מִצְרַיִם כֹּל יְמֵי חַיֶּיךָ׃

⁴ For seven days no leaven shall be found with you in all your territory, and none of the flesh of what you slaughter on the evening of the first day shall be left until morning.

ד וְלֹא־יֵרָאֶה לְךָ שְׂאֹר בְּכָל־גְּבֻלְךָ שִׁבְעַת יָמִים וְלֹא־יָלִין מִן־הַבָּשָׂר אֲשֶׁר תִּזְבַּח בָּעֶרֶב בַּיּוֹם הָרִאשׁוֹן לַבֹּקֶר׃

⁵ You are not permitted to slaughter the *Pesach* sacrifice in any of the settlements that *Hashem* your God is giving you;

ה לֹא תוּכַל לִזְבֹּחַ אֶת־הַפָּסַח בְּאַחַד שְׁעָרֶיךָ אֲשֶׁר־יְהֹוָה אֱלֹהֶיךָ נֹתֵן לָךְ׃

⁶ but at the place where *Hashem* your God will choose to establish His name, there alone shall you slaughter the *Pesach* sacrifice, in the evening, at sundown, the time of day when you departed from Egypt.

ו כִּי אִם־אֶל־הַמָּקוֹם אֲשֶׁר־יִבְחַר יְהֹוָה אֱלֹהֶיךָ לְשַׁכֵּן שְׁמוֹ שָׁם תִּזְבַּח אֶת־ הַפֶּסַח בָּעֶרֶב כְּבוֹא הַשֶּׁמֶשׁ מוֹעֵד צֵאתְךָ מִמִּצְרָיִם׃

⁷ You shall cook and eat it at the place that *Hashem* your God will choose; and in the morning you may start back on your journey home.

ז וּבִשַּׁלְתָּ וְאָכַלְתָּ בַּמָּקוֹם אֲשֶׁר יִבְחַר יְהֹוָה אֱלֹהֶיךָ בּוֹ וּפָנִיתָ בַבֹּקֶר וְהָלַכְתָּ לְאֹהָלֶיךָ׃

⁸ After eating unleavened bread six days, you shall hold a solemn gathering for *Hashem* your God on the seventh day: you shall do no work.

ח שֵׁשֶׁת יָמִים תֹּאכַל מַצּוֹת וּבַיּוֹם הַשְּׁבִיעִי עֲצֶרֶת לַיהֹוָה אֱלֹהֶיךָ לֹא תַעֲשֶׂה מְלָאכָה׃

⁹ You shall count off seven weeks; start to count the seven weeks when the sickle is first put to the standing grain.

ט שִׁבְעָה שָׁבֻעֹת תִּסְפָּר־לָךְ מֵהָחֵל חֶרְמֵשׁ בַּקָּמָה תָּחֵל לִסְפֹּר שִׁבְעָה שָׁבֻעוֹת:

¹⁰ Then you shall observe the festival of *Shavuot* for *Hashem* your God, offering your freewill contribution according as *Hashem* your God has blessed you.

י וְעָשִׂיתָ חַג שָׁבֻעוֹת לַיהוָה אֱלֹהֶיךָ מִסַּת נִדְבַת יָדְךָ אֲשֶׁר תִּתֵּן כַּאֲשֶׁר יְבָרֶכְךָ יְהוָה אֱלֹהֶיךָ:

¹¹ You shall rejoice before *Hashem* your God with your son and daughter, your male and female slave, the Levite in your communities, and the stranger, the fatherless, and the widow in your midst, at the place where *Hashem* your God will choose to establish His name.

יא וְשָׂמַחְתָּ לִפְנֵי יְהוָה אֱלֹהֶיךָ אַתָּה וּבִנְךָ וּבִתֶּךָ וְעַבְדְּךָ וַאֲמָתֶךָ וְהַלֵּוִי אֲשֶׁר בִּשְׁעָרֶיךָ וְהַגֵּר וְהַיָּתוֹם וְהָאַלְמָנָה אֲשֶׁר בְּקִרְבֶּךָ בַּמָּקוֹם אֲשֶׁר יִבְחַר יְהוָה אֱלֹהֶיךָ לְשַׁכֵּן שְׁמוֹ שָׁם:

¹² Bear in mind that you were slaves in Egypt, and take care to obey these laws.

יב וְזָכַרְתָּ כִּי־עֶבֶד הָיִיתָ בְּמִצְרָיִם וְשָׁמַרְתָּ וְעָשִׂיתָ אֶת־הַחֻקִּים הָאֵלֶּה:

¹³ After the ingathering from your threshing floor and your vat, you shall hold the festival of *Sukkot* for seven days.

יג חַג הַסֻּכֹּת תַּעֲשֶׂה לְךָ שִׁבְעַת יָמִים בְּאָסְפְּךָ מִגָּרְנְךָ וּמִיִּקְבֶךָ:

¹⁴ You shall rejoice in your festival, with your son and daughter, your male and female slave, the Levite, the stranger, the fatherless, and the widow in your communities.

יד וְשָׂמַחְתָּ בְּחַגֶּךָ אַתָּה וּבִנְךָ וּבִתֶּךָ וְעַבְדְּךָ וַאֲמָתֶךָ וְהַלֵּוִי וְהַגֵּר וְהַיָּתוֹם וְהָאַלְמָנָה אֲשֶׁר בִּשְׁעָרֶיךָ:

¹⁵ You shall hold a festival for *Hashem* your God seven days, in the place that *Hashem* will choose; for *Hashem* your God will bless all your crops and all your undertakings, and you shall have nothing but joy.

טו שִׁבְעַת יָמִים תָּחֹג לַיהוָה אֱלֹהֶיךָ בַּמָּקוֹם אֲשֶׁר־יִבְחַר יְהוָה כִּי יְבָרֶכְךָ יְהוָה אֱלֹהֶיךָ בְּכֹל תְּבוּאָתְךָ וּבְכֹל מַעֲשֵׂה יָדֶיךָ וְהָיִיתָ אַךְ שָׂמֵחַ:

¹⁶ Three times a year – on the festival of *Pesach*, on the festival of *Shavuot*, and on the festival of *Sukkot* – all your males shall appear before *Hashem* your God in the place that He will choose. They shall not appear before *Hashem* empty-handed,

טז שָׁלוֹשׁ פְּעָמִים בַּשָּׁנָה יֵרָאֶה כָל־זְכוּרְךָ אֶת־פְּנֵי יְהוָה אֱלֹהֶיךָ בַּמָּקוֹם אֲשֶׁר יִבְחָר בְּחַג הַמַּצּוֹת וּבְחַג הַשָּׁבֻעוֹת וּבְחַג הַסֻּכּוֹת וְלֹא יֵרָאֶה אֶת־פְּנֵי יְהוָה רֵיקָם:

sha-LOSH p'-a-MEEM ba-sha-NAH yay-ra-EH khol z'-khu-r'-KHA
et p'-NAY a-do-NAI e-lo-HE-kha ba-ma-KOM a-SHER yiv-KHAR
b'-KHAG ha-ma-TZOT u-v'-KHAG ha-sha-vu-OT u-v'-KHAG
ha-su-KOT v'-LO yay-ra-EH et p'-NAY a-do-NAI ray-KAM

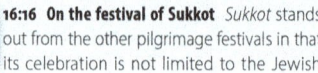

16:16 Three times a year The Hebrew word *shalosh* (שלוש) means 'three.' The number three indicates a strong unit or bond, as it says in *Megillat Kohelet* (4:12), "A threefold cord is not readily broken." Perhaps for this reason, there are three times a year when every Jew is commanded to make a pilgrimage to the *Beit Hamikdash* in *Yerushalayim* and to appear before *Hashem* in the Temple. This ensures that he will reconnect with his Creator at least three times a year, and that the bonds between them will remain strong.

שלוש

16:16 On the festival of Sukkot *Sukkot* stands out from the other pilgrimage festivals in that its celebration is not limited to the Jewish

17 but each with his own gift, according to the blessing that *Hashem* your God has bestowed upon you.

יז אִישׁ כְּמַתְּנַ֣ת יָד֑וֹ כְּבִרְכַּ֛ת יְהוָ֥ה אֱלֹהֶ֖יךָ אֲשֶׁ֥ר נָֽתַן־לָֽךְ׃

18 You shall appoint magistrates and officials for your tribes, in all the settlements that *Hashem* your God is giving you, and they shall govern the people with due justice.

יח שֹׁפְטִ֣ים וְשֹֽׁטְרִ֗ים תִּֽתֶּן־לְךָ֙ בְּכָל־שְׁעָרֶ֔יךָ אֲשֶׁ֨ר יְהוָ֧ה אֱלֹהֶ֛יךָ נֹתֵ֥ן לְךָ֖ לִשְׁבָטֶ֑יךָ וְשָֽׁפְט֥וּ אֶת־הָעָ֖ם מִשְׁפַּט־צֶֽדֶק׃

19 You shall not judge unfairly: you shall show no partiality; you shall not take bribes, for bribes blind the eyes of the discerning and upset the plea of the just.

יט לֹא־תַטֶּ֣ה מִשְׁפָּ֔ט לֹ֥א תַכִּ֖יר פָּנִ֑ים וְלֹא־תִקַּ֣ח שֹׁ֔חַד כִּ֣י הַשֹּׁ֗חַד יְעַוֵּר֙ עֵינֵ֣י חֲכָמִ֔ים וִֽיסַלֵּ֖ף דִּבְרֵ֥י צַדִּיקִֽם׃

20 Justice, justice shall you pursue, that you may thrive and occupy the land that *Hashem* your God is giving you.

כ צֶ֥דֶק צֶ֖דֶק תִּרְדֹּ֑ף לְמַ֤עַן תִּֽחְיֶה֙ וְיָֽרַשְׁתָּ֣ אֶת־הָאָ֔רֶץ אֲשֶׁר־יְהוָ֥ה אֱלֹהֶ֖יךָ נֹתֵ֥ן לָֽךְ׃

*TZE-dek TZE-dek tir-DOF l'-MA-an tikh-YEH v'-ya-rash-TA et
ha-A-retz a-sher a-do-NAI e-lo-HE-kha no-TAYN LAKH*

21 You shall not set up a sacred post – any kind of pole beside the *Mizbayach* of *Hashem* your God that you may make

כא לֹֽא־תִטַּ֥ע לְךָ֛ אֲשֵׁרָ֖ה כָּל־עֵ֑ץ אֵ֗צֶל מִזְבַּ֛ח יְהוָ֥ה אֱלֹהֶ֖יךָ אֲשֶׁ֥ר תַּֽעֲשֶׂה־לָּֽךְ׃

22 or erect a stone pillar; for such *Hashem* your God detests.

כב וְלֹֽא־תָקִ֥ים לְךָ֖ מַצֵּבָ֑ה אֲשֶׁ֥ר שָׂנֵ֖א יְהוָ֥ה אֱלֹהֶֽיךָ׃

17 1 You shall not sacrifice to *Hashem* your God an ox or a sheep that has any defect of a serious kind, for that is abhorrent to *Hashem* your God.

יז א לֹֽא־תִזְבַּח֩ לַֽיהוָ֨ה אֱלֹהֶ֜יךָ שׁ֣וֹר וָשֶׂ֗ה אֲשֶׁ֨ר יִֽהְיֶ֥ה בוֹ֙ מ֔וּם כֹּ֖ל דָּבָ֣ר רָ֑ע כִּ֧י תוֹעֲבַ֛ת יְהוָ֥ה אֱלֹהֶ֖יךָ הֽוּא׃

2 If there is found among you, in one of the settlements that *Hashem* your God is giving you, a man or woman who has affronted *Hashem* your God and transgressed His covenant

ב כִּֽי־יִמָּצֵ֤א בְקִרְבְּךָ֙ בְּאַחַ֣ד שְׁעָרֶ֔יךָ אֲשֶׁר־יְהוָ֥ה אֱלֹהֶ֖יךָ נֹתֵ֣ן לָ֑ךְ אִ֣ישׁ אֽוֹ־אִשָּׁ֗ה אֲשֶׁ֨ר יַֽעֲשֶׂ֧ה אֶת־הָרַ֛ע בְּעֵינֵ֥י יְהוָ֖ה אֱלֹהֶ֖יךָ לַֽעֲבֹ֥ר בְּרִיתֽוֹ׃

3 turning to the worship of other gods and bowing down to them, to the sun or the moon or any of the heavenly host, something I never commanded

ג וַיֵּ֗לֶךְ וַיַּֽעֲבֹד֙ אֱלֹהִ֣ים אֲחֵרִ֔ים וַיִּשְׁתַּ֖חוּ לָהֶ֑ם וְלַשֶּׁ֣מֶשׁ ׀ א֣וֹ לַיָּרֵ֗חַ א֛וֹ לְכָל־צְבָ֥א הַשָּׁמַ֖יִם אֲשֶׁ֥ר לֹא־צִוִּֽיתִי׃

The Chinese delegation at the Jerusalem March, Sukkot 2013

people. Rather, the Sages explain (*Sukkah* 55b) that a total of seventy bulls were brought as burnt-offerings throughout the Feast of Booths, on behalf of all seventy nations of the world. This served as a mighty display of universal solidarity and worship of the one true God of Israel. The Sages of the *Midrash* conclude that had the Babylonians and Romans understood the universal benefit that the *Beit Hamikdash* provided, they would never

have destroyed it and would even have built a protective fortress around it. The prophet *Zecharya* promises that in the time of *Mashiach*, *Sukkot* will once again be celebrated in *Yerushalayim* by all the nations of the world: "All who survive of all those nations that came up against *Yerushalayim* shall make a pilgrimage year by year to bow low to the King Lord of Hosts, and to observe the festival of *Sukkot*" (Zechariah 14:16). This prophecy has begun to be fulfilled through the thousands of non-Jewish visitors from all over the world who come to *Yerushalayim* each year for *Sukkot*.

4 and you have been informed or have learned of it, then you shall make a thorough inquiry. If it is true, the fact is established, that abhorrent thing was perpetrated in *Yisrael*,

ד וְהֻגַּד־לְךָ וְשָׁמָעְתָּ וְדָרַשְׁתָּ הֵיטֵב וְהִנֵּה אֱמֶת נָכוֹן הַדָּבָר נֶעֶשְׂתָה הַתּוֹעֵבָה הַזֹּאת בְּיִשְׂרָאֵל:

5 you shall take the man or the woman who did that wicked thing out to the public place, and you shall stone them, man or woman, to death.

ה וְהוֹצֵאתָ אֶת־הָאִישׁ הַהוּא אוֹ אֶת־ הָאִשָּׁה הַהִוא אֲשֶׁר עָשׂוּ אֶת־הַדָּבָר הָרָע הַזֶּה אֶל־שְׁעָרֶיךָ אֶת־הָאִישׁ אוֹ אֶת־הָאִשָּׁה וּסְקַלְתָּם בָּאֲבָנִים וָמֵתוּ:

6 A person shall be put to death only on the testimony of two or more witnesses; he must not be put to death on the testimony of a single witness.

ו עַל־פִּי שְׁנַיִם עֵדִים אוֹ שְׁלֹשָׁה עֵדִים יוּמַת הַמֵּת לֹא יוּמַת עַל־פִּי עֵד אֶחָד:

7 Let the hands of the witnesses be the first against him to put him to death, and the hands of the rest of the people thereafter. Thus you will sweep out evil from your midst.

ז יַד הָעֵדִים תִּהְיֶה־בּוֹ בָרִאשֹׁנָה לַהֲמִיתוֹ וְיַד כָּל־הָעָם בָּאַחֲרֹנָה וּבִעַרְתָּ הָרָע מִקִּרְבֶּךָ:

8 If a case is too baffling for you to decide, be it a controversy over homicide, civil law, or assault – matters of dispute in your courts – you shall promptly repair to the place that *Hashem* your God will have chosen,

ח כִּי יִפָּלֵא מִמְּךָ דָבָר לַמִּשְׁפָּט בֵּין־דָּם לְדָם בֵּין־דִּין לְדִין וּבֵין נֶגַע לָנֶגַע דִּבְרֵי רִיבֹת בִּשְׁעָרֶיךָ וְקַמְתָּ וְעָלִיתָ אֶל־ הַמָּקוֹם אֲשֶׁר יִבְחַר יְהוָה אֱלֹהֶיךָ בּוֹ:

9 and appear before the levitical *Kohanim*, or the magistrate in charge at the time, and present your problem. When they have announced to you the verdict in the case,

ט וּבָאתָ אֶל־הַכֹּהֲנִים הַלְוִיִּם וְאֶל־הַשֹּׁפֵט אֲשֶׁר יִהְיֶה בַּיָּמִים הָהֵם וְדָרַשְׁתָּ וְהִגִּידוּ לְךָ אֵת דְּבַר הַמִּשְׁפָּט:

10 you shall carry out the verdict that is announced to you from that place that *Hashem* chose, observing scrupulously all their instructions to you.

י וְעָשִׂיתָ עַל־פִּי הַדָּבָר אֲשֶׁר יַגִּידוּ לְךָ מִן־הַמָּקוֹם הַהוּא אֲשֶׁר יִבְחַר יְהוָה וְשָׁמַרְתָּ לַעֲשׂוֹת כְּכֹל אֲשֶׁר יוֹרוּךָ:

11 You shall act in accordance with the instructions given you and the ruling handed down to you; you must not deviate from the verdict that they announce to you either to the right or to the left.

יא עַל־פִּי הַתּוֹרָה אֲשֶׁר יוֹרוּךָ וְעַל־ הַמִּשְׁפָּט אֲשֶׁר־יֹאמְרוּ לְךָ תַּעֲשֶׂה לֹא תָסוּר מִן־הַדָּבָר אֲשֶׁר־יַגִּידוּ לְךָ יָמִין וּשְׂמֹאל:

12 Should a man act presumptuously and disregard the *Kohen* charged with serving there *Hashem* your God, or the magistrate, that man shall die. Thus you will sweep out evil from *Yisrael*:

יב וְהָאִישׁ אֲשֶׁר־יַעֲשֶׂה בְזָדוֹן לְבִלְתִּי שְׁמֹעַ אֶל־הַכֹּהֵן הָעֹמֵד לְשָׁרֶת שָׁם אֶת־יְהוָה אֱלֹהֶיךָ אוֹ אֶל־הַשֹּׁפֵט וּמֵת הָאִישׁ הַהוּא וּבִעַרְתָּ הָרָע מִיִּשְׂרָאֵל:

13 all the people will hear and be afraid and will not act presumptuously again.

יג וְכָל־הָעָם יִשְׁמְעוּ וְיִרָאוּ וְלֹא יְזִידוּן עוֹד:

14 If, after you have entered the land that *Hashem* your God has assigned to you, and taken possession of it and settled in it, you decide, "I will set a king over me, as do all the nations about me,"

יד כִּי־תָבֹא אֶל־הָאָרֶץ אֲשֶׁר יְהוָה אֱלֹהֶיךָ נֹתֵן לָךְ וִירִשְׁתָּהּ וְיָשַׁבְתָּה בָּהּ וְאָמַרְתָּ אָשִׂימָה עָלַי מֶלֶךְ כְּכָל־הַגּוֹיִם אֲשֶׁר סְבִיבֹתָי:

15 you shall be free to set a king over yourself, one chosen by *Hashem* your God. Be sure to set as king over yourself one of your own people; you must not set a foreigner over you, one who is not your kinsman.

טו שׂוֹם תָּשִׂים עָלֶיךָ מֶלֶךְ אֲשֶׁר יִבְחַר יְהוָה אֱלֹהֶיךָ בּוֹ מִקֶּרֶב אַחֶיךָ תָּשִׂים עָלֶיךָ מֶלֶךְ לֹא תוּכַל לָתֵת עָלֶיךָ אִישׁ נָכְרִי אֲשֶׁר לֹא־אָחִיךָ הוּא׃

16 Moreover, he shall not keep many horses or send people back to Egypt to add to his horses, since *Hashem* has warned you, "You must not go back that way again."

טז רַק לֹא־יַרְבֶּה־לּוֹ סוּסִים וְלֹא־יָשִׁיב אֶת־הָעָם מִצְרַיְמָה לְמַעַן הַרְבּוֹת סוּס וַיהוָה אָמַר לָכֶם לֹא תֹסִפוּן לָשׁוּב בַּדֶּרֶךְ הַזֶּה עוֹד׃

17 And he shall not have many wives, lest his heart go astray; nor shall he amass silver and gold to excess.

יז וְלֹא יַרְבֶּה־לּוֹ נָשִׁים וְלֹא יָסוּר לְבָבוֹ וְכֶסֶף וְזָהָב לֹא יַרְבֶּה־לּוֹ מְאֹד׃

18 When he is seated on his royal throne, he shall have a copy of this *Torah* written for him on a scroll by the levitical *Kohanim*.

יח וְהָיָה כְשִׁבְתּוֹ עַל כִּסֵּא מַמְלַכְתּוֹ וְכָתַב לוֹ אֶת־מִשְׁנֵה הַתּוֹרָה הַזֹּאת עַל־סֵפֶר מִלִּפְנֵי הַכֹּהֲנִים הַלְוִיִּם׃

19 Let it remain with him and let him read in it all his life, so that he may learn to revere *Hashem* his God, to observe faithfully every word of this Teaching as well as these laws.

יט וְהָיְתָה עִמּוֹ וְקָרָא בוֹ כָּל־יְמֵי חַיָּיו לְמַעַן יִלְמַד לְיִרְאָה אֶת־יְהוָה אֱלֹהָיו לִשְׁמֹר אֶת־כָּל־דִּבְרֵי הַתּוֹרָה הַזֹּאת וְאֶת־הַחֻקִּים הָאֵלֶּה לַעֲשֹׂתָם׃

20 Thus he will not act haughtily toward his fellows or deviate from the Instruction to the right or to the left, to the end that he and his descendants may reign long in the midst of *Yisrael*.

כ לְבִלְתִּי רוּם־לְבָבוֹ מֵאֶחָיו וּלְבִלְתִּי סוּר מִן־הַמִּצְוָה יָמִין וּשְׂמֹאול לְמַעַן יַאֲרִיךְ יָמִים עַל־מַמְלַכְתּוֹ הוּא וּבָנָיו בְּקֶרֶב יִשְׂרָאֵל׃

l'-vil-TEE rum l'-va-VO may-e-KHAV u-l'-vil-TEE SUR min
ha-mitz-VAH ya-MIN us-MOL l'-MA-an ya-a-REEKH ya-MEEM
al mam-lakh-TO HU u-va-NAV b'-KE-rev yis-ra-AYL

18 1 The levitical *Kohanim*, the whole tribe of *Levi*, shall have no territorial portion with *Yisrael*. They shall live only off *Hashem*'s offerings by fire as their portion,

יח א לֹא־יִהְיֶה לַכֹּהֲנִים הַלְוִיִּם כָּל־שֵׁבֶט לֵוִי חֵלֶק וְנַחֲלָה עִם־יִשְׂרָאֵל אִשֵּׁי יְהוָה וְנַחֲלָתוֹ יֹאכֵלוּן׃

2 and shall have no portion among their brother tribes: *Hashem* is their portion, as He promised them.

ב וְנַחֲלָה לֹא־יִהְיֶה־לּוֹ בְּקֶרֶב אֶחָיו יְהוָה הוּא נַחֲלָתוֹ כַּאֲשֶׁר דִּבֶּר־לוֹ׃

Man carrying a *Torah* scroll at the Western Wall

17:20 Thus he will not act haughtily Verses 14–20 discuss the command for the People of Israel to appoint a king, and the subsequent restrictions the *Torah* places on the kings of Israel. Appointing a king is one of the three commandments that the Jews were instructed to perform after settling the land. Without leadership, chaos ensues, as the verse implies "In those days there was no king in *Yisrael*; everyone did as he pleased" (Judges 21:25). However, there is a risk that the king will forget the source of his strength and attribute his successes to his own wisdom and power. Therefore, the Bible places three special restrictions upon the kings, and also requires that they carry a copy of the *Torah* with them at all times. The laws of the kings remind us that we all must recognize the true source of blessing and success in our lives.

3 This then shall be the *Kohanim's* due from the people: Everyone who offers a sacrifice, whether an ox or a sheep, must give the shoulder, the cheeks, and the stomach to the *Kohen.*

ג וְזֶה יִהְיֶה מִשְׁפַּט הַכֹּהֲנִים מֵאֵת הָעָם מֵאֵת זֹבְחֵי הַזֶּבַח אִם־שׁוֹר אִם־שֶׂה וְנָתַן לַכֹּהֵן הַזְּרֹעַ וְהַלְּחָיַיִם וְהַקֵּבָה:

4 You shall also give him the first fruits of your new grain and wine and oil, and the first shearing of your sheep.

ד רֵאשִׁית דְּגָנְךָ תִּירֹשְׁךָ וְיִצְהָרֶךָ וְרֵאשִׁית גֵּז צֹאנְךָ תִּתֶּן־לוֹ:

5 For *Hashem* your God has chosen him and his descendants, out of all your tribes, to be in attendance for service in the name of *Hashem* for all time.

ה כִּי בוֹ בָּחַר יְהֹוָה אֱלֹהֶיךָ מִכָּל־שְׁבָטֶיךָ לַעֲמֹד לְשָׁרֵת בְּשֵׁם־יְהֹוָה הוּא וּבָנָיו כָּל־הַיָּמִים:

6 If a Levite would go, from any of the settlements throughout *Yisrael* where he has been residing, to the place that *Hashem* has chosen, he may do so whenever he pleases.

ו וְכִי־יָבֹא הַלֵּוִי מֵאַחַד שְׁעָרֶיךָ מִכָּל־יִשְׂרָאֵל אֲשֶׁר־הוּא גָּר שָׁם וּבָא בְּכָל־אַוַּת נַפְשׁוֹ אֶל־הַמָּקוֹם אֲשֶׁר־יִבְחַר יְהֹוָה:

7 He may serve in the name of *Hashem* his God like all his fellow *Leviim* who are there in attendance before *Hashem.*

ז וְשֵׁרֵת בְּשֵׁם יְהֹוָה אֱלֹהָיו כְּכָל־אֶחָיו הַלְוִיִּם הָעֹמְדִים שָׁם לִפְנֵי יְהֹוָה:

8 They shall receive equal shares of the dues, without regard to personal gifts or patrimonies.

ח חֵלֶק כְּחֵלֶק יֹאכֵלוּ לְבַד מִמְכָּרָיו עַל־הָאָבוֹת:

9 When you enter the land that *Hashem* your God is giving you, you shall not learn to imitate the abhorrent practices of those nations.

ט כִּי אַתָּה בָּא אֶל־הָאָרֶץ אֲשֶׁר־יְהֹוָה אֱלֹהֶיךָ נֹתֵן לָךְ לֹא־תִלְמַד לַעֲשׂוֹת כְּתוֹעֲבֹת הַגּוֹיִם הָהֵם:

KEE a-TAH BA el ha-A-retz a-sher a-do-NAI e-lo-HE-kha no-TAYN LAKH lo til-MAD la-a-SOT k'-to-a-VOT ha-go-YIM ha-HAYM

10 Let no one be found among you who consigns his son or daughter to the fire, or who is an augur, a soothsayer, a diviner, a sorcerer,

י לֹא־יִמָּצֵא בְךָ מַעֲבִיר בְּנוֹ־וּבִתּוֹ בָּאֵשׁ קֹסֵם קְסָמִים מְעוֹנֵן וּמְנַחֵשׁ וּמְכַשֵּׁף:

11 one who casts spells, or one who consults ghosts or familiar spirits, or one who inquires of the dead.

יא וְחֹבֵר חָבֶר וְשֹׁאֵל אוֹב וְיִדְּעֹנִי וְדֹרֵשׁ אֶל־הַמֵּתִים:

12 For anyone who does such things is abhorrent to *Hashem*, and it is because of these abhorrent things that *Hashem* your God is dispossessing them before you.

יב כִּי־תוֹעֲבַת יְהֹוָה כָּל־עֹשֵׂה אֵלֶּה וּבִגְלַל הַתּוֹעֵבֹת הָאֵלֶּה יְהֹוָה אֱלֹהֶיךָ מוֹרִישׁ אוֹתָם מִפָּנֶיךָ:

18:9 The land that *Hashem* your God is giving you This verse teaches that *Hashem* promises the land to 'you,' written in the singular form *lach* (לך). Every individual in the nation has a place in the Land of Israel, and everyone needs to be mindful of the fact that remaining in the land depends on his or her moral character. Therefore, in the continuation of the verse, *Hashem* warns the people not to learn from and mimic the abominations of the peoples already living there, as doing so would jeopardize their right to be rulers of their land. The Jewish people are charged to live up to a high moral standard, and to serve as models of morality and ethics for the rest of the world.

A view of the land in northern Israel

Deuteronomy

¹³ You must be wholehearted with *Hashem* your God.

יג תָּמִים תִּהְיֶ֔ה עִ֖ם יְהֹוָ֥ה אֱלֹהֶֽיךָ׃

¹⁴ Those nations that you are about to dispossess do indeed resort to soothsayers and augurs; to you, however, *Hashem* your God has not assigned the like.

יד כִּ֣י הַגּוֹיִ֣ם הָאֵ֗לֶּה אֲשֶׁ֤ר אַתָּה֙ יוֹרֵ֣שׁ אוֹתָ֔ם אֶל־מְעֹנְנִ֥ים וְאֶל־קֹסְמִ֖ים יִשְׁמָ֑עוּ וְאַתָּ֕ה לֹ֣א כֵ֔ן נָ֣תַן לְךָ֔ יְהֹוָ֥ה אֱלֹהֶֽיךָ׃

¹⁵ *Hashem* your God will raise up for you a *navi* from among your own people, like myself; him you shall heed.

טו נָבִ֨יא מִקִּרְבְּךָ֤ מֵאַחֶ֨יךָ֙ כָּמֹ֔נִי יָקִ֥ים לְךָ֖ יְהֹוָ֣ה אֱלֹהֶ֑יךָ אֵלָ֖יו תִּשְׁמָעֽוּן׃

¹⁶ This is just what you asked of *Hashem* your God at Horeb, on the day of the Assembly, saying, "Let me not hear the voice of *Hashem* my God any longer or see this wondrous fire any more, lest I die."

טז כְּכֹ֨ל אֲשֶׁר־שָׁאַ֜לְתָּ מֵעִ֨ם יְהֹוָ֤ה אֱלֹהֶ֨יךָ֙ בְּחֹרֵ֔ב בְּי֥וֹם הַקָּהָ֖ל לֵאמֹ֑ר לֹ֣א אֹסֵ֗ף לִשְׁמֹ֨עַ֙ אֶת־קוֹל֙ יְהֹוָ֣ה אֱלֹהָ֔י וְאֶת־הָאֵ֨שׁ הַגְּדֹלָ֤ה הַזֹּאת֙ לֹֽא־אֶרְאֶ֣ה ע֔וֹד וְלֹ֖א אָמֽוּת׃

¹⁷ Whereupon *Hashem* said to me, "They have done well in speaking thus.

יז וַיֹּ֥אמֶר יְהֹוָ֖ה אֵלָ֑י הֵיטִ֖יבוּ אֲשֶׁ֥ר דִּבֵּֽרוּ׃

¹⁸ I will raise up a *navi* for them from among their own people, like yourself: I will put My words in his mouth and he will speak to them all that I command him;

יח נָבִ֨יא אָקִ֥ים לָהֶ֛ם מִקֶּ֥רֶב אֲחֵיהֶ֖ם כָּמ֑וֹךָ וְנָתַתִּ֤י דְבָרַי֙ בְּפִ֔יו וְדִבֶּ֣ר אֲלֵיהֶ֔ם אֵ֖ת כָּל־אֲשֶׁ֥ר אֲצַוֶּֽנּוּ׃

¹⁹ and if anybody fails to heed the words he speaks in My name, I Myself will call him to account.

יט וְהָיָ֣ה הָאִ֔ישׁ אֲשֶׁ֤ר לֹֽא־יִשְׁמַע֙ אֶל־דְּבָרַ֔י אֲשֶׁ֥ר יְדַבֵּ֖ר בִּשְׁמִ֑י אָנֹכִ֖י אֶדְרֹ֥שׁ מֵֽעִמּֽוֹ׃

²⁰ But any *navi* who presumes to speak in My name an oracle that I did not command him to utter, or who speaks in the name of other gods – that *navi* shall die."

כ אַ֣ךְ הַנָּבִ֡יא אֲשֶׁ֣ר יָזִיד֩ לְדַבֵּ֨ר דָּבָ֜ר בִּשְׁמִ֗י אֵ֣ת אֲשֶׁ֤ר לֹֽא־צִוִּיתִיו֙ לְדַבֵּ֔ר וַֽאֲשֶׁ֣ר יְדַבֵּ֔ר בְּשֵׁ֖ם אֱלֹהִ֣ים אֲחֵרִ֑ים וּמֵ֖ת הַנָּבִ֥יא הַהֽוּא׃

²¹ And should you ask yourselves, "How can we know that the oracle was not spoken by *Hashem*?"

כא וְכִ֥י תֹאמַ֖ר בִּלְבָבֶ֑ךָ אֵיכָה֙ נֵדַ֣ע אֶת־הַדָּבָ֔ר אֲשֶׁ֥ר לֹֽא־דִבְּר֖וֹ יְהֹוָֽה׃

²² if the *navi* speaks in the name of *Hashem* and the oracle does not come true, that oracle was not spoken by *Hashem*; the *navi* has uttered it presumptuously: do not stand in dread of him.

כב אֲשֶׁר֩ יְדַבֵּ֨ר הַנָּבִ֜יא בְּשֵׁ֣ם יְהֹוָ֗ה וְלֹֽא־יִֽהְיֶ֤ה הַדָּבָר֙ וְלֹ֣א יָב֔וֹא ה֣וּא הַדָּבָ֔ר אֲשֶׁ֥ר לֹֽא־דִבְּר֖וֹ יְהֹוָ֑ה בְּזָדוֹן֙ דִּבְּר֣וֹ הַנָּבִ֔יא לֹ֥א תָג֖וּר מִמֶּֽנּוּ׃

19 ¹ When *Hashem* your God has cut down the nations whose land *Hashem* your God is assigning to you, and you have dispossessed them and settled in their towns and homes,

יט א כִּֽי־יַכְרִ֞ית יְהֹוָ֤ה אֱלֹהֶ֨יךָ֙ אֶת־הַגּוֹיִ֔ם אֲשֶׁר֙ יְהֹוָ֣ה אֱלֹהֶ֔יךָ נֹתֵ֥ן לְךָ֖ אֶת־אַרְצָ֑ם וִֽירִשְׁתָּ֕ם וְיָֽשַׁבְתָּ֥ בְעָֽרֵיהֶ֖ם וּבְבָֽתֵּיהֶֽם׃

² you shall set aside three cities in the land that *Hashem* your God is giving you to possess.

ב שָׁל֥וֹשׁ עָרִ֖ים תַּבְדִּ֣יל לָ֑ךְ בְּת֣וֹךְ אַרְצְךָ֔ אֲשֶׁר֙ יְהֹוָ֣ה אֱלֹהֶ֔יךָ נֹתֵ֥ן לְךָ֖ לְרִשְׁתָּֽהּ׃

³ You shall survey the distances, and divide into three parts the territory of the country that *Hashem* your God has allotted to you, so that any manslayer may have a place to flee to.

ג תָּכִ֣ין לְךָ֮ הַדֶּ֒רֶךְ֒ וְשִׁלַּשְׁתָּ֙ אֶת־גְּב֣וּל אַרְצְךָ֔ אֲשֶׁ֥ר יַנְחִֽילְךָ֖ יְהֹוָ֣ה אֱלֹהֶ֑יךָ וְהָיָ֕ה לָנ֥וּס שָׁ֖מָּה כָּל־רֹצֵֽחַ׃

Deuteronomy

4 Now this is the case of the manslayer who may flee there and live: one who has killed another unwittingly, without having been his enemy in the past.

ד וְזֶה דְּבַר הָרֹצֵחַ אֲשֶׁר־יָנוּס שָׁמָּה וָחָי אֲשֶׁר יַכֶּה אֶת־רֵעֵהוּ בִּבְלִי־דַעַת וְהוּא לֹא־שֹׂנֵא לוֹ מִתְּמֹל שִׁלְשֹׁם:

5 For instance, a man goes with his neighbor into a grove to cut wood; as his hand swings the ax to cut down a tree, the ax-head flies off the handle and strikes the other so that he dies. That man shall flee to one of these cities and live.

ה וַאֲשֶׁר יָבֹא אֶת־רֵעֵהוּ בַיַּעַר לַחְטֹב עֵצִים וְנִדְּחָה יָדוֹ בַגַּרְזֶן לִכְרֹת הָעֵץ וְנָשַׁל הַבַּרְזֶל מִן־הָעֵץ וּמָצָא אֶת־רֵעֵהוּ וָמֵת הוּא יָנוּס אֶל־אַחַת הֶעָרִים־הָאֵלֶּה וָחָי:

6 Otherwise, when the distance is great, the blood-avenger, pursuing the manslayer in hot anger, may overtake him and kill him; yet he did not incur the death penalty, since he had never been the other's enemy.

ו פֶּן־יִרְדֹּף גֹּאֵל הַדָּם אַחֲרֵי הָרֹצֵחַ כִּי־יֵחַם לְבָבוֹ וְהִשִּׂיגוֹ כִּי־יִרְבֶּה הַדֶּרֶךְ וְהִכָּהוּ נָפֶשׁ וְלוֹ אֵין מִשְׁפַּט־מָוֶת כִּי לֹא שֹׂנֵא הוּא לוֹ מִתְּמוֹל שִׁלְשׁוֹם:

7 That is why I command you: set aside three cities.

ז עַל־כֵּן אָנֹכִי מְצַוְּךָ לֵאמֹר שָׁלֹשׁ עָרִים תַּבְדִּיל לָךְ:

8 And when *Hashem* your God enlarges your territory, as He swore to your fathers, and gives you all the land that He promised to give your fathers

ח וְאִם־יַרְחִיב יְהֹוָה אֱלֹהֶיךָ אֶת־גְּבֻלְךָ כַּאֲשֶׁר נִשְׁבַּע לַאֲבֹתֶיךָ וְנָתַן לְךָ אֶת־כָּל־הָאָרֶץ אֲשֶׁר דִּבֶּר לָתֵת לַאֲבֹתֶיךָ:

*v'-im yar-KHEEV a-do-NAI e-lo-HE-kha et g'-VU-l'-KHA
ka-a-SHER nish-BA la-a-vo-TE-kha v'-na-TAN l'-KHA et kol
ha-A-retz a-SHER di-BAYR la-TAYT la-a-vo-TE-kha*

9 if you faithfully observe all this Instruction that I enjoin upon you this day, to love *Hashem* your God and to walk in His ways at all times – then you shall add three more towns to those three.

ט כִּי־תִשְׁמֹר אֶת־כָּל־הַמִּצְוָה הַזֹּאת לַעֲשֹׂתָהּ אֲשֶׁר אָנֹכִי מְצַוְּךָ הַיּוֹם לְאַהֲבָה אֶת־יְהֹוָה אֱלֹהֶיךָ וְלָלֶכֶת בִּדְרָכָיו כָּל־הַיָּמִים וְיָסַפְתָּ לְךָ עוֹד שָׁלֹשׁ עָרִים עַל הַשָּׁלֹשׁ הָאֵלֶּה:

10 Thus blood of the innocent will not be shed, bringing bloodguilt upon you in the land that *Hashem* your God is allotting to you.

י וְלֹא יִשָּׁפֵךְ דָּם נָקִי בְּקֶרֶב אַרְצְךָ אֲשֶׁר יְהֹוָה אֱלֹהֶיךָ נֹתֵן לְךָ נַחֲלָה וְהָיָה עָלֶיךָ דָּמִים:

11 If, however, a person who is the enemy of another lies in wait for him and sets upon him and strikes him a fatal blow and then flees to one of these towns,

יא וְכִי־יִהְיֶה אִישׁ שֹׂנֵא לְרֵעֵהוּ וְאָרַב לוֹ וְקָם עָלָיו וְהִכָּהוּ נֶפֶשׁ וָמֵת וְנָס אֶל־אַחַת הֶעָרִים הָאֵל:

12 the elders of his town shall have him brought back from there and shall hand him over to the blood-avenger to be put to death;

יב וְשָׁלְחוּ זִקְנֵי עִירוֹ וְלָקְחוּ אֹתוֹ מִשָּׁם וְנָתְנוּ אֹתוֹ בְּיַד גֹּאֵל הַדָּם וָמֵת:

13 you must show him no pity. Thus you will purge *Yisrael* of the blood of the innocent, and it will go well with you.

יג לֹא־תָחוֹס עֵינְךָ עָלָיו וּבִעַרְתָּ דַם־הַנָּקִי מִיִּשְׂרָאֵל וְטוֹב לָךְ:

Deuteronomy

14 You shall not move your countryman's landmarks, set up by previous generations, in the property that will be allotted to you in the land that *Hashem* your God is giving you to possess.

יד לֹא תַסִּיג גְּבוּל רֵעֲךָ אֲשֶׁר גָּבְלוּ רִאשֹׁנִים בְּנַחֲלָתְךָ אֲשֶׁר תִּנְחַל בָּאָרֶץ אֲשֶׁר יְהוָה אֱלֹהֶיךָ נֹתֵן לְךָ לְרִשְׁתָּהּ:

*LO ta-SEEG g'-VUL ray-a-KHA a-SHER ga-v'-LU ri-sho-NEEM
b'-na-kha-la-t'-KHA a-SHER tin-KHAL ba-A-retz a-SHER
a-do-NAI e-lo-HE-kha no-TAYN l'-KHA l'-rish-TAH*

15 A single witness may not validate against a person any guilt or blame for any offense that may be committed; a case can be valid only on the testimony of two witnesses or more.

טו לֹא־יָקוּם עֵד אֶחָד בְּאִישׁ לְכָל־עָוֹן וּלְכָל־חַטָּאת בְּכָל־חֵטְא אֲשֶׁר יֶחֱטָא עַל־פִּי שְׁנֵי עֵדִים אוֹ עַל־פִּי שְׁלֹשָׁה־עֵדִים יָקוּם דָּבָר:

16 If a man appears against another to testify maliciously and gives false testimony against him,

טז כִּי־יָקוּם עֵד־חָמָס בְּאִישׁ לַעֲנוֹת בּוֹ סָרָה:

17 the two parties to the dispute shall appear before *Hashem*, before the *Kohanim* or magistrates in authority at the time,

יז וְעָמְדוּ שְׁנֵי־הָאֲנָשִׁים אֲשֶׁר־לָהֶם הָרִיב לִפְנֵי יְהוָה לִפְנֵי הַכֹּהֲנִים וְהַשֹּׁפְטִים אֲשֶׁר יִהְיוּ בַּיָּמִים הָהֵם:

18 and the magistrates shall make a thorough investigation. If the man who testified is a false witness, if he has testified falsely against his fellow,

יח וְדָרְשׁוּ הַשֹּׁפְטִים הֵיטֵב וְהִנֵּה עֵד־שֶׁקֶר הָעֵד שֶׁקֶר עָנָה בְאָחִיו:

19 you shall do to him as he schemed to do to his fellow. Thus you will sweep out evil from your midst;

יט וַעֲשִׂיתֶם לוֹ כַּאֲשֶׁר זָמַם לַעֲשׂוֹת לְאָחִיו וּבִעַרְתָּ הָרָע מִקִּרְבֶּךָ:

20 others will hear and be afraid, and such evil things will not again be done in your midst.

כ וְהַנִּשְׁאָרִים יִשְׁמְעוּ וְיִרָאוּ וְלֹא־יֹסִפוּ לַעֲשׂוֹת עוֹד כַּדָּבָר הָרָע הַזֶּה בְּקִרְבֶּךָ:

21 Nor must you show pity: life for life, eye for eye, tooth for tooth, hand for hand, foot for foot.

כא וְלֹא תָחוֹס עֵינֶךָ נֶפֶשׁ בְּנֶפֶשׁ עַיִן בְּעַיִן שֵׁן בְּשֵׁן יָד בְּיָד רֶגֶל בְּרָגֶל:

20 ¹ When you take the field against your enemies, and see horses and chariots – forces larger than yours – have no fear of them, for *Hashem* your God, who brought you from the land of Egypt, is with you.

כ א כִּי־תֵצֵא לַמִּלְחָמָה עַל־אֹיְבֶךָ וְרָאִיתָ סוּס וָרֶכֶב עַם רַב מִמְּךָ לֹא תִירָא מֵהֶם כִּי־יְהוָה אֱלֹהֶיךָ עִמָּךְ הַמַּעַלְךָ מֵאֶרֶץ מִצְרָיִם:

² Before you join battle, the *Kohen* shall come forward and address the troops.

ב וְהָיָה כְּקָרָבְכֶם אֶל־הַמִּלְחָמָה וְנִגַּשׁ הַכֹּהֵן וְדִבֶּר אֶל־הָעָם:

19:14 You shall not move your countryman's landmarks In this verse, the *Torah* prohibits moving the borders of one's property in order to secretly and illegitimately incorporate some of his neighbor's land into his own. *Hashem* gave *Eretz Yisrael* to the Israelites, and He expects them to live in it fairly and justly, without taking even one inch of land that does not belong to them. It is therefore particularly painful today to see those who deny the Bible accuse the Jewish people of "occupation," and of stealing someone else's land. Over and over, the *Tanakh* establishes the deep connection between the Jewish People and *Eretz Yisrael*, yet this fundamental fact has been attacked in recent years with increasing hostility. It is incumbent upon students of the Bible to point to verses such as this as evidence of the fairness and honesty that underpins the historic relationship between the People of Israel and the Land of Israel.

Rakafot Hill neighborhood in Kiriat Blalik, Israel

3 He shall say to them, "Hear, O *Yisrael*! You are about to join battle with your enemy. Let not your courage falter. Do not be in fear, or in panic, or in dread of them.

ג וְאָמַר אֲלֵהֶם שְׁמַע יִשְׂרָאֵל אַתֶּם קְרֵבִים הַיּוֹם לַמִּלְחָמָה עַל־אֹיְבֵיכֶם אַל־יֵרַךְ לְבַבְכֶם אַל־תִּירְאוּ וְאַל־תַּחְפְּזוּ וְאַל־תַּעַרְצוּ מִפְּנֵיהֶם:

4 For it is *Hashem* your God who marches with you to do battle for you against your enemy, to bring you victory."

ד כִּי יְהוָֹה אֱלֹהֵיכֶם הַהֹלֵךְ עִמָּכֶם לְהִלָּחֵם לָכֶם עִם־אֹיְבֵיכֶם לְהוֹשִׁיעַ אֶתְכֶם:

KEE a-do-NAI e-lo-hay-KHEM ha-ho-LAYKH i-ma-KHEM
l'-hi-la-KHAYM la-KHEM im o-y'-vay-KHEM l'-ho-SHEE-a et-KHEM

5 Then the officials shall address the troops, as follows: "Is there anyone who has built a new house but has not dedicated it? Let him go back to his home, lest he die in battle and another dedicate it.

ה וְדִבְּרוּ הַשֹּׁטְרִים אֶל־הָעָם לֵאמֹר מִי־ הָאִישׁ אֲשֶׁר בָּנָה בַיִת־חָדָשׁ וְלֹא חֲנָכוֹ יֵלֵךְ וְיָשֹׁב לְבֵיתוֹ פֶּן־יָמוּת בַּמִּלְחָמָה וְאִישׁ אַחֵר יַחְנְכֶנּוּ:

6 Is there anyone who has planted a vineyard but has never harvested it? Let him go back to his home, lest he die in battle and another harvest it.

ו וּמִי־הָאִישׁ אֲשֶׁר־נָטַע כֶּרֶם וְלֹא חִלְּלוֹ יֵלֵךְ וְיָשֹׁב לְבֵיתוֹ פֶּן־יָמוּת בַּמִּלְחָמָה וְאִישׁ אַחֵר יְחַלְּלֶנּוּ:

7 Is there anyone who has paid the bride-price for a wife, but who has not yet married her? Let him go back to his home, lest he die in battle and another marry her."

ז וּמִי־הָאִישׁ אֲשֶׁר־אֵרַשׂ אִשָּׁה וְלֹא לְקָחָהּ יֵלֵךְ וְיָשֹׁב לְבֵיתוֹ פֶּן־יָמוּת בַּמִּלְחָמָה וְאִישׁ אַחֵר יִקָּחֶנָּה:

8 The officials shall go on addressing the troops and say, "Is there anyone afraid and disheartened? Let him go back to his home, lest the courage of his comrades flag like his."

ח וְיָסְפוּ הַשֹּׁטְרִים לְדַבֵּר אֶל־הָעָם וְאָמְרוּ מִי־הָאִישׁ הַיָּרֵא וְרַךְ הַלֵּבָב יֵלֵךְ וְיָשֹׁב לְבֵיתוֹ וְלֹא יִמַּס אֶת־לְבַב אֶחָיו כִּלְבָבוֹ:

9 When the officials have finished addressing the troops, army commanders shall assume command of the troops.

ט וְהָיָה כְּכַלֹּת הַשֹּׁטְרִים לְדַבֵּר אֶל־הָעָם וּפָקְדוּ שָׂרֵי צְבָאוֹת בְּרֹאשׁ הָעָם:

10 When you approach a town to attack it, you shall offer it terms of peace.

י כִּי־תִקְרַב אֶל־עִיר לְהִלָּחֵם עָלֶיהָ וְקָרָאתָ אֵלֶיהָ לְשָׁלוֹם:

kee tik-RAV el EER l'-hi-la-KHAYM a-LE-ha v'-ka-RA-ta ay-LE-ha l'-sha-LOM

11 If it responds peaceably and lets you in, all the people present there shall serve you at forced labor.

יא וְהָיָה אִם־שָׁלוֹם תַּעַנְךָ וּפָתְחָה לָךְ וְהָיָה כָּל־הָעָם הַנִּמְצָא־בָהּ יִהְיוּ לְךָ לָמַס וַעֲבָדוּךָ:

12 If it does not surrender to you, but would join battle with you, you shall lay siege to it;

יב וְאִם־לֹא תַשְׁלִים עִמָּךְ וְעָשְׂתָה עִמְּךָ מִלְחָמָה וְצַרְתָּ עָלֶיהָ:

20:10 You shall offer it terms of peace Before going to war, the Children of Israel are required to first offer their enemies the opportunity to make peace. According to some commentators, this applies even to the nations living in the parts of the Land of Israel promised to *B'nei Yisrael*. The land was given to the People of Israel as an inheritance, but first and foremost they must try to live there in peace with their neighbors. The State of Israel has taken the quest for peace very seriously. It has even returned land captured in a defensive war, and offered to return more, in exchange for peace with its neighbors.

Girl waving the Israeli flag

Deuteronomy

13 and when *Hashem* your God delivers it into your hand, you shall put all its males to the sword.

14 You may, however, take as your booty the women, the children, the livestock, and everything in the town – all its spoil – and enjoy the use of the spoil of your enemy, which *Hashem* your God gives you.

15 Thus you shall deal with all towns that lie very far from you, towns that do not belong to nations hereabout.

16 In the towns of the latter peoples, however, which *Hashem* your God is giving you as a heritage, you shall not let a soul remain alive.

17 No, you must proscribe them – the Hittites and the Amorites, the Canaanites and the Perizzites, the Hivites and the Jebusites – as *Hashem* your God has commanded you,

18 lest they lead you into doing all the abhorrent things that they have done for their gods and you stand guilty before *Hashem* your God.

19 When in your war against a city you have to besiege it a long time in order to capture it, you must not destroy its trees, wielding the ax against them. You may eat of them, but you must not cut them down. Are trees of the field human to withdraw before you into the besieged city?

20 Only trees that you know do not yield food may be destroyed; you may cut them down for constructing siegeworks against the city that is waging war on you, until it has been reduced.

21 1 If, in the land that *Hashem* your God is assigning you to possess, someone slain is found lying in the open, the identity of the slayer not being known,

יג וּנְתָנָהּ יהוה אֱלֹהֶיךָ בְּיָדֶךָ וְהִכִּיתָ אֶת־כָּל־זְכוּרָהּ לְפִי־חָרֶב:

יד רַק הַנָּשִׁים וְהַטַּף וְהַבְּהֵמָה וְכֹל אֲשֶׁר יִהְיֶה בָעִיר כָּל־שְׁלָלָהּ תָּבֹז לָךְ וְאָכַלְתָּ אֶת־שְׁלַל אֹיְבֶיךָ אֲשֶׁר נָתַן יהוה אֱלֹהֶיךָ לָךְ:

טו כֵּן תַּעֲשֶׂה לְכָל־הֶעָרִים הָרְחֹקֹת מִמְּךָ מְאֹד אֲשֶׁר לֹא־מֵעָרֵי הַגּוֹיִם־הָאֵלֶּה הֵנָּה:

טז רַק מֵעָרֵי הָעַמִּים הָאֵלֶּה אֲשֶׁר יהוה אֱלֹהֶיךָ נֹתֵן לְךָ נַחֲלָה לֹא תְחַיֶּה כָּל־נְשָׁמָה:

יז כִּי־הַחֲרֵם תַּחֲרִימֵם הַחִתִּי וְהָאֱמֹרִי הַכְּנַעֲנִי וְהַפְּרִזִּי הַחִוִּי וְהַיְבוּסִי כַּאֲשֶׁר צִוְּךָ יהוה אֱלֹהֶיךָ:

יח לְמַעַן אֲשֶׁר לֹא־יְלַמְּדוּ אֶתְכֶם לַעֲשׂוֹת כְּכֹל תּוֹעֲבֹתָם אֲשֶׁר עָשׂוּ לֵאלֹהֵיהֶם וַחֲטָאתֶם לַיהוה אֱלֹהֵיכֶם:

יט כִּי־תָצוּר אֶל־עִיר יָמִים רַבִּים לְהִלָּחֵם עָלֶיהָ לְתָפְשָׂהּ לֹא־תַשְׁחִית אֶת־עֵצָהּ לִנְדֹּחַ עָלָיו גַּרְזֶן כִּי מִמֶּנּוּ תֹאכֵל וְאֹתוֹ לֹא תִכְרֹת כִּי הָאָדָם עֵץ הַשָּׂדֶה לָבֹא מִפָּנֶיךָ בַּמָּצוֹר:

כ רַק עֵץ אֲשֶׁר־תֵּדַע כִּי־לֹא־עֵץ מַאֲכָל הוּא אֹתוֹ תַשְׁחִית וְכָרָתָּ וּבָנִיתָ מָצוֹר עַל־הָעִיר אֲשֶׁר־הִוא עֹשָׂה עִמְּךָ מִלְחָמָה עַד רִדְתָּהּ:

א כא כִּי־יִמָּצֵא חָלָל בָּאֲדָמָה אֲשֶׁר יהוה אֱלֹהֶיךָ נֹתֵן לְךָ לְרִשְׁתָּהּ נֹפֵל בַּשָּׂדֶה לֹא נוֹדַע מִי הִכָּהוּ:

kee yi-ma-TZAY kha-LAL ba-a-da-MAH a-SHER a-do-NAI e-lo-HE-kha
no-TAYN l'-KHA l'-rish-TAH no-FAYL ba-sa-DEH LO no-DA MEE hi-KA-hu

Rabbi Joseph B.
Soloveitchik
(1903–1993)

21:1 In the land that *Hashem* your God is assigning you The axed heifer is one of the few biblical commandments that can be performed only in *Eretz Yisrael* even though it is not an agricultural law. Rabbi Joseph B. Soloveitchik explains that the reason for this is that this law is incumbent on the 'Congregation of Israel', not on individual members of the nation, and the Israelites are only considered the 'Congregation of Israel' when residing in their land. This highlights the centrality of the Land of Israel to the People of Israel: They are considered the Congregation of Israel in every sense of the term only when they live in their land. The ability to fulfill national biblical commands such as this is one of the reasons it is so important for Jews from all over the world to come on *aliyah*, to move to Israel.

² your elders and magistrates shall go out and measure the distances from the corpse to the nearby towns.

³ The elders of the town nearest to the corpse shall then take a heifer which has never been worked, which has never pulled in a yoke;

⁴ and the elders of that town shall bring the heifer down to an everflowing wadi, which is not tilled or sown. There, in the wadi, they shall break the heifer's neck.

⁵ The *Kohanim*, sons of *Levi*, shall come forward; for *Hashem* your God has chosen them to minister to Him and to pronounce blessing in the name of *Hashem*, and every lawsuit and case of assault is subject to their ruling.

⁶ Then all the elders of the town nearest to the corpse shall wash their hands over the heifer whose neck was broken in the wadi.

⁷ And they shall make this declaration: "Our hands did not shed this blood, nor did our eyes see it done.

⁸ Absolve, *Hashem*, Your people *Yisrael* whom You redeemed, and do not let guilt for the blood of the innocent remain among Your people *Yisrael*." And they will be absolved of bloodguilt.

⁹ Thus you will remove from your midst guilt for the blood of the innocent, for you will be doing what is right in the sight of *Hashem*.

¹⁰ When you take the field against your enemies, and *Hashem* your God delivers them into your power and you take some of them captive,

¹¹ and you see among the captives a beautiful woman and you desire her and would take her to wife,

¹² you shall bring her into your house, and she shall trim her hair, pare her nails,

¹³ and discard her captive's garb. She shall spend a month's time in your house lamenting her father and mother; after that you may come to her and possess her, and she shall be your wife.

¹⁴ Then, should you no longer want her, you must release her outright. You must not sell her for money: since you had your will of her, you must not enslave her.

ב וְיָצְא֣וּ זְקֵנֶ֔יךָ וְשֹׁפְטֶ֑יךָ וּמָדְד֖וּ אֶל־
הֶעָרִ֔ים אֲשֶׁ֖ר סְבִיבֹ֥ת הֶחָלָֽל׃

ג וְהָיָ֣ה הָעִ֔יר הַקְּרֹבָ֖ה אֶל־הֶחָלָ֑ל וְלָקְח֡וּ
זִקְנֵי֩ הָעִ֨יר הַהִ֜וא עֶגְלַ֣ת בָּקָ֗ר אֲשֶׁ֤ר לֹֽא־
עֻבַּד֙ בָּ֔הּ אֲשֶׁ֥ר לֹא־מָשְׁכָ֖ה בְּעֹֽל׃

ד וְהוֹרִ֡דוּ זִקְנֵי֩ הָעִ֨יר הַהִ֤וא אֶת־הָֽעֶגְלָה֙
אֶל־נַ֣חַל אֵיתָ֔ן אֲשֶׁ֛ר לֹא־יֵעָבֵ֥ד בּ֖וֹ וְלֹ֣א
יִזָּרֵ֑עַ וְעָ֥רְפוּ־שָׁ֛ם אֶת־הָעֶגְלָ֖ה בַּנָּֽחַל׃

ה וְנִגְּשׁ֣וּ הַכֹּֽהֲנִים֮ בְּנֵ֣י לֵוִי֒ כִּ֣י בָ֗ם בָּחַ֞ר יְהֹוָ֤ה
אֱלֹהֶ֙יךָ֙ לְשָׁ֣רְת֔וֹ וּלְבָרֵ֖ךְ בְּשֵׁ֣ם יְהֹוָ֑ה וְעַל־
פִּיהֶ֥ם יִהְיֶ֖ה כׇּל־רִ֥יב וְכׇל־נָֽגַע׃

ו וְכֹ֗ל זִקְנֵי֙ הָעִ֣יר הַהִ֔וא הַקְּרֹבִ֖ים אֶל־
הֶחָלָ֑ל יִרְחֲצוּ֙ אֶת־יְדֵיהֶ֔ם עַל־הָעֶגְלָ֖ה
הָעֲרוּפָ֥ה בַנָּֽחַל׃

ז וְעָנ֖וּ וְאָֽמְר֑וּ יָדֵ֗ינוּ לֹ֤א שׁפכה [שָֽׁפְכוּ֙]
אֶת־הַדָּ֣ם הַזֶּ֔ה וְעֵינֵ֖ינוּ לֹ֥א רָאֽוּ׃

ח כַּפֵּר֩ לְעַמְּךָ֙ יִשְׂרָאֵ֤ל אֲשֶׁר־פָּדִ֙יתָ֙ יְהֹוָ֔ה
וְאַל־תִּתֵּן֙ דָּ֣ם נָקִ֔י בְּקֶ֖רֶב עַמְּךָ֣ יִשְׂרָאֵ֑ל
וְנִכַּפֵּ֥ר לָהֶ֖ם הַדָּֽם׃

ט וְאַתָּ֗ה תְּבַעֵ֛ר הַדָּ֥ם הַנָּקִ֖י מִקִּרְבֶּ֑ךָ כִּֽי־
תַעֲשֶׂ֥ה הַיָּשָׁ֖ר בְּעֵינֵ֥י יְהֹוָֽה׃

🔶 כִּֽי־תֵצֵ֤א לַמִּלְחָמָה֙ עַל־אֹ֣יְבֶ֔יךָ וּנְתָנ֞וֹ
יְהֹוָ֧ה אֱלֹהֶ֛יךָ בְּיָדֶ֖ךָ וְשָׁבִ֥יתָ שִׁבְיֽוֹ׃

יא וְרָאִ֙יתָ֙ בַּשִּׁבְיָ֔ה אֵ֖שֶׁת יְפַת־תֹּ֑אַר
וְחָשַׁקְתָּ֣ בָ֔הּ וְלָקַחְתָּ֥ לְךָ֖ לְאִשָּֽׁה׃

יב וַהֲבֵאתָ֖הּ אֶל־תּ֣וֹךְ בֵּיתֶ֑ךָ וְגִלְּחָה֙ אֶת־
רֹאשָׁ֔הּ וְעָשְׂתָ֖ה אֶת־צִפׇּרְנֶֽיהָ׃

יג וְהֵסִ֩ירָה֩ אֶת־שִׂמְלַ֨ת שִׁבְיָ֜הּ מֵעָלֶ֗יהָ
וְיָֽשְׁבָה֙ בְּבֵיתֶ֔ךָ וּבָֽכְתָ֛ה אֶת־אָבִ֥יהָ וְאֶת־
אִמָּ֖הּ יֶ֣רַח יָמִ֑ים וְאַ֨חַר כֵּ֜ן תָּב֤וֹא אֵלֶ֙יהָ֙
וּבְעַלְתָּ֔הּ וְהָֽיְתָ֥ה לְךָ֖ לְאִשָּֽׁה׃

יד וְהָיָ֞ה אִם־לֹ֧א חָפַ֣צְתָּ בָּ֗הּ וְשִׁלַּחְתָּהּ֙
לְנַפְשָׁ֔הּ וּמָכֹ֤ר לֹֽא־תִמְכְּרֶ֙נָּה֙ בַּכָּ֑סֶף לֹֽא־
תִתְעַמֵּ֣ר בָּ֔הּ תַּ֖חַת אֲשֶׁ֥ר עִנִּיתָֽהּ׃

Deuteronomy

15 If a man has two wives, one loved and the other unloved, and both the loved and the unloved have borne him sons, but the first-born is the son of the unloved one

טו כִּי־תִהְיֶיןָ לְאִישׁ שְׁתֵּי נָשִׁים הָאַחַת אֲהוּבָה וְהָאַחַת שְׂנוּאָה וְיָלְדוּ־לוֹ בָנִים הָאֲהוּבָה וְהַשְּׂנוּאָה וְהָיָה הַבֵּן הַבְּכוֹר לַשְּׂנִיאָה:

16 when he wills his property to his sons, he may not treat as first-born the son of the loved one in disregard of the son of the unloved one who is older.

טז וְהָיָה בְּיוֹם הַנְחִילוֹ אֶת־בָּנָיו אֵת אֲשֶׁר־יִהְיֶה לוֹ לֹא יוּכַל לְבַכֵּר אֶת־בֶּן־ הָאֲהוּבָה עַל־פְּנֵי בֶן־הַשְּׂנוּאָה הַבְּכֹר:

17 Instead, he must accept the first-born, the son of the unloved one, and allot to him a double portion of all he possesses; since he is the first fruit of his vigor, the birthright is his due.

יז כִּי אֶת־הַבְּכֹר בֶּן־הַשְּׂנוּאָה יַכִּיר לָתֶת לוֹ פִּי שְׁנַיִם בְּכֹל אֲשֶׁר־יִמָּצֵא לוֹ כִּי־הוּא רֵאשִׁית אֹנוֹ לוֹ מִשְׁפַּט הַבְּכֹרָה:

18 If a man has a wayward and defiant son, who does not heed his father or mother and does not obey them even after they discipline him,

יח כִּי־יִהְיֶה לְאִישׁ בֵּן סוֹרֵר וּמוֹרֶה אֵינֶנּוּ שֹׁמֵעַ בְּקוֹל אָבִיו וּבְקוֹל אִמּוֹ וְיִסְּרוּ אֹתוֹ וְלֹא יִשְׁמַע אֲלֵיהֶם:

19 his father and mother shall take hold of him and bring him out to the elders of his town at the public place of his community.

יט וְתָפְשׂוּ בוֹ אָבִיו וְאִמּוֹ וְהוֹצִיאוּ אֹתוֹ אֶל־זִקְנֵי עִירוֹ וְאֶל־שַׁעַר מְקֹמוֹ:

20 They shall say to the elders of his town, "This son of ours is disloyal and defiant; he does not heed us. He is a glutton and a drunkard."

כ וְאָמְרוּ אֶל־זִקְנֵי עִירוֹ בְּנֵנוּ זֶה סוֹרֵר וּמֹרֶה אֵינֶנּוּ שֹׁמֵעַ בְּקֹלֵנוּ זוֹלֵל וְסֹבֵא:

21 Thereupon the men of his town shall stone him to death. Thus you will sweep out evil from your midst: all *Yisrael* will hear and be afraid.

כא וּרְגָמֻהוּ כָּל־אַנְשֵׁי עִירוֹ בָאֲבָנִים וָמֵת וּבִעַרְתָּ הָרָע מִקִּרְבֶּךָ וְכָל־יִשְׂרָאֵל יִשְׁמְעוּ וְיִרָאוּ:

22 If a man is guilty of a capital offense and is put to death, and you impale him on a stake,

כב וְכִי־יִהְיֶה בְאִישׁ חֵטְא מִשְׁפַּט־מָוֶת וְהוּמָת וְתָלִיתָ אֹתוֹ עַל־עֵץ:

23 you must not let his corpse remain on the stake overnight, but must bury him the same day. For an impaled body is an affront to *Hashem*: you shall not defile the land that *Hashem* your God is giving you to possess.

כג לֹא־תָלִין נִבְלָתוֹ עַל־הָעֵץ כִּי־קָבוֹר תִּקְבְּרֶנּוּ בַּיּוֹם הַהוּא כִּי־קִלְלַת אֱלֹהִים תָּלוּי וְלֹא תְטַמֵּא אֶת־אַדְמָתְךָ אֲשֶׁר יְהֹוָה אֱלֹהֶיךָ נֹתֵן לְךָ נַחֲלָה:

22 1 If you see your fellow's ox or sheep gone astray, do not ignore it; you must take it back to your fellow.

כב א לֹא־תִרְאֶה אֶת־שׁוֹר אָחִיךָ אוֹ אֶת־שֵׂיוֹ נִדָּחִים וְהִתְעַלַּמְתָּ מֵהֶם הָשֵׁב תְּשִׁיבֵם לְאָחִיךָ:

2 If your fellow does not live near you or you do not know who he is, you shall bring it home and it shall remain with you until your fellow claims it; then you shall give it back to him.

ב וְאִם־לֹא קָרוֹב אָחִיךָ אֵלֶיךָ וְלֹא יְדַעְתּוֹ וַאֲסַפְתּוֹ אֶל־תּוֹךְ בֵּיתֶךָ וְהָיָה עִמְּךָ עַד דְּרֹשׁ אָחִיךָ אֹתוֹ וַהֲשֵׁבֹתוֹ לוֹ:

3 You shall do the same with his ass; you shall do the same with his garment; and so too shall you do with anything that your fellow loses and you find: you must not remain indifferent.

ג וְכֵן תַּעֲשֶׂה לַחֲמֹרוֹ וְכֵן תַּעֲשֶׂה לְשִׂמְלָתוֹ וְכֵן תַּעֲשֶׂה לְכָל־אֲבֵדַת אָחִיךָ אֲשֶׁר־תֹּאבַד מִמֶּנּוּ וּמְצָאתָהּ לֹא תוּכַל לְהִתְעַלֵּם:

Deuteronomy

⁴ If you see your fellow's ass or ox fallen on the road, do not ignore it; you must help him raise it.

ד לֹא־תִרְאֶה אֶת־חֲמוֹר אָחִיךָ אוֹ שׁוֹרוֹ נֹפְלִים בַּדֶּרֶךְ וְהִתְעַלַּמְתָּ מֵהֶם הָקֵם תָּקִים עִמּוֹ:

⁵ A woman must not put on man's apparel, nor shall a man wear woman's clothing; for whoever does these things is abhorrent to *Hashem* your God.

ה לֹא־יִהְיֶה כְלִי־גֶבֶר עַל־אִשָּׁה וְלֹא־יִלְבַּשׁ גֶּבֶר שִׂמְלַת אִשָּׁה כִּי תוֹעֲבַת יְהֹוָה אֱלֹהֶיךָ כָּל־עֹשֵׂה אֵלֶּה:

⁶ If, along the road, you chance upon a bird's nest, in any tree or on the ground, with fledglings or eggs and the mother sitting over the fledglings or on the eggs, do not take the mother together with her young.

ו כִּי יִקָּרֵא קַן־צִפּוֹר לְפָנֶיךָ בַּדֶּרֶךְ בְּכָל־ עֵץ אוֹ עַל־הָאָרֶץ אֶפְרֹחִים אוֹ בֵיצִים וְהָאֵם רֹבֶצֶת עַל־הָאֶפְרֹחִים אוֹ עַל־ הַבֵּיצִים לֹא־תִקַּח הָאֵם עַל־הַבָּנִים:

⁷ Let the mother go, and take only the young, in order that you may fare well and have a long life.

ז שַׁלֵּחַ תְּשַׁלַּח אֶת־הָאֵם וְאֶת־הַבָּנִים תִּקַּח־לָךְ לְמַעַן יִיטַב לָךְ וְהַאֲרַכְתָּ יָמִים:

*sha-LAY-akh t'-sha-LAKH et ha-AYM v'-et ha-ba-NEEM ti-kakh
LAKH l'-MA-an YEE-tav LAKH v'-ha-a-rakh-TA ya-MEEM*

⁸ When you build a new house, you shall make a parapet for your roof, so that you do not bring bloodguilt on your house if anyone should fall from it.

ח כִּי תִבְנֶה בַּיִת חָדָשׁ וְעָשִׂיתָ מַעֲקֶה לְגַגֶּךָ וְלֹא־תָשִׂים דָּמִים בְּבֵיתֶךָ כִּי־יִפֹּל הַנֹּפֵל מִמֶּנּוּ:

⁹ You shall not sow your vineyard with a second kind of seed, else the crop – from the seed you have sown – and the yield of the vineyard may not be used.

ט לֹא־תִזְרַע כַּרְמְךָ כִּלְאָיִם פֶּן־תִּקְדַּשׁ הַמְלֵאָה הַזֶּרַע אֲשֶׁר תִּזְרָע וּתְבוּאַת הַכָּרֶם:

¹⁰ You shall not plow with an ox and an ass together.

י לֹא־תַחֲרֹשׁ בְּשׁוֹר־וּבַחֲמֹר יַחְדָּו:

¹¹ You shall not wear cloth combining wool and linen.

יא לֹא תִלְבַּשׁ שַׁעַטְנֵז צֶמֶר וּפִשְׁתִּים יַחְדָּו:

¹² You shall make tassels on the four corners of the garment with which you cover yourself.

יב גְּדִלִים תַּעֲשֶׂה־לָּךְ עַל־אַרְבַּע כַּנְפוֹת כְּסוּתְךָ אֲשֶׁר תְּכַסֶּה־בָּהּ:

¹³ A man marries a woman and cohabits with her. Then he takes an aversion to her

יג כִּי־יִקַּח אִישׁ אִשָּׁה וּבָא אֵלֶיהָ וּשְׂנֵאָהּ:

22:7 Let the mother go This verse instructs one to chase a mother bird from its nest before taking its fledglings. On a deeper level, this law reflects the state of the Jewish people in exile. According to the mystical work *Zohar*, the mother bird who has been chased away cries about the separation from her children. When her cries are heard on high, the angels ask *Hashem* why He has commanded that the mother bird suffer such a sad fate. God answers that He shares the same fate as the mother bird: His presence has been driven from the *Beit Hamikdash*, and His children have been taken into exile. God asks that the angels sympathize with His plight and the plight of the Jewish people. He demands that they pray for the return of the Jewish people to their homeland and for the restoration of the *Beit Hamikdash* so that His presence can once again dwell in *Yerushalayim*.

Migrating birds over the Hula lake nature reserve

Deuteronomy

14 and makes up charges against her and defames her, saying, "I married this woman; but when I approached her, I found that she was not a virgin."

יד וְשָׂם לָהּ עֲלִילֹת דְּבָרִים וְהוֹצִיא עָלֶיהָ שֵׁם רָע וְאָמַר אֶת־הָאִשָּׁה הַזֹּאת לָקַחְתִּי וָאֶקְרַב אֵלֶיהָ וְלֹא־מָצָאתִי לָהּ בְּתוּלִים:

15 In such a case, the girl's father and mother shall produce the evidence of the girl's virginity before the elders of the town at the gate.

טו וְלָקַח אֲבִי הַנַּעֲרָ [הַנַּעֲרָה] וְאִמָּהּ וְהוֹצִיאוּ אֶת־בְּתוּלֵי הַנַּעֲרָ [הַנַּעֲרָה] אֶל־זִקְנֵי הָעִיר הַשָּׁעְרָה:

16 And the girl's father shall say to the elders, "I gave this man my daughter to wife, but he has taken an aversion to her;

טז וְאָמַר אֲבִי הַנַּעֲרָ [הַנַּעֲרָה] אֶל־הַזְּקֵנִים אֶת־בִּתִּי נָתַתִּי לָאִישׁ הַזֶּה לְאִשָּׁה וַיִּשְׂנָאֶהָ:

17 so he has made up charges, saying, 'I did not find your daughter a virgin.' But here is the evidence of my daughter's virginity!" And they shall spread out the cloth before the elders of the town.

יז וְהִנֵּה־הוּא שָׂם עֲלִילֹת דְּבָרִים לֵאמֹר לֹא־מָצָאתִי לְבִתְּךָ בְּתוּלִים וְאֵלֶּה בְּתוּלֵי בִתִּי וּפָרְשׂוּ הַשִּׂמְלָה לִפְנֵי זִקְנֵי הָעִיר:

18 The elders of that town shall then take the man and flog him,

יח וְלָקְחוּ זִקְנֵי הָעִיר־הַהִוא אֶת־הָאִישׁ וְיִסְּרוּ אֹתוֹ:

19 and they shall fine him a hundred [*shekalim* of] silver and give it to the girl's father; for the man has defamed a virgin in *Yisrael*. Moreover, she shall remain his wife; he shall never have the right to divorce her.

יט וְעָנְשׁוּ אֹתוֹ מֵאָה כֶסֶף וְנָתְנוּ לַאֲבִי הַנַּעֲרָה כִּי הוֹצִיא שֵׁם רָע עַל בְּתוּלַת יִשְׂרָאֵל וְלוֹ־תִהְיֶה לְאִשָּׁה לֹא־יוּכַל לְשַׁלְּחָהּ כָּל־יָמָיו:

20 But if the charge proves true, the girl was found not to have been a virgin,

כ וְאִם־אֱמֶת הָיָה הַדָּבָר הַזֶּה לֹא־נִמְצְאוּ בְתוּלִים לַנַּעֲרָ [לַנַּעֲרָה]:

21 then the girl shall be brought out to the entrance of her father's house, and the men of her town shall stone her to death; for she did a shameful thing in *Yisrael*, committing fornication while under her father's authority. Thus you will sweep away evil from your midst.

כא וְהוֹצִיאוּ אֶת־הַנַּעֲרָ [הַנַּעֲרָה] אֶל־פֶּתַח בֵּית־אָבִיהָ וּסְקָלוּהָ אַנְשֵׁי עִירָהּ בָּאֲבָנִים וָמֵתָה כִּי־עָשְׂתָה נְבָלָה בְּיִשְׂרָאֵל לִזְנוֹת בֵּית אָבִיהָ וּבִעַרְתָּ הָרָע מִקִּרְבֶּךָ:

22 If a man is found lying with another man's wife, both of them – the man and the woman with whom he lay – shall die. Thus you will sweep away evil from *Yisrael*.

כב כִּי־יִמָּצֵא אִישׁ שֹׁכֵב עִם־אִשָּׁה בְעֻלַת־בַּעַל וּמֵתוּ גַּם־שְׁנֵיהֶם הָאִישׁ הַשֹּׁכֵב עִם־הָאִשָּׁה וְהָאִשָּׁה וּבִעַרְתָּ הָרָע מִיִּשְׂרָאֵל:

23 In the case of a virgin who is engaged to a man – if a man comes upon her in town and lies with her,

כג כִּי יִהְיֶה נַעֲרָ [נַעֲרָה] בְתוּלָה מְאֹרָשָׂה לְאִישׁ וּמְצָאָהּ אִישׁ בָּעִיר וְשָׁכַב עִמָּהּ:

24 you shall take the two of them out to the gate of that town and stone them to death: the girl because she did not cry for help in the town, and the man because he violated another man's wife. Thus you will sweep away evil from your midst.

כד וְהוֹצֵאתֶם אֶת־שְׁנֵיהֶם אֶל־שַׁעַר הָעִיר הַהִוא וּסְקַלְתֶּם אֹתָם בָּאֲבָנִים וָמֵתוּ אֶת־הַנַּעֲרָ [הַנַּעֲרָה] עַל־דְּבַר אֲשֶׁר לֹא־צָעֲקָה בָעִיר וְאֶת־הָאִישׁ עַל־דְּבַר אֲשֶׁר־עִנָּה אֶת־אֵשֶׁת רֵעֵהוּ וּבִעַרְתָּ הָרָע מִקִּרְבֶּךָ:

25 But if the man comes upon the engaged girl in the open country, and the man lies with her by force, only the man who lay with her shall die,

כה וְאִם־בַּשָּׂדֶ֣ה יִמְצָ֣א הָאִ֗ישׁ אֶת־הַֽנַּעֲרָ֙ [הַֽנַּעֲרָ֔ה] הַמְאֹ֣רָשָׂ֔ה וְהֶחֱזִֽיק־בָּ֥הּ הָאִ֖ישׁ וְשָׁכַ֣ב עִמָּ֑הּ וּמֵ֗ת הָאִ֛ישׁ אֲשֶׁר־שָׁכַ֥ב עִמָּ֖הּ לְבַדּֽוֹ:

26 but you shall do nothing to the girl. The girl did not incur the death penalty, for this case is like that of a man attacking another and murdering him.

כו וְלַֽנַּעֲרָ֙ [וְלַֽנַּעֲרָ֔ה] לֹא־תַעֲשֶׂ֣ה דָבָ֔ר אֵ֥ין לַֽנַּעֲרָ֖ [לַֽנַּעֲרָ֖ה] חֵ֣טְא מָ֑וֶת כִּ֡י כַּאֲשֶׁר֩ יָק֨וּם אִ֤ישׁ עַל־רֵעֵ֙הוּ֙ וּרְצָח֣וֹ נֶ֔פֶשׁ כֵּ֖ן הַדָּבָ֥ר הַזֶּֽה:

27 He came upon her in the open; though the engaged girl cried for help, there was no one to save her.

כז כִּ֥י בַשָּׂדֶ֖ה מְצָאָ֑הּ צָעֲקָ֗ה הַֽנַּעֲרָ֙ [הַֽנַּעֲרָ֔ה] הַמְאֹ֣רָשָׂ֔ה וְאֵ֥ין מוֹשִׁ֖יעַ לָֽהּ:

28 If a man comes upon a virgin who is not engaged and he seizes her and lies with her, and they are discovered,

כח כִּֽי־יִמְצָ֣א אִ֗ישׁ נַעֲרָ֤ [נַעֲרָה֙] בְתוּלָ֔ה אֲשֶׁ֖ר לֹא־אֹרָ֑שָׂה וּתְפָשָׂ֥הּ וְשָׁכַ֣ב עִמָּ֖הּ וְנִמְצָֽאוּ:

29 the man who lay with her shall pay the girl's father fifty [*shekalim* of] silver, and she shall be his wife. Because he has violated her, he can never have the right to divorce her.

כט וְנָתַ֠ן הָאִ֨ישׁ הַשֹּׁכֵ֥ב עִמָּ֛הּ לַאֲבִ֥י הַֽנַּעֲרָ֖ [הַֽנַּעֲרָ֖ה] חֲמִשִּׁ֣ים כָּ֑סֶף וְלֽוֹ־תִהְיֶ֣ה לְאִשָּׁ֗ה תַּ֚חַת אֲשֶׁ֣ר עִנָּ֔הּ לֹא־יוּכַ֥ל שַׁלְּחָ֖הּ כָּל־יָמָֽיו:

23 1 No man shall marry his father's former wife, so as to remove his father's garment.

כג א לֹא־יִקַּ֥ח אִ֖ישׁ אֶת־אֵ֣שֶׁת אָבִ֑יו וְלֹ֥א יְגַלֶּ֖ה כְּנַ֥ף אָבִֽיו:

2 No one whose testes are crushed or whose member is cut off shall be admitted into the congregation of *Hashem*.

ב לֹֽא־יָבֹ֧א פְצֽוּעַ־דַּכָּ֛א וּכְר֥וּת שָׁפְכָ֖ה בִּקְהַ֥ל יְהֹוָֽה:

3 No one misbegotten shall be admitted into the congregation of *Hashem*; none of his descendants, even in the tenth generation, shall be admitted into the congregation of *Hashem*.

ג לֹא־יָבֹ֥א מַמְזֵ֖ר בִּקְהַ֣ל יְהֹוָ֑ה גַּ֚ם דּ֣וֹר עֲשִׂירִ֔י לֹא־יָ֥בֹא ל֖וֹ בִּקְהַ֥ל יְהֹוָֽה:

4 No Amonite or Moabite shall be admitted into the congregation of *Hashem*; none of their descendants, even in the tenth generation, shall ever be admitted into the congregation of *Hashem*,

ד לֹֽא־יָבֹ֧א עַמּוֹנִ֛י וּמוֹאָבִ֖י בִּקְהַ֣ל יְהֹוָ֑ה גַּ֚ם דּ֣וֹר עֲשִׂירִ֔י לֹא־יָבֹ֥א לָהֶ֛ם בִּקְהַ֥ל יְהֹוָ֖ה עַד־עוֹלָֽם:

5 because they did not meet you with food and water on your journey after you left Egypt, and because they hired Balaam son of Beor, from Pethor of Aram-Naharaim, to curse you.

ה עַל־דְּבַ֞ר אֲשֶׁ֨ר לֹא־קִדְּמ֤וּ אֶתְכֶם֙ בַּלֶּ֣חֶם וּבַמַּ֔יִם בַּדֶּ֖רֶךְ בְּצֵאתְכֶ֣ם מִמִּצְרָ֑יִם וַאֲשֶׁר֩ שָׂכַ֨ר עָלֶ֜יךָ אֶת־בִּלְעָ֣ם בֶּן־בְּע֗וֹר מִפְּת֛וֹר אֲרַ֥ם נַהֲרַ֖יִם לְקַֽלְלֶֽךָּ:

6 But *Hashem* your God refused to heed Balaam; instead, *Hashem* your God turned the curse into a blessing for you, for *Hashem* your God loves you.

ו וְלֹֽא־אָבָ֞ה יְהֹוָ֤ה אֱלֹהֶ֙יךָ֙ לִשְׁמֹ֣עַ אֶל־בִּלְעָ֔ם וַיַּהֲפֹךְ֩ יְהֹוָ֨ה אֱלֹהֶ֧יךָ לְּךָ֛ אֶת־הַקְּלָלָ֖ה לִבְרָכָ֑ה כִּ֥י אֲהֵֽבְךָ֖ יְהֹוָ֥ה אֱלֹהֶֽיךָ:

7 You shall never concern yourself with their welfare or benefit as long as you live.

ז לֹא־תִדְרֹ֥שׁ שְׁלֹמָ֖ם וְטֹבָתָ֑ם כָּל־יָמֶ֖יךָ לְעוֹלָֽם:

8 You shall not abhor an Edomite, for he is your kinsman. You shall not abhor an Egyptian, for you were a stranger in his land.

ח לֹא־תְתַעֵב אֲדֹמִי כִּי אָחִיךָ הוּא לֹא־תְתַעֵב מִצְרִי כִּי־גֵר הָיִיתָ בְאַרְצוֹ:

lo t'-ta-AYV a-do-MEE KEE a-KHEE-kha HU lo t'-ta-AYV
mitz-REE kee GAYR ha-YEE-ta v'-ar-TZO

9 Children born to them may be admitted into the congregation of *Hashem* in the third generation.

ט בָּנִים אֲשֶׁר־יִוָּלְדוּ לָהֶם דּוֹר שְׁלִישִׁי יָבֹא לָהֶם בִּקְהַל יְהֹוָה:

10 When you go out as a troop against your enemies, be on your guard against anything untoward.

י כִּי־תֵצֵא מַחֲנֶה עַל־אֹיְבֶיךָ וְנִשְׁמַרְתָּ מִכֹּל דָּבָר רָע:

11 If anyone among you has been rendered unclean by a nocturnal emission, he must leave the camp, and he must not reenter the camp.

יא כִּי־יִהְיֶה בְךָ אִישׁ אֲשֶׁר לֹא־יִהְיֶה טָהוֹר מִקְּרֵה־לָיְלָה וְיָצָא אֶל־מִחוּץ לַמַּחֲנֶה לֹא יָבֹא אֶל־תּוֹךְ הַמַּחֲנֶה:

12 Toward evening he shall bathe in water, and at sundown he may reenter the camp.

יב וְהָיָה לִפְנוֹת־עֶרֶב יִרְחַץ בַּמָּיִם וּכְבֹא הַשֶּׁמֶשׁ יָבֹא אֶל־תּוֹךְ הַמַּחֲנֶה:

13 Further, there shall be an area for you outside the camp, where you may relieve yourself.

יג וְיָד תִּהְיֶה לְךָ מִחוּץ לַמַּחֲנֶה וְיָצָאתָ שָׁמָּה חוּץ:

14 With your gear you shall have a spike, and when you have squatted you shall dig a hole with it and cover up your excrement.

יד וְיָתֵד תִּהְיֶה לְךָ עַל־אֲזֵנֶךָ וְהָיָה בְּשִׁבְתְּךָ חוּץ וְחָפַרְתָּה בָהּ וְשַׁבְתָּ וְכִסִּיתָ אֶת־צֵאָתֶךָ:

15 Since *Hashem* your God moves about in your camp to protect you and to deliver your enemies to you, let your camp be holy; let Him not find anything unseemly among you and turn away from you.

טו כִּי יְהֹוָה אֱלֹהֶיךָ מִתְהַלֵּךְ בְּקֶרֶב מַחֲנֶךָ לְהַצִּילְךָ וְלָתֵת אֹיְבֶיךָ לְפָנֶיךָ וְהָיָה מַחֲנֶיךָ קָדוֹשׁ וְלֹא־יִרְאֶה בְךָ עֶרְוַת דָּבָר וְשָׁב מֵאַחֲרֶיךָ:

KEE a-do-NAI e-lo-HE-kha mit-ha-LAYKH b'-KE-rev
ma-kha-NE-kha l'-ha-TZEE-l'-kha v'-la-TAYT o-y'-VE-kha
l'-fa-NE-kha v'-ha-YAH ma-kha-NE-khah ka-DOSH v'-lo yir-EH
v'-KHA er-VAT da-VAR v'-SHAV may-a-kha-RE-kha

16 You shall not turn over to his master a slave who seeks refuge with you from his master.

טז לֹא־תַסְגִּיר עֶבֶד אֶל־אֲדֹנָיו אֲשֶׁר־יִנָּצֵל אֵלֶיךָ מֵעִם אֲדֹנָיו:

17 He shall live with you in any place he may choose among the settlements in your midst, wherever he pleases; you must not ill-treat him.

יז עִמְּךָ יֵשֵׁב בְּקִרְבְּךָ בַּמָּקוֹם אֲשֶׁר־יִבְחַר בְּאַחַד שְׁעָרֶיךָ בַּטּוֹב לוֹ לֹא תוֹנֶנּוּ:

23:8 You shall not abhor an *Egyptian* Despite the bitter slavery the nation suffered at the hand of the Egyptians, the *Torah* teaches that we must care for all of *Hashem*'s children, even our persecutors, and not treat them the same way they treated us. In fact, the *Torah* emphasizes universal feelings of sympathy and compassion for all, and warns against rejoicing at the downfall of our enemies. It is for this reason that at the *Seder* meal every *Pesach*, when the Jewish people celebrate their salvation from the hands of their Egyptian oppressors, they spill symbolic drops of wine from their cups while mentioning the ten plagues, to indicate that their joy is diminished due the suffering caused to their enemies. The State of Israel has also demonstrated great sympathy towards its military enemies and towards the civilian populations of neighboring countries, despite their hostility. The field hospitals the IDF has maintained for Syrian refugees provide one example of the fact that the Israeli army is the most humanitarian one in the world.

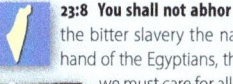

IDF field hospital for wounded Syrian civilians

18 No Israelite woman shall be a cult prostitute, nor shall any Israelite man be a cult prostitute.

19 You shall not bring the fee of a whore or the pay of a dog into the house of *Hashem* your God in fulfillment of any vow, for both are abhorrent to *Hashem* your God.

20 You shall not deduct interest from loans to your countrymen, whether in money or food or anything else that can be deducted as interest;

21 but you may deduct interest from loans to foreigners. Do not deduct interest from loans to your countrymen, so that *Hashem* your God may bless you in all your undertakings in the land that you are about to enter and possess.

22 When you make a vow to *Hashem* your God, do not put off fulfilling it, for *Hashem* your God will require it of you, and you will have incurred guilt;

23 whereas you incur no guilt if you refrain from vowing.

24 You must fulfill what has crossed your lips and perform what you have voluntarily vowed to *Hashem* your God, having made the promise with your own mouth.

25 When you enter another man's vineyard, you may eat as many grapes as you want, until you are full, but you must not put any in your vessel.

26 When you enter another man's field of standing grain, you may pluck ears with your hand; but you must not put a sickle to your neighbor's grain.

24 1 A man takes a wife and possesses her. She fails to please him because he finds something obnoxious about her, and he writes her a bill of divorcement, hands it to her, and sends her away from his house;

2 she leaves his household and becomes the wife of another man;

3 then this latter man rejects her, writes her a bill of divorcement, hands it to her, and sends her away from his house; or the man who married her last dies.

4 Then the first husband who divorced her shall not take her to wife again, since she has been defiled – for that would be abhorrent to *Hashem*. You must not bring sin upon the land that *Hashem* your God is giving you as a heritage.

יח לֹא־תִהְיֶ֥ה קְדֵשָׁ֖ה מִבְּנ֣וֹת יִשְׂרָאֵ֑ל וְלֹֽא־יִהְיֶ֥ה קָדֵ֖שׁ מִבְּנֵ֥י יִשְׂרָאֵֽל׃

יט לֹא־תָבִיא֩ אֶתְנַ֨ן זוֹנָ֜ה וּמְחִ֣יר כֶּ֗לֶב בֵּ֛ית יְהֹוָ֥ה אֱלֹהֶ֖יךָ לְכׇל־נֶ֑דֶר כִּ֧י תוֹעֲבַ֛ת יְהֹוָ֥ה אֱלֹהֶ֖יךָ גַּם־שְׁנֵיהֶֽם׃

כ לֹא־תַשִּׁ֣יךְ לְאָחִ֔יךָ נֶ֥שֶׁךְ כֶּ֖סֶף נֶ֣שֶׁךְ אֹ֑כֶל נֶ֕שֶׁךְ כׇּל־דָּבָ֖ר אֲשֶׁ֥ר יִשָּֽׁךְ׃

כא לַנׇּכְרִ֣י תַשִּׁ֔יךְ וּלְאָחִ֖יךָ לֹ֣א תַשִּׁ֑יךְ לְמַ֨עַן יְבָרֶכְךָ֜ יְהֹוָ֣ה אֱלֹהֶ֗יךָ בְּכֹל֙ מִשְׁלַ֣ח יָדֶ֔ךָ עַל־הָאָ֕רֶץ אֲשֶׁר־אַתָּ֥ה בָא־שָׁ֖מָּה לְרִשְׁתָּֽהּ׃

כב כִּֽי־תִדֹּ֥ר נֶ֙דֶר֙ לַֽיהֹוָ֣ה אֱלֹהֶ֔יךָ לֹ֥א תְאַחֵ֖ר לְשַׁלְּמ֑וֹ כִּֽי־דָּרֹ֨שׁ יִדְרְשֶׁ֜נּוּ יְהֹוָ֤ה אֱלֹהֶ֙יךָ֙ מֵֽעִמָּ֔ךְ וְהָיָ֥ה בְךָ֖ חֵֽטְא׃

כג וְכִ֥י תֶחְדַּ֖ל לִנְדֹּ֑ר לֹֽא־יִהְיֶ֥ה בְךָ֖ חֵֽטְא׃

כד מוֹצָ֥א שְׂפָתֶ֖יךָ תִּשְׁמֹ֣ר וְעָשִׂ֑יתָ כַּאֲשֶׁ֣ר נָדַ֗רְתָּ לַֽיהֹוָ֤ה אֱלֹהֶ֙יךָ֙ נְדָבָ֔ה אֲשֶׁ֥ר דִּבַּ֖רְתָּ בְּפִֽיךָ׃

כה כִּ֤י תָבֹא֙ בְּכֶ֣רֶם רֵעֶ֔ךָ וְאָכַלְתָּ֧ עֲנָבִ֛ים כְּנַפְשְׁךָ֖ שׇׂבְעֶ֑ךָ וְאֶֽל־כֶּלְיְךָ֖ לֹ֥א תִתֵּֽן׃

כו כִּ֤י תָבֹא֙ בְּקָמַ֣ת רֵעֶ֔ךָ וְקָטַפְתָּ֥ מְלִילֹ֖ת בְּיָדֶ֑ךָ וְחֶרְמֵשׁ֙ לֹ֣א תָנִ֔יף עַ֖ל קָמַ֥ת רֵעֶֽךָ׃

כד א כִּֽי־יִקַּ֥ח אִ֛ישׁ אִשָּׁ֖ה וּבְעָלָ֑הּ וְהָיָ֞ה אִם־לֹ֧א תִמְצָא־חֵ֣ן בְּעֵינָ֗יו כִּי־מָ֤צָא בָהּ֙ עֶרְוַ֣ת דָּבָ֔ר וְכָ֨תַב לָ֜הּ סֵ֤פֶר כְּרִיתֻת֙ וְנָתַ֣ן בְּיָדָ֔הּ וְשִׁלְּחָ֖הּ מִבֵּיתֽוֹ׃

ב וְיָצְאָ֖ה מִבֵּית֑וֹ וְהָלְכָ֖ה וְהָיְתָ֥ה לְאִישׁ־אַחֵֽר׃

ג וּשְׂנֵאָהּ֮ הָאִ֣ישׁ הָאַחֲרוֹן֒ וְכָ֨תַב לָ֜הּ סֵ֤פֶר כְּרִיתֻת֙ וְנָתַ֣ן בְּיָדָ֔הּ וְשִׁלְּחָ֖הּ מִבֵּית֑וֹ א֣וֹ כִ֤י יָמוּת֙ הָאִ֣ישׁ הָאַחֲר֔וֹן אֲשֶׁר־לְקָחָ֥הּ ל֖וֹ לְאִשָּֽׁה׃

ד לֹא־יוּכַ֣ל בַּעְלָ֣הּ הָרִאשׁ֣וֹן אֲשֶֽׁר־שִׁ֠לְּחָ֠הּ לָשׁ֨וּב לְקַחְתָּ֜הּ לִהְי֧וֹת ל֣וֹ לְאִשָּׁ֗ה אַחֲרֵי֙ אֲשֶׁ֣ר הֻטַּמָּ֔אָה כִּֽי־תוֹעֵבָ֥ה הִ֖וא לִפְנֵ֣י יְהֹוָ֑ה וְלֹ֤א תַחֲטִיא֙ אֶת־הָאָ֔רֶץ אֲשֶׁר֙ יְהֹוָ֣ה אֱלֹהֶ֔יךָ נֹתֵ֥ן לְךָ֖ נַחֲלָֽה׃

Deuteronomy

5 When a man has taken a bride, he shall not go out with the army or be assigned to it for any purpose; he shall be exempt one year for the sake of his household, to give happiness to the woman he has married.

ה כִּי־יִקַּח אִישׁ אִשָּׁה חֲדָשָׁה לֹא יֵצֵא בַּצָּבָא וְלֹא־יַעֲבֹר עָלָיו לְכָל־דָּבָר נָקִי יִהְיֶה לְבֵיתוֹ שָׁנָה אֶחָת וְשִׂמַּח אֶת־אִשְׁתּוֹ אֲשֶׁר־לָקָח:

6 A handmill or an upper millstone shall not be taken in pawn, for that would be taking someone's life in pawn.

ו לֹא־יַחֲבֹל רֵחַיִם וָרָכֶב כִּי־נֶפֶשׁ הוּא חֹבֵל:

7 If a man is found to have kidnapped a fellow Israelite, enslaving him or selling him, that kidnapper shall die; thus you will sweep out evil from your midst.

ז כִּי־יִמָּצֵא אִישׁ גֹּנֵב נֶפֶשׁ מֵאֶחָיו מִבְּנֵי יִשְׂרָאֵל וְהִתְעַמֶּר־בּוֹ וּמְכָרוֹ וּמֵת הַגַּנָּב הַהוּא וּבִעַרְתָּ הָרָע מִקִּרְבֶּךָ:

8 In cases of a skin affection be most careful to do exactly as the levitical *Kohanim* instruct you. Take care to do as I have commanded them.

ח הִשָּׁמֶר בְּנֶגַע־הַצָּרַעַת לִשְׁמֹר מְאֹד וְלַעֲשׂוֹת כְּכֹל אֲשֶׁר־יוֹרוּ אֶתְכֶם הַכֹּהֲנִים הַלְוִיִּם כַּאֲשֶׁר צִוִּיתִם תִּשְׁמְרוּ לַעֲשׂוֹת:

9 Remember what *Hashem* your God did to *Miriam* on the journey after you left Egypt.

ט זָכוֹר אֵת אֲשֶׁר־עָשָׂה יְהֹוָה אֱלֹהֶיךָ לְמִרְיָם בַּדֶּרֶךְ בְּצֵאתְכֶם מִמִּצְרָיִם:

10 When you make a loan of any sort to your countryman, you must not enter his house to seize his pledge.

י כִּי־תַשֶּׁה בְרֵעֲךָ מַשַּׁאת מְאוּמָה לֹא־תָבֹא אֶל־בֵּיתוֹ לַעֲבֹט עֲבֹטוֹ:

11 You must remain outside, while the man to whom you made the loan brings the pledge out to you.

יא בַּחוּץ תַּעֲמֹד וְהָאִישׁ אֲשֶׁר אַתָּה נֹשֶׁה בוֹ יוֹצִיא אֵלֶיךָ אֶת־הַעֲבוֹט הַחוּצָה:

12 If he is a needy man, you shall not go to sleep in his pledge;

יב וְאִם־אִישׁ עָנִי הוּא לֹא תִשְׁכַּב בַּעֲבֹטוֹ:

13 you must return the pledge to him at sundown, that he may sleep in his cloth and bless you; and it will be to your merit before *Hashem* your God.

יג הָשֵׁב תָּשִׁיב לוֹ אֶת־הַעֲבוֹט כְּבֹא הַשֶּׁמֶשׁ וְשָׁכַב בְּשַׂלְמָתוֹ וּבֵרֲכֶךָּ וּלְךָ תִּהְיֶה צְדָקָה לִפְנֵי יְהֹוָה אֱלֹהֶיךָ:

14 You shall not abuse a needy and destitute laborer, whether a fellow countryman or a stranger in one of the communities of your land.

יד לֹא־תַעֲשֹׁק שָׂכִיר עָנִי וְאֶבְיוֹן מֵאַחֶיךָ אוֹ מִגֵּרְךָ אֲשֶׁר בְּאַרְצְךָ בִּשְׁעָרֶיךָ:

15 You must pay him his wages on the same day, before the sun sets, for he is needy and urgently depends on it; else he will cry to *Hashem* against you and you will incur guilt.

טו בְּיוֹמוֹ תִתֵּן שְׂכָרוֹ וְלֹא־תָבוֹא עָלָיו הַשֶּׁמֶשׁ כִּי עָנִי הוּא וְאֵלָיו הוּא נֹשֵׂא אֶת־נַפְשׁוֹ וְלֹא־יִקְרָא עָלֶיךָ אֶל־יְהֹוָה וְהָיָה בְךָ חֵטְא:

16 Parents shall not be put to death for children, nor children be put to death for parents: a person shall be put to death only for his own crime.

טז לֹא־יוּמְתוּ אָבוֹת עַל־בָּנִים וּבָנִים לֹא־יוּמְתוּ עַל־אָבוֹת אִישׁ בְּחֶטְאוֹ יוּמָתוּ:

17 You shall not subvert the rights of the stranger or the fatherless; you shall not take a widow's garment in pawn.

יז לֹא תַטֶּה מִשְׁפַּט גֵּר יָתוֹם וְלֹא תַחֲבֹל בֶּגֶד אַלְמָנָה:

18 Remember that you were a slave in Egypt and that *Hashem* your God redeemed you from there; therefore do I enjoin you to observe this commandment.

יח וְזָכַרְתָּ כִּי עֶבֶד הָיִיתָ בְּמִצְרַיִם וַיִּפְדְּךָ יְהֹוָה אֱלֹהֶיךָ מִשָּׁם עַל־כֵּן אָנֹכִי מְצַוְּךָ לַעֲשׂוֹת אֶת־הַדָּבָר הַזֶּה:

19 When you reap the harvest in your field and overlook a sheaf in the field, do not turn back to get it; it shall go to the stranger, the fatherless, and the widow – in order that *Hashem* your God may bless you in all your undertakings.

יט כִּי תִקְצֹר קְצִירְךָ בְשָׂדֶךָ וְשָׁכַחְתָּ עֹמֶר בַּשָּׂדֶה לֹא תָשׁוּב לְקַחְתּוֹ לַגֵּר לַיָּתוֹם וְלָאַלְמָנָה יִהְיֶה לְמַעַן יְבָרֶכְךָ יְהֹוָה אֱלֹהֶיךָ בְּכֹל מַעֲשֵׂה יָדֶיךָ:

20 When you beat down the fruit of your olive trees, do not go over them again; that shall go to the stranger, the fatherless, and the widow.

כ כִּי תַחְבֹּט זֵיתְךָ לֹא תְפָאֵר אַחֲרֶיךָ לַגֵּר לַיָּתוֹם וְלָאַלְמָנָה יִהְיֶה:

KEE takh-BOT zay-t'-KHA LO t'-fa-AYR a-kha-RE-kha
la-GAYR la-ya-TOM v'-la-al-ma-NAH yih-YEH

21 When you gather the grapes of your vineyard, do not pick it over again; that shall go to the stranger, the fatherless, and the widow.

כא כִּי תִבְצֹר כַּרְמְךָ לֹא תְעוֹלֵל אַחֲרֶיךָ לַגֵּר לַיָּתוֹם וְלָאַלְמָנָה יִהְיֶה:

22 Always remember that you were a slave in the land of Egypt; therefore do I enjoin you to observe this commandment.

כב וְזָכַרְתָּ כִּי עֶבֶד הָיִיתָ בְּאֶרֶץ מִצְרָיִם עַל־כֵּן אָנֹכִי מְצַוְּךָ לַעֲשׂוֹת אֶת־הַדָּבָר הַזֶּה:

25 1 When there is a dispute between men and they go to law, and a decision is rendered declaring the one in the right and the other in the wrong

כה א כִּי־יִהְיֶה רִיב בֵּין אֲנָשִׁים וְנִגְּשׁוּ אֶל־הַמִּשְׁפָּט וּשְׁפָטוּם וְהִצְדִּיקוּ אֶת־הַצַּדִּיק וְהִרְשִׁיעוּ אֶת־הָרָשָׁע:

2 if the guilty one is to be flogged, the magistrate shall have him lie down and be given lashes in his presence, by count, as his guilt warrants.

ב וְהָיָה אִם־בִּן הַכּוֹת הָרָשָׁע וְהִפִּילוֹ הַשֹּׁפֵט וְהִכָּהוּ לְפָנָיו כְּדֵי רִשְׁעָתוֹ בְּמִסְפָּר:

3 He may be given up to forty lashes, but not more, lest being flogged further, to excess, your brother be degraded before your eyes.

ג אַרְבָּעִים יַכֶּנּוּ לֹא יֹסִיף פֶּן־יֹסִיף לְהַכֹּתוֹ עַל־אֵלֶּה מַכָּה רַבָּה וְנִקְלָה אָחִיךָ לְעֵינֶיךָ:

4 You shall not muzzle an ox while it is threshing.

ד לֹא־תַחְסֹם שׁוֹר בְּדִישׁוֹ:

5 When brothers dwell together and one of them dies and leaves no son, the wife of the deceased shall not be married to a stranger, outside the family. Her husband's brother shall unite with her: he shall take her as his wife and perform the levir's duty.

ה כִּי־יֵשְׁבוּ אַחִים יַחְדָּו וּמֵת אַחַד מֵהֶם וּבֵן אֵין־לוֹ לֹא־תִהְיֶה אֵשֶׁת־הַמֵּת הַחוּצָה לְאִישׁ זָר יְבָמָהּ יָבֹא עָלֶיהָ וּלְקָחָהּ לוֹ לְאִשָּׁה וְיִבְּמָהּ:

24:20 When you beat down the fruit of your olive trees Just as grain must be left in the fields for the poor during the time of the harvest, so too fruit must be left on the trees. In describing the process of removing the fruit from the olive tree, the verse says "when you beat down the fruit of your olive trees." In ancient times, olive trees were harvested by beating the branches with a stick, causing the olives to fall to the ground. According to Jewish tradition, this command hints to the blessing of abundance in the Land of Israel. There will be so much produce that the farmers will only need to harvest what falls off with the beating of the tree branches; they will not even need to bother climbing a ladder to reach the fruit at the top of the tree.

Harvesting olives in the Upper Galilee

Deuteronomy

6 The first son that she bears shall be accounted to the dead brother, that his name may not be blotted out in *Yisrael*.

ו וְהָיָ֗ה הַבְּכוֹר֙ אֲשֶׁ֣ר תֵּלֵ֔ד יָק֕וּם עַל־שֵׁ֥ם אָחִ֖יו הַמֵּ֑ת וְלֹֽא־יִמָּחֶ֥ה שְׁמ֖וֹ מִיִּשְׂרָאֵֽל׃

7 But if the man does not want to marry his brother's widow, his brother's widow shall appear before the elders in the gate and declare, "My husband's brother refuses to establish a name in *Yisrael* for his brother; he will not perform the duty of a levir."

ז וְאִם־לֹ֤א יַחְפֹּץ֙ הָאִ֔ישׁ לָקַ֖חַת אֶת־יְבִמְתּ֑וֹ וְעָלְתָה֩ יְבִמְתּ֨וֹ הַשַּׁ֜עְרָה אֶל־הַזְּקֵנִ֗ים וְאָֽמְרָה֙ מֵאֵ֨ן יְבָמִ֜י לְהָקִ֨ים לְאָחִ֥יו שֵׁם֙ בְּיִשְׂרָאֵ֔ל לֹ֥א אָבָ֖ה יַבְּמִֽי׃

8 The elders of his town shall then summon him and talk to him. If he insists, saying, "I do not want to marry her,"

ח וְקָֽרְאוּ־ל֥וֹ זִקְנֵֽי־עִיר֖וֹ וְדִבְּר֣וּ אֵלָ֑יו וְעָמַ֣ד וְאָמַ֔ר לֹ֥א חָפַ֖צְתִּי לְקַחְתָּֽהּ׃

9 his brother's widow shall go up to him in the presence of the elders, pull the sandal off his foot, spit in his face, and make this declaration: Thus shall be done to the man who will not build up his brother's house!

ט וְנִגְּשָׁ֨ה יְבִמְתּ֣וֹ אֵלָיו֮ לְעֵינֵ֣י הַזְּקֵנִים֒ וְחָֽלְצָ֤ה נַֽעֲלוֹ֙ מֵעַ֣ל רַגְל֔וֹ וְיָֽרְקָ֖ה בְּפָנָ֑יו וְעָֽנְתָה֙ וְאָ֣מְרָ֔ה כָּ֚כָה יֵֽעָשֶׂ֣ה לָאִ֔ישׁ אֲשֶׁ֥ר לֹֽא־יִבְנֶ֖ה אֶת־בֵּ֥ית אָחִֽיו׃

10 And he shall go in *Yisrael* by the name of "the family of the unsandaled one."

י וְנִקְרָ֥א שְׁמ֖וֹ בְּיִשְׂרָאֵ֑ל בֵּ֖ית חֲל֥וּץ הַנָּֽעַל׃

11 If two men get into a fight with each other, and the wife of one comes up to save her husband from his antagonist and puts out her hand and seizes him by his genitals,

יא כִּֽי־יִנָּצ֨וּ אֲנָשִׁ֤ים יַחְדָּו֙ אִ֣ישׁ וְאָחִ֔יו וְקָֽרְבָה֙ אֵ֣שֶׁת הָֽאֶחָ֔ד לְהַצִּ֥יל אֶת־אִישָׁ֖הּ מִיַּ֣ד מַכֵּ֑הוּ וְשָֽׁלְחָ֣ה יָדָ֔הּ וְהֶֽחֱזִ֖יקָה בִּמְבֻשָֽׁיו׃

12 you shall cut off her hand; show no pity.

יב וְקַצֹּתָ֖ה אֶת־כַּפָּ֑הּ לֹ֥א תָח֖וֹס עֵינֶֽךָ׃

13 You shall not have in your pouch alternate weights, larger and smaller.

יג לֹֽא־יִהְיֶ֥ה לְךָ֛ בְּכִֽיסְךָ֖ אֶ֣בֶן וָאָ֑בֶן גְּדוֹלָ֖ה וּקְטַנָּֽה׃

14 You shall not have in your house alternate measures, a larger and a smaller.

יד לֹֽא־יִהְיֶ֥ה לְךָ֛ בְּבֵֽיתְךָ֖ אֵיפָ֣ה וְאֵיפָ֑ה גְּדוֹלָ֖ה וּקְטַנָּֽה׃

15 You must have completely honest weights and completely honest measures, if you are to endure long on the soil that *Hashem* your God is giving you.

טו אֶ֣בֶן שְׁלֵמָ֤ה וָצֶ֨דֶק֙ יִֽהְיֶה־לָּ֔ךְ אֵיפָ֧ה שְׁלֵמָ֛ה וָצֶ֖דֶק יִֽהְיֶה־לָּ֑ךְ לְמַ֨עַן֙ יַֽאֲרִ֣יכוּ יָמֶ֔יךָ עַ֚ל הָֽאֲדָמָ֔ה אֲשֶׁר־יְהֹוָ֥ה אֱלֹהֶ֖יךָ נֹתֵ֥ן לָֽךְ׃

16 For everyone who does those things, everyone who deals dishonestly, is abhorrent to *Hashem* your God.

טז כִּ֧י תֽוֹעֲבַ֛ת יְהֹוָ֥ה אֱלֹהֶ֖יךָ כָּל־עֹ֣שֵׂה אֵ֑לֶּה כֹּ֖ל עֹ֥שֵׂה עָֽוֶל׃

17 Remember what Amalek did to you on your journey, after you left Egypt

יז זָכ֕וֹר אֵ֛ת אֲשֶׁר־עָשָׂ֥ה לְךָ֖ עֲמָלֵ֑ק בַּדֶּ֖רֶךְ בְּצֵֽאתְכֶ֥ם מִמִּצְרָֽיִם׃

18 how, undeterred by fear of *Hashem*, he surprised you on the march, when you were famished and weary, and cut down all the stragglers in your rear.

יח אֲשֶׁ֨ר קָֽרְךָ֜ בַּדֶּ֗רֶךְ וַיְזַנֵּ֤ב בְּךָ֙ כָּל־הַנֶּֽחֱשָׁלִ֣ים אַֽחֲרֶ֔יךָ וְאַתָּ֖ה עָיֵ֣ף וְיָגֵ֑עַ וְלֹ֥א יָרֵ֖א אֱלֹהִֽים׃

Deuteronomy

19 Therefore, when *Hashem* your God grants you safety from all your enemies around you, in the land that *Hashem* your God is giving you as a hereditary portion, you shall blot out the memory of Amalek from under heaven. Do not forget!

יט וְהָיָה בְּהָנִיחַ יְהֹוָה אֱלֹהֶיךָ לְךָ מִכָּל־
אֹיְבֶיךָ מִסָּבִיב בָּאָרֶץ אֲשֶׁר יְהֹוָה
אֱלֹהֶיךָ נֹתֵן לְךָ נַחֲלָה לְרִשְׁתָּהּ תִּמְחֶה
אֶת־זֵכֶר עֲמָלֵק מִתַּחַת הַשָּׁמָיִם לֹא
תִּשְׁכָּח:

v'-ha-YAH b'-ha-NEE-akh a-do-NAI e-lo-HE-kha l'-KHA mi-kol
O-y'-VE-kha mi-sa-VEEV ba-A-retz a-sher a-do-NAI e-lo-HE-kha
no-TAYN l'-KHA na-kha-LAH l'-rish-TAH tim-KHEH et ZAY-kher
a-ma-LAYK mi-TA-khat ha-sh-MA-yim LO tish-KAKH

26 ¹ When you enter the land that *Hashem* your God is giving you as a heritage, and you possess it and settle in it,

כו וְהָיָה כִּי־תָבוֹא אֶל־הָאָרֶץ אֲשֶׁר יְהֹוָה
אֱלֹהֶיךָ נֹתֵן לְךָ נַחֲלָה וִירִשְׁתָּהּ וְיָשַׁבְתָּ
בָּהּ:

v'-ha-YAH kee ta-VO el ha-A-retz a-SHER a-do-NAI e-lo-HE-kha
no-TAYN l'-KHA na-kha-LAH vee-rish-TAH v'-ya-SHAV-ta BAH

² you shall take some of every first fruit of the soil, which you harvest from the land that *Hashem* your God is giving you, put it in a basket and go to the place where *Hashem* your God will choose to establish His name.

ב וְלָקַחְתָּ מֵרֵאשִׁית כָּל־פְּרִי הָאֲדָמָה
אֲשֶׁר תָּבִיא מֵאַרְצְךָ אֲשֶׁר יְהֹוָה
אֱלֹהֶיךָ נֹתֵן לָךְ וְשַׂמְתָּ בַטֶּנֶא וְהָלַכְתָּ
אֶל־הַמָּקוֹם אֲשֶׁר יִבְחַר יְהֹוָה אֱלֹהֶיךָ
לְשַׁכֵּן שְׁמוֹ שָׁם:

v-la-kakh-TA may-ray-SHEET kol p'-REE ha-a-da-MAH a-SHER
ta-VEE may-ar-tz'-KHA a-SHER a-do-NAY e-lo-HE-kha no-TAYN
LKAH v'-sam-TA va-TE-ne v'-ha-lakh-TA el ha-ma-KOM a-SHER
yiv-KHAR a-do-NAI e-lo-HE-kha l'-sha-KAYN sh'-MO SHAM

³ You shall go to the *Kohen* in charge at that time and say to him, "I acknowledge this day before *Hashem* your God that I have entered the land that *Hashem* swore to our fathers to assign us."

ג וּבָאתָ אֶל־הַכֹּהֵן אֲשֶׁר יִהְיֶה בַּיָּמִים
הָהֵם וְאָמַרְתָּ אֵלָיו הִגַּדְתִּי הַיּוֹם לַיהֹוָה
אֱלֹהֶיךָ כִּי־בָאתִי אֶל־הָאָרֶץ אֲשֶׁר
נִשְׁבַּע יְהֹוָה לַאֲבֹתֵינוּ לָתֶת לָנוּ:

25:19 When *Hashem* your God grants you safety from all your enemies around you One of the three commandments that the People of Israel are to fulfill after successfully conquering the Land of Israel is the obliteration of the Amalekites. The Amalekites are descendants of Esau and were the first to attack the Children of Israel after the exodus from Egypt. Amalek is more than just a nation – it represents an ideology antithetical to that of Israel: Absolute denial of Godliness in this world and a total lack of morality. For this reason, once the land is conquered and the People of Israel are settled, Israel was required to wage war against Amalek, and against their system of belief.

26:1 The land that *Hashem* your God is giving you as a heritage The 1917 Balfour Declaration is one of the most significant documents in modern Jewish history, articulating the historic right of the Jewish people to reestablish their homeland in Israel. Written by foreign secretary Arthur James Balfour and approved by the government of Great Britain, the declaration states clearly and unequivocally that Britain's leaders "view with favor the establishment in Palestine of a national home for the Jewish people, and will use their best endeavors to facilitate the achievement of this object." Lord Balfour was a deeply religious Christian Zionist, whose biblical upbringing led to his pivotal support for the return of the Jewish people to the Land of Israel. This verse promises the Jewish people that *Eretz Yisrael* is their inheritance, their birthright and heritage forever. Throughout history, *Hashem* has used individuals such as Balfour as His agents in returning His people back to Israel.

Arthur James Balfour
(1848–1930)

The Balfour Declaration

⁴ The *Kohen* shall take the basket from your hand and set it down in front of the *Mizbayach* of *Hashem* your God.

ד וְלָקַח הַכֹּהֵן הַטֶּנֶא מִיָּדֶךָ וְהִנִּיחוֹ לִפְנֵי מִזְבַּח יְהֹוָה אֱלֹהֶיךָ:

⁵ You shall then recite as follows before *Hashem* your God: "My father was a fugitive Aramean. He went down to Egypt with meager numbers and sojourned there; but there he became a great and very populous nation.

ה וְעָנִיתָ וְאָמַרְתָּ לִפְנֵי יְהֹוָה אֱלֹהֶיךָ אֲרַמִּי אֹבֵד אָבִי וַיֵּרֶד מִצְרַיְמָה וַיָּגָר שָׁם בִּמְתֵי מְעָט וַיְהִי־שָׁם לְגוֹי גָּדוֹל עָצוּם וָרָב:

⁶ The Egyptians dealt harshly with us and oppressed us; they imposed heavy labor upon us.

ו וַיָּרֵעוּ אֹתָנוּ הַמִּצְרִים וַיְעַנּוּנוּ וַיִּתְּנוּ עָלֵינוּ עֲבֹדָה קָשָׁה:

va-ya-RAY-u o-TA-nu ha-mitz-REEM vai-a-NU-nu
va-yi-t'-NU a-LAY-nu a-vo-DAH ka-SHAH

⁷ We cried to *Hashem*, the God of our fathers, and *Hashem* heard our plea and saw our plight, our misery, and our oppression.

ז וַנִּצְעַק אֶל־יְהֹוָה אֱלֹהֵי אֲבֹתֵינוּ וַיִּשְׁמַע יְהֹוָה אֶת־קֹלֵנוּ וַיַּרְא אֶת־עָנְיֵנוּ וְאֶת־עֲמָלֵנוּ וְאֶת־לַחֲצֵנוּ:

⁸ *Hashem* freed us from Egypt by a mighty hand, by an outstretched arm and awesome power, and by signs and portents.

ח וַיּוֹצִאֵנוּ יְהֹוָה מִמִּצְרַיִם בְּיָד חֲזָקָה וּבִזְרֹעַ נְטוּיָה וּבְמֹרָא גָּדֹל וּבְאֹתוֹת וּבְמֹפְתִים:

⁹ He brought us to this place and gave us this land, a land flowing with milk and honey.

ט וַיְבִאֵנוּ אֶל־הַמָּקוֹם הַזֶּה וַיִּתֶּן־לָנוּ אֶת־הָאָרֶץ הַזֹּאת אֶרֶץ זָבַת חָלָב וּדְבָשׁ:

vai-vi-AY-nu el ha-ma-KOM ha-ZEH va-yi-ten LA-nu et
ha-A-retz ha-ZOT E-retz za-VAT kha-LAV ud-VASH

¹⁰ Wherefore I now bring the first fruits of the soil which You, *Hashem*, have given me." You shall leave it before *Hashem* your God and bow low before *Hashem* your God.

י וְעַתָּה הִנֵּה הֵבֵאתִי אֶת־רֵאשִׁית פְּרִי הָאֲדָמָה אֲשֶׁר־נָתַתָּה לִּי יְהֹוָה וְהִנַּחְתּוֹ לִפְנֵי יְהֹוָה אֱלֹהֶיךָ וְהִשְׁתַּחֲוִיתָ לִפְנֵי יְהֹוָה אֱלֹהֶיךָ:

¹¹ And you shall enjoy, together with the Levite and the stranger in your midst, all the bounty that *Hashem* your God has bestowed upon you and your household.

יא וְשָׂמַחְתָּ בְכָל־הַטּוֹב אֲשֶׁר נָתַן־לְךָ יְהֹוָה אֱלֹהֶיךָ וּלְבֵיתֶךָ אַתָּה וְהַלֵּוִי וְהַגֵּר אֲשֶׁר בְּקִרְבֶּךָ:

¹² When you have set aside in full the tenth part of your yield – in the third year, the year of the tithe – and have given it to the Levite, the stranger, the fatherless, and the widow, that they may eat their fill in your settlements,

יב כִּי תְכַלֶּה לַעְשֵׂר אֶת־כָּל־מַעְשַׂר תְּבוּאָתְךָ בַּשָּׁנָה הַשְּׁלִישִׁת שְׁנַת הַמַּעֲשֵׂר וְנָתַתָּה לַלֵּוִי לַגֵּר לַיָּתוֹם וְלָאַלְמָנָה וְאָכְלוּ בִשְׁעָרֶיךָ וְשָׂבֵעוּ:

ויֵרעו

26:6 The Egyptians dealt harshly with us Ironically, the Hebrew word in this verse for 'dealt harshly with us,' *vayareiu* (ויֵרעו), also contains the word for 'friendship,' *reiut* (רעות). By choosing this term, the *Torah* is making a subtle observation about the origins of Hebrew slavery. At first, the Egyptians befriended the Jews. It was only later on that they gradually began to institute discriminatory laws, persecution and finally slavery. This pattern, where a host nation invites Jews in and offers protection, but as time goes on the hospitality runs out and anti-Semitism creeps in, has repeated itself throughout Jewish history. Only in the State of Israel can safety and security be guaranteed to the Jewish people permanently.

Israel365's Josh Wander with a Ukrainian refugee and Holocaust survivor preparing for *aliyah*

13 you shall declare before *Hashem* your God: "I have cleared out the consecrated portion from the house; and I have given it to the Levite, the stranger, the fatherless, and the widow, just as You commanded me; I have neither transgressed nor neglected any of Your commandments:

14 I have not eaten of it while in mourning, I have not cleared out any of it while I was unclean, and I have not deposited any of it with the dead. I have obeyed *Hashem* my God; I have done just as You commanded me.

15 Look down from Your holy abode, from heaven, and bless Your people *Yisrael* and the soil You have given us, a land flowing with milk and honey, as You swore to our fathers."

יג וְאָמַרְתָּ לִפְנֵי יְהֹוָה אֱלֹהֶיךָ בִּעַרְתִּי הַקֹּדֶשׁ מִן־הַבַּיִת וְגַם נְתַתִּיו לַלֵּוִי וְלַגֵּר לַיָּתוֹם וְלָאַלְמָנָה כְּכָל־מִצְוָתְךָ אֲשֶׁר צִוִּיתָנִי לֹא־עָבַרְתִּי מִמִּצְוֹתֶיךָ וְלֹא שָׁכָחְתִּי:

יד לֹא־אָכַלְתִּי בְאֹנִי מִמֶּנּוּ וְלֹא־בִעַרְתִּי מִמֶּנּוּ בְּטָמֵא וְלֹא־נָתַתִּי מִמֶּנּוּ לְמֵת שָׁמַעְתִּי בְּקוֹל יְהֹוָה אֱלֹהָי עָשִׂיתִי כְּכֹל אֲשֶׁר צִוִּיתָנִי:

טו הַשְׁקִיפָה מִמְּעוֹן קָדְשְׁךָ מִן־הַשָּׁמַיִם וּבָרֵךְ אֶת־עַמְּךָ אֶת־יִשְׂרָאֵל וְאֵת הָאֲדָמָה אֲשֶׁר נָתַתָּה לָנוּ כַּאֲשֶׁר נִשְׁבַּעְתָּ לַאֲבֹתֵינוּ אֶרֶץ זָבַת חָלָב וּדְבָשׁ:

hash-KEE-fah mi-m'-ON kod-sh'-KHA min ha-sha-MA-yim u-va-RAYKH
et a-m'-KHA et yis-ra-AYL ve-AYT ha-a-da-MAH a-SHER na-TA-ta LA-nu
ka-a-SHER nish-BA-ta la-a-vo-TAY-nu E-retz za-VAT kha-LAV ud-VASH

16 *Hashem* your God commands you this day to observe these laws and rules; observe them faithfully with all your heart and soul.

17 You have affirmed this day that *Hashem* is your God, that you will walk in His ways, that you will observe His laws and commandments and rules, and that you will obey Him.

18 And *Hashem* has affirmed this day that you are, as He promised you, His treasured people who shall observe all His commandments,

19 and that He will set you, in fame and renown and glory, high above all the nations that He has made; and that you shall be, as He promised, a holy people to *Hashem* your God.

טז הַיּוֹם הַזֶּה יְהֹוָה אֱלֹהֶיךָ מְצַוְּךָ לַעֲשׂוֹת אֶת־הַחֻקִּים הָאֵלֶּה וְאֶת־הַמִּשְׁפָּטִים וְשָׁמַרְתָּ וְעָשִׂיתָ אוֹתָם בְּכָל־לְבָבְךָ וּבְכָל־נַפְשֶׁךָ:

יז אֶת־יְהֹוָה הֶאֱמַרְתָּ הַיּוֹם לִהְיוֹת לְךָ לֵאלֹהִים וְלָלֶכֶת בִּדְרָכָיו וְלִשְׁמֹר חֻקָּיו וּמִצְוֹתָיו וּמִשְׁפָּטָיו וְלִשְׁמֹעַ בְּקֹלוֹ:

יח וַיהֹוָה הֶאֱמִירְךָ הַיּוֹם לִהְיוֹת לוֹ לְעַם סְגֻלָּה כַּאֲשֶׁר דִּבֶּר־לָךְ וְלִשְׁמֹר כָּל־מִצְוֹתָיו:

יט וּלְתִתְּךָ עֶלְיוֹן עַל כָּל־הַגּוֹיִם אֲשֶׁר עָשָׂה לִתְהִלָּה וּלְשֵׁם וּלְתִפְאָרֶת וְלִהְיֹתְךָ עַם־קָדֹשׁ לַיהֹוָה אֱלֹהֶיךָ כַּאֲשֶׁר דִּבֵּר:

27 1 *Moshe* and the elders of *Yisrael* charged the people, saying: Observe all the Instruction that I enjoin upon you this day.

כז א וַיְצַו מֹשֶׁה וְזִקְנֵי יִשְׂרָאֵל אֶת־הָעָם לֵאמֹר שָׁמֹר אֶת־כָּל־הַמִּצְוָה אֲשֶׁר אָנֹכִי מְצַוֶּה אֶתְכֶם הַיּוֹם:

 26:15 And bless Your people *Yisrael* and the soil You have given us In Hebrew, the name 'Israel,' *Yisrael* (ישראל), refers to both the land and the people. It also has a deeper meaning. In his book *The Secrets of Hebrew Words*, Rabbi Benjamin Blech points out that, "the smallest letter in the Hebrew alphabet

The portion of *Shema Yisrael*, "Hear O Israel," in a *Torah* scroll

is the *yud* (י). The largest letter is the *lamed* (ל). The very name of the Jewish people, *Yisrael* (ישראל), alludes to both its humble beginnings as well as its glorious destiny." There is no other language like Hebrew, where every word is infused with such deep meaning.

ישראל

Deuteronomy

² As soon as you have crossed the *Yarden* into the land that *Hashem* your God is giving you, you shall set up large stones. Coat them with plaster

ב וְהָיָה בַּיּוֹם אֲשֶׁר תַּעַבְרוּ אֶת־הַיַּרְדֵּן אֶל־הָאָרֶץ אֲשֶׁר־יְהוָֹה אֱלֹהֶיךָ נֹתֵן לָךְ וַהֲקֵמֹתָ לְךָ אֲבָנִים גְּדֹלוֹת וְשַׂדְתָּ אֹתָם בַּשִּׂיד:

³ and inscribe upon them all the words of this Teaching. When you cross over to enter the land that *Hashem* your God is giving you, a land flowing with milk and honey, as *Hashem*, the God of your fathers, promised you

ג וְכָתַבְתָּ עֲלֵיהֶן אֶת־כָּל־דִּבְרֵי הַתּוֹרָה הַזֹּאת בְּעָבְרֶךָ לְמַעַן אֲשֶׁר תָּבֹא אֶל־ הָאָרֶץ אֲשֶׁר־יְהוָֹה אֱלֹהֶיךָ נֹתֵן לְךָ אֶרֶץ זָבַת חָלָב וּדְבַשׁ כַּאֲשֶׁר דִּבֶּר יְהוָֹה אֱלֹהֵי־אֲבֹתֶיךָ לָךְ:

⁴ upon crossing the *Yarden*, you shall set up these stones, about which I charge you this day, on *Har Eival*, and coat them with plaster.

ד וְהָיָה בְּעָבְרְכֶם אֶת־הַיַּרְדֵּן תָּקִימוּ אֶת־הָאֲבָנִים הָאֵלֶּה אֲשֶׁר אָנֹכִי מְצַוֶּה אֶתְכֶם הַיּוֹם בְּהַר עֵיבָל וְשַׂדְתָּ אוֹתָם בַּשִּׂיד:

⁵ There, too, you shall build a *Mizbayach* to *Hashem* your God, a *Mizbayach* of stones. Do not wield an iron tool over them;

ה וּבָנִיתָ שָּׁם מִזְבֵּחַ לַיהוָֹה אֱלֹהֶיךָ מִזְבַּח אֲבָנִים לֹא־תָנִיף עֲלֵיהֶם בַּרְזֶל:

u-va-NEE-ta SHAM miz-BAY-akh la-do-NAI e-lo-HE-kha miz-BAKH a-va-NEEM lo ta-NEEF a-lay-HEM bar-ZEL

⁶ you must build the *Mizbayach* of *Hashem* your God of unhewn stones. You shall offer on it burnt offerings to *Hashem* your God,

ו אֲבָנִים שְׁלֵמוֹת תִּבְנֶה אֶת־מִזְבַּח יְהוָֹה אֱלֹהֶיךָ וְהַעֲלִיתָ עָלָיו עוֹלֹת לַיהוָֹה אֱלֹהֶיךָ:

⁷ and you shall sacrifice there offerings of well-being and eat them, rejoicing before *Hashem* your God.

ז וְזָבַחְתָּ שְׁלָמִים וְאָכַלְתָּ שָּׁם וְשָׂמַחְתָּ לִפְנֵי יְהוָֹה אֱלֹהֶיךָ:

⁸ And on those stones you shall inscribe every word of this Teaching most distinctly.

ח וְכָתַבְתָּ עַל־הָאֲבָנִים אֶת־כָּל־דִּבְרֵי הַתּוֹרָה הַזֹּאת בַּאֵר הֵיטֵב:

⁹ *Moshe* and the levitical *Kohanim* spoke to all *Yisrael*, saying: Silence! Hear, O *Yisrael*! Today you have become the people of *Hashem* your God:

ט וַיְדַבֵּר מֹשֶׁה וְהַכֹּהֲנִים הַלְוִיִּם אֶל כָּל־ יִשְׂרָאֵל לֵאמֹר הַסְכֵּת וּשְׁמַע יִשְׂרָאֵל הַיּוֹם הַזֶּה נִהְיֵיתָ לְעָם לַיהוָֹה אֱלֹהֶיךָ:

27:5 There, too, you shall build a *Mizbayach*
Moshe commands the Israelites that upon entry into the land, they are to perform a ceremony recommitting themselves to *Hashem* and His *Torah*. This ceremony is to take place on Mount *Gerizim* and Mount *Eival*, located near the city of *Shechem*, also known today as Nablus. Indeed, the fulfilment of this command is documented in *Sefer Yehoshua* (8:30–35). In addition to the ceremony, the Jewish people are commanded to build an altar on Mount *Eival*. They are to inscribe the *Torah* on its stones and, according to the Sages, then dismantle the altar and place the stones in *Gilgal*, their first station in the Land of Israel (Sotah

200 New Israeli Shekel banknote featuring Zalman Shazar

36a). According to Rabbi Yitzchak Abrabanel, these stones inscribed with the *Torah* text, placed at the entry to the land, indicated to all that this is the land of the *Torah*. They served as a reminder that the purpose of living in *Eretz Yisrael* is to practice the *Torah*'s commandments, and that all success in the land comes from *Hashem*. In the modern State of Israel, Bible studies are a mandatory part of the curriculum in the state's educational system. As Zalman Shazar, third president of the State of Israel and then minister of education, said in his address to Knesset after the passing of the Compulsory Education Law in 1949, "Rich or poor, only children or large families, single or married – we must all carry the burden of *Torah* study." This quote, as well as a portrait of President Shazar, are featured on the 200 shekel bill first printed in 1999.

President Zalman Shazar, 1959

10 Heed *Hashem* your God and observe His commandments and His laws, which I enjoin upon you this day.

י וְשָׁמַעְתָּ בְּקוֹל יְהֹוָה אֱלֹהֶיךָ וְעָשִׂיתָ אֶת־מִצְוֺתָו וְאֶת־חֻקָּיו אֲשֶׁר אָנֹכִי מְצַוְּךָ הַיּוֹם:

11 Thereupon *Moshe* charged the people, saying:

יא וַיְצַו מֹשֶׁה אֶת־הָעָם בַּיּוֹם הַהוּא לֵאמֹר:

12 After you have crossed the *Yarden*, the following shall stand on *Har Gerizim* when the blessing for the people is spoken: *Shimon, Levi, Yehuda, Yissachar, Yosef,* and *Binyamin.*

יב אֵלֶּה יַעַמְדוּ לְבָרֵךְ אֶת־הָעָם עַל־הַר גְּרִזִים בְּעָבְרְכֶם אֶת־הַיַּרְדֵּן שִׁמְעוֹן וְלֵוִי וִיהוּדָה וְיִשָּׂשכָר וְיוֹסֵף וּבִנְיָמִן:

13 And for the curse, the following shall stand on *Har Eival: Reuven, Gad, Asher, Zevulun, Dan,* and *Naftali.*

יג וְאֵלֶּה יַעַמְדוּ עַל־הַקְּלָלָה בְּהַר עֵיבָל רְאוּבֵן גָּד וְאָשֵׁר וּזְבוּלֻן דָּן וְנַפְתָּלִי:

14 The *Leviim* shall then proclaim in a loud voice to all the people of *Yisrael:*

יד וְעָנוּ הַלְוִיִּם וְאָמְרוּ אֶל־כָּל־אִישׁ יִשְׂרָאֵל קוֹל רָם:

15 Cursed be anyone who makes a sculptured or molten image, abhorred by *Hashem,* a craftsman's handiwork, and sets it up in secret. – And all the people shall respond, *Amen.*

טו אָרוּר הָאִישׁ אֲשֶׁר יַעֲשֶׂה פֶסֶל וּמַסֵּכָה תּוֹעֲבַת יְהֹוָה מַעֲשֵׂה יְדֵי חָרָשׁ וְשָׂם בַּסָּתֶר וְעָנוּ כָל־הָעָם וְאָמְרוּ אָמֵן:

16 Cursed be he who insults his father or mother. – And all the people shall say, *Amen.*

טז אָרוּר מַקְלֶה אָבִיו וְאִמּוֹ וְאָמַר כָּל־הָעָם אָמֵן:

17 Cursed be he who moves his fellow countryman's landmark. – And all the people shall say, *Amen.*

יז אָרוּר מַסִּיג גְּבוּל רֵעֵהוּ וְאָמַר כָּל־הָעָם אָמֵן:

18 Cursed be he who misdirects a blind person on his way. – And all the people shall say, *Amen.*

יח אָרוּר מַשְׁגֶּה עִוֵּר בַּדָּרֶךְ וְאָמַר כָּל־הָעָם אָמֵן:

19 Cursed be he who subverts the rights of the stranger, the fatherless, and the widow. – And all the people shall say, *Amen.*

יט אָרוּר מַטֶּה מִשְׁפַּט גֵּר־יָתוֹם וְאַלְמָנָה וְאָמַר כָּל־הָעָם אָמֵן:

20 Cursed be he who lies with his father's wife, for he has removed his father's garment. – And all the people shall say, *Amen.*

כ אָרוּר שֹׁכֵב עִם־אֵשֶׁת אָבִיו כִּי גִלָּה כְּנַף אָבִיו וְאָמַר כָּל־הָעָם אָמֵן:

21 Cursed be he who lies with any beast. – And all the people shall say, *Amen.*

כא אָרוּר שֹׁכֵב עִם־כָּל־בְּהֵמָה וְאָמַר כָּל־הָעָם אָמֵן:

22 Cursed be he who lies with his sister, whether daughter of his father or of his mother. – And all the people shall say, *Amen.*

כב אָרוּר שֹׁכֵב עִם־אֲחֹתוֹ בַּת־אָבִיו אוֹ בַת־אִמּוֹ וְאָמַר כָּל־הָעָם אָמֵן:

23 Cursed be he who lies with his mother-in-law. – And all the people shall say, *Amen.*

כג אָרוּר שֹׁכֵב עִם־חֹתַנְתּוֹ וְאָמַר כָּל־הָעָם אָמֵן:

24 Cursed be he who strikes down his fellow countryman in secret. – And all the people shall say, *Amen.*

כד אָרוּר מַכֵּה רֵעֵהוּ בַּסָּתֶר וְאָמַר כָּל־הָעָם אָמֵן:

Deuteronomy

25 Cursed be he who accepts a bribe in the case of the murder of an innocent person. – And all the people shall say, *Amen.*

כה אָרוּר לֹקֵחַ שֹׁחַד לְהַכּוֹת נֶפֶשׁ דָּם נָקִי וְאָמַר כָּל־הָעָם אָמֵן:

26 Cursed be he who will not uphold the terms of this Teaching and observe them. – And all the people shall say, *Amen.*

כו אָרוּר אֲשֶׁר לֹא־יָקִים אֶת־דִּבְרֵי הַתּוֹרָה־הַזֹּאת לַעֲשׂוֹת אוֹתָם וְאָמַר כָּל־הָעָם אָמֵן:

28 1 Now, if you obey *Hashem* your God, to observe faithfully all His commandments which I enjoin upon you this day, *Hashem* your God will set you high above all the nations of the earth.

כח א וְהָיָה אִם־שָׁמוֹעַ תִּשְׁמַע בְּקוֹל יְהוָה אֱלֹהֶיךָ לִשְׁמֹר לַעֲשׂוֹת אֶת־כָּל־מִצְוֺתָיו אֲשֶׁר אָנֹכִי מְצַוְּךָ הַיּוֹם וּנְתָנְךָ יְהוָה אֱלֹהֶיךָ עֶלְיוֹן עַל כָּל־גּוֹיֵי הָאָרֶץ:

2 All these blessings shall come upon you and take effect, if you will but heed the word of *Hashem* your God:

ב וּבָאוּ עָלֶיךָ כָּל־הַבְּרָכוֹת הָאֵלֶּה וְהִשִּׂיגֻךָ כִּי תִשְׁמַע בְּקוֹל יְהוָה אֱלֹהֶיךָ:

3 Blessed shall you be in the city and blessed shall you be in the country.

ג בָּרוּךְ אַתָּה בָּעִיר וּבָרוּךְ אַתָּה בַּשָּׂדֶה:

4 Blessed shall be the issue of your womb, the produce of your soil, and the offspring of your cattle, the calving of your herd and the lambing of your flock.

ד בָּרוּךְ פְּרִי־בִטְנְךָ וּפְרִי אַדְמָתְךָ וּפְרִי בְהֶמְתֶּךָ שְׁגַר אֲלָפֶיךָ וְעַשְׁתְּרוֹת צֹאנֶךָ:

5 Blessed shall be your basket and your kneading bowl.

ה בָּרוּךְ טַנְאֲךָ וּמִשְׁאַרְתֶּךָ:

6 Blessed shall you be in your comings and blessed shall you be in your goings.

ו בָּרוּךְ אַתָּה בְּבֹאֶךָ וּבָרוּךְ אַתָּה בְּצֵאתֶךָ:

7 *Hashem* will put to rout before you the enemies who attack you; they will march out against you by a single road, but flee from you by many roads.

ז יִתֵּן יְהוָה אֶת־אֹיְבֶיךָ הַקָּמִים עָלֶיךָ נִגָּפִים לְפָנֶיךָ בְּדֶרֶךְ אֶחָד יֵצְאוּ אֵלֶיךָ וּבְשִׁבְעָה דְרָכִים יָנוּסוּ לְפָנֶיךָ:

8 *Hashem* will ordain blessings for you upon your barns and upon all your undertakings: He will bless you in the land that *Hashem* your God is giving you.

ח יְצַו יְהוָה אִתְּךָ אֶת־הַבְּרָכָה בַּאֲסָמֶיךָ וּבְכֹל מִשְׁלַח יָדֶךָ וּבֵרַכְךָ בָּאָרֶץ אֲשֶׁר־יְהוָה אֱלֹהֶיךָ נֹתֵן לָךְ:

9 *Hashem* will establish you as His holy people, as He swore to you, if you keep the commandments of *Hashem* your God and walk in His ways.

ט יְקִימְךָ יְהוָה לוֹ לְעַם קָדוֹשׁ כַּאֲשֶׁר נִשְׁבַּע־לָךְ כִּי תִשְׁמֹר אֶת־מִצְוֺת יְהוָה אֱלֹהֶיךָ וְהָלַכְתָּ בִּדְרָכָיו:

10 And all the peoples of the earth shall see that *Hashem*'s name is proclaimed over you, and they shall stand in fear of you.

י וְרָאוּ כָּל־עַמֵּי הָאָרֶץ כִּי שֵׁם יְהוָה נִקְרָא עָלֶיךָ וְיָרְאוּ מִמֶּךָּ:

11 *Hashem* will give you abounding prosperity in the issue of your womb, the offspring of your cattle, and the produce of your soil in the land that *Hashem* swore to your fathers to assign to you.

יא וְהוֹתִרְךָ יְהוָה לְטוֹבָה בִּפְרִי בִטְנְךָ וּבִפְרִי בְהֶמְתְּךָ וּבִפְרִי אַדְמָתֶךָ עַל הָאֲדָמָה אֲשֶׁר נִשְׁבַּע יְהוָה לַאֲבֹתֶיךָ לָתֶת לָךְ:

12 *Hashem* will open for you His bounteous store, the heavens, to provide rain for your land in season and to bless all your undertakings. You will be creditor to many nations, but debtor to none.

יב יִפְתַּח יְהוָה ׀ לְךָ אֶת־אוֹצָרוֹ הַטּוֹב אֶת־הַשָּׁמַיִם לָתֵת מְטַר־אַרְצְךָ בְּעִתּוֹ וּלְבָרֵךְ אֵת כָּל־מַעֲשֵׂה יָדֶךָ וְהִלְוִיתָ גּוֹיִם רַבִּים וְאַתָּה לֹא תִלְוֶה:

yif-TAKH a-do-NAI l'-KHA et o-tza-RO ha-TOV et ha-sha-MA-yim
la-TAYT m'-tar ar-tz'-KHA b'-i-TO u-l'-va-RAYKH AYT kol ma-a-SAY
ya-DE-kha v'-hil-VEE-ta go-YIM ra-BEEM v'-a-TA lo til-VEH

13 *Hashem* will make you the head, not the tail; you will always be at the top and never at the bottom – if only you obey and faithfully observe the commandments of *Hashem* your God that I enjoin upon you this day,

יג וּנְתָנְךָ יְהוָה לְרֹאשׁ וְלֹא לְזָנָב וְהָיִיתָ רַק לְמַעְלָה וְלֹא תִהְיֶה לְמָטָּה כִּי־תִשְׁמַע אֶל־מִצְוֹת ׀ יְהוָה אֱלֹהֶיךָ אֲשֶׁר אָנֹכִי מְצַוְּךָ הַיּוֹם לִשְׁמֹר וְלַעֲשׂוֹת:

14 and do not deviate to the right or to the left from any of the commandments that I enjoin upon you this day and turn to the worship of other gods.

יד וְלֹא תָסוּר מִכָּל־הַדְּבָרִים אֲשֶׁר אָנֹכִי מְצַוֶּה אֶתְכֶם הַיּוֹם יָמִין וּשְׂמֹאול לָלֶכֶת אַחֲרֵי אֱלֹהִים אֲחֵרִים לְעָבְדָם:

15 But if you do not obey *Hashem* your God to observe faithfully all His commandments and laws which I enjoin upon you this day, all these curses shall come upon you and take effect:

טו וְהָיָה אִם־לֹא תִשְׁמַע בְּקוֹל יְהוָה אֱלֹהֶיךָ לִשְׁמֹר לַעֲשׂוֹת אֶת־כָּל־מִצְוֹתָיו וְחֻקֹּתָיו אֲשֶׁר אָנֹכִי מְצַוְּךָ הַיּוֹם וּבָאוּ עָלֶיךָ כָּל־הַקְּלָלוֹת הָאֵלֶּה וְהִשִּׂיגוּךָ:

16 Cursed shall you be in the city and cursed shall you be in the country.

טז אָרוּר אַתָּה בָּעִיר וְאָרוּר אַתָּה בַּשָּׂדֶה:

17 Cursed shall be your basket and your kneading bowl.

יז אָרוּר טַנְאֲךָ וּמִשְׁאַרְתֶּךָ:

18 Cursed shall be the issue of your womb and the produce of your soil, the calving of your herd and the lambing of your flock.

יח אָרוּר פְּרִי־בִטְנְךָ וּפְרִי אַדְמָתֶךָ שְׁגַר אֲלָפֶיךָ וְעַשְׁתְּרֹת צֹאנֶךָ:

19 Cursed shall you be in your comings and cursed shall you be in your goings.

יט אָרוּר אַתָּה בְּבֹאֶךָ וְאָרוּר אַתָּה בְּצֵאתֶךָ:

20 *Hashem* will let loose against you calamity, panic, and frustration in all the enterprises you undertake, so that you shall soon be utterly wiped out because of your evildoing in forsaking Me.

כ יְשַׁלַּח יְהוָה ׀ בְּךָ אֶת־הַמְּאֵרָה אֶת־הַמְּהוּמָה וְאֶת־הַמִּגְעֶרֶת בְּכָל־מִשְׁלַח יָדְךָ אֲשֶׁר תַּעֲשֶׂה עַד הִשָּׁמֶדְךָ וְעַד־אֲבָדְךָ מַהֵר מִפְּנֵי רֹעַ מַעֲלָלֶיךָ אֲשֶׁר עֲזַבְתָּנִי:

28:12 To provide rain for your land in season One of the blessings promised as a reward for observing God's commandments in the Holy Land is the promise of rain *bíto* (בעתו), 'in its time,' or 'in season.' While the Land of Israel is dependent on rainfall for water and irrigation, rain is valuable only if it falls at the right time. While at the right time, even a small amount of rain can be the source of much blessing, when it is not needed rain can be a curse, as it can ruin the crops. Because *Eretz Yisrael* does not have sufficient water sources, rain "in season" is a most significant blessing.

Raindrops on flowers in the Galilee

Deuteronomy

²¹ *Hashem* will make pestilence cling to you, until He has put an end to you in the land that you are entering to possess.

כא יַדְבֵּק יְהֹוָה בְּךָ אֶת־הַדָּבֶר עַד כַּלֹּתוֹ אֹתְךָ מֵעַל הָאֲדָמָה אֲשֶׁר־אַתָּה בָא־שָׁמָּה לְרִשְׁתָּהּ:

²² *Hashem* will strike you with consumption, fever, and inflammation, with scorching heat and drought, with blight and mildew; they shall hound you until you perish.

כב יַכְּכָה יְהֹוָה בַּשַּׁחֶפֶת וּבַקַּדַּחַת וּבַדַּלֶּקֶת וּבַחַרְחֻר וּבַחֶרֶב וּבַשִּׁדָּפוֹן וּבַיֵּרָקוֹן וּרְדָפוּךָ עַד אָבְדֶךָ:

²³ The skies above your head shall be copper and the earth under you iron.

כג וְהָיוּ שָׁמֶיךָ אֲשֶׁר עַל־רֹאשְׁךָ נְחֹשֶׁת וְהָאָרֶץ אֲשֶׁר־תַּחְתֶּיךָ בַּרְזֶל:

²⁴ *Hashem* will make the rain of your land dust, and sand shall drop on you from the sky, until you are wiped out.

כד יִתֵּן יְהֹוָה אֶת־מְטַר אַרְצְךָ אָבָק וְעָפָר מִן־הַשָּׁמַיִם יֵרֵד עָלֶיךָ עַד הִשָּׁמְדָךְ:

²⁵ *Hashem* will put you to rout before your enemies; you shall march out against them by a single road, but flee from them by many roads; and you shall become a horror to all the kingdoms of the earth.

כה יִתֶּנְךָ יְהֹוָה נִגָּף לִפְנֵי אֹיְבֶיךָ בְּדֶרֶךְ אֶחָד תֵּצֵא אֵלָיו וּבְשִׁבְעָה דְרָכִים תָּנוּס לְפָנָיו וְהָיִיתָ לְזַעֲוָה לְכֹל מַמְלְכוֹת הָאָרֶץ:

²⁶ Your carcasses shall become food for all the birds of the sky and all the beasts of the earth, with none to frighten them off.

כו וְהָיְתָה נִבְלָתְךָ לְמַאֲכָל לְכָל־עוֹף הַשָּׁמַיִם וּלְבֶהֱמַת הָאָרֶץ וְאֵין מַחֲרִיד:

²⁷ *Hashem* will strike you with the Egyptian inflammation, with hemorrhoids, boil-scars, and itch, from which you shall never recover.

כז יַכְּכָה יְהֹוָה בִּשְׁחִין מִצְרַיִם וּבַעְפֹלִים [וּבַטְּחֹרִים] וּבַגָּרָב וּבֶחָרֶס אֲשֶׁר לֹא־תוּכַל לְהֵרָפֵא:

²⁸ *Hashem* will strike you with madness, blindness, and dismay.

כח יַכְּכָה יְהֹוָה בְּשִׁגָּעוֹן וּבְעִוָּרוֹן וּבְתִמְהוֹן לֵבָב:

²⁹ You shall grope at noon as a blind man gropes in the dark; you shall not prosper in your ventures, but shall be constantly abused and robbed, with none to give help.

כט וְהָיִיתָ מְמַשֵּׁשׁ בַּצָּהֳרַיִם כַּאֲשֶׁר יְמַשֵּׁשׁ הָעִוֵּר בָּאֲפֵלָה וְלֹא תַצְלִיחַ אֶת־דְּרָכֶיךָ וְהָיִיתָ אַךְ עָשׁוּק וְגָזוּל כָּל־הַיָּמִים וְאֵין מוֹשִׁיעַ:

³⁰ If you pay the bride-price for a wife, another man shall enjoy her. If you build a house, you shall not live in it. If you plant a vineyard, you shall not harvest it.

ל אִשָּׁה תְאָרֵשׂ וְאִישׁ אַחֵר יִשְׁגָּלֶנָּה [יִשְׁכָּבֶנָּה] בַּיִת תִּבְנֶה וְלֹא־תֵשֵׁב בּוֹ כֶּרֶם תִּטַּע וְלֹא תְחַלְּלֶנּוּ:

³¹ Your ox shall be slaughtered before your eyes, but you shall not eat of it; your ass shall be seized in front of you, and it shall not be returned to you; your flock shall be delivered to your enemies, with none to help you.

לא שׁוֹרְךָ טָבוּחַ לְעֵינֶיךָ וְלֹא תֹאכַל מִמֶּנּוּ חֲמֹרְךָ גָּזוּל מִלְּפָנֶיךָ וְלֹא יָשׁוּב לָךְ צֹאנְךָ נְתֻנוֹת לְאֹיְבֶיךָ וְאֵין לְךָ מוֹשִׁיעַ:

³² Your sons and daughters shall be delivered to another people, while you look on; and your eyes shall strain for them constantly, but you shall be helpless.

לב בָּנֶיךָ וּבְנֹתֶיךָ נְתֻנִים לְעַם אַחֵר וְעֵינֶיךָ רֹאוֹת וְכָלוֹת אֲלֵיהֶם כָּל־הַיּוֹם וְאֵין לְאֵל יָדֶךָ:

33 A people you do not know shall eat up the produce of your soil and all your gains; you shall be abused and downtrodden continually,

לג פְּרִי אַדְמָתְךָ וְכָל־יְגִיעֲךָ יֹאכַל עַם אֲשֶׁר לֹא־יָדָעְתָּ וְהָיִיתָ רַק עָשׁוּק וְרָצוּץ כָּל־הַיָּמִים:

34 until you are driven mad by what your eyes behold.

לד וְהָיִיתָ מְשֻׁגָּע מִמַּרְאֵה עֵינֶיךָ אֲשֶׁר תִּרְאֶה:

35 *Hashem* will afflict you at the knees and thighs with a severe inflammation, from which you shall never recover – from the sole of your foot to the crown of your head.

לה יַכְּכָה יְהֹוָה בִּשְׁחִין רָע עַל־הַבִּרְכַּיִם וְעַל־הַשֹּׁקַיִם אֲשֶׁר לֹא־תוּכַל לְהֵרָפֵא מִכַּף רַגְלְךָ וְעַד קָדְקֳדֶךָ:

36 *Hashem* will drive you, and the king you have set over you, to a nation unknown to you or your fathers, where you shall serve other gods, of wood and stone.

לו יוֹלֵךְ יְהֹוָה אֹתְךָ וְאֶת־מַלְכְּךָ אֲשֶׁר תָּקִים עָלֶיךָ אֶל־גּוֹי אֲשֶׁר לֹא־יָדַעְתָּ אַתָּה וַאֲבֹתֶיךָ וְעָבַדְתָּ שָּׁם אֱלֹהִים אֲחֵרִים עֵץ וָאָבֶן:

37 You shall be a consternation, a proverb, and a byword among all the peoples to which *Hashem* will drive you.

לז וְהָיִיתָ לְשַׁמָּה לְמָשָׁל וְלִשְׁנִינָה בְּכֹל הָעַמִּים אֲשֶׁר־יְנַהֶגְךָ יְהֹוָה שָׁמָּה:

38 Though you take much seed out to the field, you shall gather in little, for the locust shall consume it.

לח זֶרַע רַב תּוֹצִיא הַשָּׂדֶה וּמְעַט תֶּאֱסֹף כִּי יַחְסְלֶנּוּ הָאַרְבֶּה:

39 Though you plant vineyards and till them, you shall have no wine to drink or store, for the worm shall devour them.

לט כְּרָמִים תִּטַּע וְעָבָדְתָּ וְיַיִן לֹא־תִשְׁתֶּה וְלֹא תֶאֱגֹר כִּי תֹאכְלֶנּוּ הַתֹּלָעַת:

40 Though you have olive trees throughout your territory, you shall have no oil for anointment, for your olives shall drop off.

מ זֵיתִים יִהְיוּ לְךָ בְּכָל־גְּבוּלֶךָ וְשֶׁמֶן לֹא תָסוּךְ כִּי יִשַּׁל זֵיתֶךָ:

41 Though you beget sons and daughters, they shall not remain with you, for they shall go into captivity.

מא בָּנִים וּבָנוֹת תּוֹלִיד וְלֹא־יִהְיוּ לָךְ כִּי יֵלְכוּ בַּשֶּׁבִי:

42 The cricket shall take over all the trees and produce of your land.

מב כָּל־עֵצְךָ וּפְרִי אַדְמָתֶךָ יְיָרֵשׁ הַצְּלָצַל:

43 The stranger in your midst shall rise above you higher and higher, while you sink lower and lower:

מג הַגֵּר אֲשֶׁר בְּקִרְבְּךָ יַעֲלֶה עָלֶיךָ מַעְלָה מָּעְלָה וְאַתָּה תֵרֵד מַטָּה מָּטָּה:

44 he shall be your creditor, but you shall not be his; he shall be the head and you the tail.

מד הוּא יַלְוְךָ וְאַתָּה לֹא תַלְוֶנּוּ הוּא יִהְיֶה לְרֹאשׁ וְאַתָּה תִּהְיֶה לְזָנָב:

45 All these curses shall befall you; they shall pursue you and overtake you, until you are wiped out, because you did not heed *Hashem* your God and keep the commandments and laws that He enjoined upon you.

מה וּבָאוּ עָלֶיךָ כָּל־הַקְּלָלוֹת הָאֵלֶּה וּרְדָפוּךָ וְהִשִּׂיגוּךָ עַד הִשָּׁמְדָךְ כִּי־לֹא שָׁמַעְתָּ בְּקוֹל יְהֹוָה אֱלֹהֶיךָ לִשְׁמֹר מִצְוֺתָיו וְחֻקֹּתָיו אֲשֶׁר צִוָּךְ:

46 They shall serve as signs and proofs against you and your offspring for all time.

מו וְהָיוּ בְךָ לְאוֹת וּלְמוֹפֵת וּבְזַרְעֲךָ עַד־עוֹלָם:

47 Because you would not serve *Hashem* your God in joy and gladness over the abundance of everything,

מז תַּחַת אֲשֶׁר לֹא־עָבַדְתָּ אֶת־יְהֹוָה אֱלֹהֶיךָ בְּשִׂמְחָה וּבְטוּב לֵבָב מֵרֹב כֹּל:

48 you shall have to serve – in hunger and thirst, naked and lacking everything – the enemies whom *Hashem* will let loose against you. He will put an iron yoke upon your neck until He has wiped you out.

מח וְעָבַדְתָּ אֶת־אֹיְבֶיךָ אֲשֶׁר יְשַׁלְּחֶנּוּ יְהוָה בְּךָ בְּרָעָב וּבְצָמָא וּבְעֵירֹם וּבְחֹסֶר כֹּל וְנָתַן עֹל בַּרְזֶל עַל־צַוָּארֶךָ עַד הִשְׁמִידוֹ אֹתָךְ:

49 *Hashem* will bring a nation against you from afar, from the end of the earth, which will swoop down like the eagle – a nation whose language you do not understand,

מט יִשָּׂא יְהוָה עָלֶיךָ גּוֹי מֵרָחֹק מִקְצֵה הָאָרֶץ כַּאֲשֶׁר יִדְאֶה הַנָּשֶׁר גּוֹי אֲשֶׁר לֹא־תִשְׁמַע לְשֹׁנוֹ:

50 a ruthless nation, that will show the old no regard and the young no mercy.

נ גּוֹי עַז פָּנִים אֲשֶׁר לֹא־יִשָּׂא פָנִים לְזָקֵן וְנַעַר לֹא יָחֹן:

51 It shall devour the offspring of your cattle and the produce of your soil, until you have been wiped out, leaving you nothing of new grain, wine, or oil, of the calving of your herds and the lambing of your flocks, until it has brought you to ruin.

נא וְאָכַל פְּרִי בְהֶמְתְּךָ וּפְרִי־אַדְמָתְךָ עַד הִשָּׁמְדָךְ אֲשֶׁר לֹא־יַשְׁאִיר לְךָ דָּגָן תִּירוֹשׁ וְיִצְהָר שְׁגַר אֲלָפֶיךָ וְעַשְׁתְּרֹת צֹאנֶךָ עַד הַאֲבִידוֹ אֹתָךְ:

52 It shall shut you up in all your towns throughout your land until every mighty, towering wall in which you trust has come down. And when you are shut up in all your towns throughout your land that *Hashem* your God has assigned to you,

נב וְהֵצַר לְךָ בְּכָל־שְׁעָרֶיךָ עַד רֶדֶת חֹמֹתֶיךָ הַגְּבֹהוֹת וְהַבְּצֻרוֹת אֲשֶׁר אַתָּה בֹּטֵחַ בָּהֵן בְּכָל־אַרְצֶךָ וְהֵצַר לְךָ בְּכָל־שְׁעָרֶיךָ בְּכָל־אַרְצֶךָ אֲשֶׁר נָתַן יְהוָה אֱלֹהֶיךָ לָךְ:

53 you shall eat your own issue, the flesh of your sons and daughters that *Hashem* your God has assigned to you, because of the desperate straits to which your enemy shall reduce you.

נג וְאָכַלְתָּ פְרִי־בִטְנְךָ בְּשַׂר בָּנֶיךָ וּבְנֹתֶיךָ אֲשֶׁר נָתַן־לְךָ יְהוָה אֱלֹהֶיךָ בְּמָצוֹר וּבְמָצוֹק אֲשֶׁר־יָצִיק לְךָ אֹיְבֶךָ:

54 He who is most tender and fastidious among you shall be too mean to his brother and the wife of his bosom and the children he has spared

נד הָאִישׁ הָרַךְ בְּךָ וְהֶעָנֹג מְאֹד תֵּרַע עֵינוֹ בְאָחִיו וּבְאֵשֶׁת חֵיקוֹ וּבְיֶתֶר בָּנָיו אֲשֶׁר יוֹתִיר:

55 to share with any of them the flesh of the children that he eats, because he has nothing else left as a result of the desperate straits to which your enemy shall reduce you in all your towns.

נה מִתֵּת לְאַחַד מֵהֶם מִבְּשַׂר בָּנָיו אֲשֶׁר יֹאכֵל מִבְּלִי הִשְׁאִיר־לוֹ כֹּל בְּמָצוֹר וּבְמָצוֹק אֲשֶׁר יָצִיק לְךָ אֹיִבְךָ בְּכָל־שְׁעָרֶיךָ:

56 And she who is most tender and dainty among you, so tender and dainty that she would never venture to set a foot on the ground, shall begrudge the husband of her bosom, and her son and her daughter,

נו הָרַכָּה בְךָ וְהָעֲנֻגָּה אֲשֶׁר לֹא־נִסְּתָה כַף־רַגְלָהּ הַצֵּג עַל־הָאָרֶץ מֵהִתְעַנֵּג וּמֵרֹךְ תֵּרַע עֵינָהּ בְּאִישׁ חֵיקָהּ וּבִבְנָהּ וּבְבִתָּהּ:

57 the afterbirth that issues from between her legs and the babies she bears; she shall eat them secretly, because of utter want, in the desperate straits to which your enemy shall reduce you in your towns.

נז וּבְשִׁלְיָתָהּ הַיּוֹצֵת מִבֵּין רַגְלֶיהָ וּבְבָנֶיהָ אֲשֶׁר תֵּלֵד כִּי־תֹאכְלֵם בְּחֹסֶר־כֹּל בַּסָּתֶר בְּמָצוֹר וּבְמָצוֹק אֲשֶׁר יָצִיק לְךָ אֹיִבְךָ בִּשְׁעָרֶיךָ:

58 If you fail to observe faithfully all the terms of this Teaching that are written in this book, to reverence this honored and awesome Name, *Hashem* your God,

נח אִם־לֹא תִשְׁמֹר לַעֲשׂוֹת אֶת־כָּל־דִּבְרֵי הַתּוֹרָה הַזֹּאת הַכְּתוּבִים בַּסֵּפֶר הַזֶּה לְיִרְאָה אֶת־הַשֵּׁם הַנִּכְבָּד וְהַנּוֹרָא הַזֶּה אֵת יְהֹוָה אֱלֹהֶיךָ:

59 *Hashem* will inflict extraordinary plagues upon you and your offspring, strange and lasting plagues, malignant and chronic diseases.

נט וְהִפְלָא יְהֹוָה אֶת־מַכֹּתְךָ וְאֵת מַכּוֹת זַרְעֶךָ מַכּוֹת גְּדֹלֹת וְנֶאֱמָנוֹת וָחֳלָיִם רָעִים וְנֶאֱמָנִים:

60 He will bring back upon you all the sicknesses of Egypt that you dreaded so, and they shall cling to you.

ס וְהֵשִׁיב בְּךָ אֵת כָּל־מַדְוֵה מִצְרַיִם אֲשֶׁר יָגֹרְתָּ מִפְּנֵיהֶם וְדָבְקוּ בָּךְ:

61 Moreover, *Hashem* will bring upon you all the other diseases and plagues that are not mentioned in this book of Teaching, until you are wiped out.

סא גַּם כָּל־חֳלִי וְכָל־מַכָּה אֲשֶׁר לֹא כָתוּב בְּסֵפֶר הַתּוֹרָה הַזֹּאת יַעְלֵם יְהֹוָה עָלֶיךָ עַד הִשָּׁמְדָךְ:

62 You shall be left a scant few, after having been as numerous as the stars in the skies, because you did not heed the command of *Hashem* your God.

סב וְנִשְׁאַרְתֶּם בִּמְתֵי מְעָט תַּחַת אֲשֶׁר הֱיִיתֶם כְּכוֹכְבֵי הַשָּׁמַיִם לָרֹב כִּי־לֹא שָׁמַעְתָּ בְּקוֹל יְהֹוָה אֱלֹהֶיךָ:

63 And as *Hashem* once delighted in making you prosperous and many, so will *Hashem* now delight in causing you to perish and in wiping you out; you shall be torn from the land that you are about to enter and possess.

סג וְהָיָה כַּאֲשֶׁר־שָׂשׂ יְהֹוָה עֲלֵיכֶם לְהֵיטִיב אֶתְכֶם וּלְהַרְבּוֹת אֶתְכֶם כֵּן יָשִׂישׂ יְהֹוָה עֲלֵיכֶם לְהַאֲבִיד אֶתְכֶם וּלְהַשְׁמִיד אֶתְכֶם וְנִסַּחְתֶּם מֵעַל הָאֲדָמָה אֲשֶׁר־אַתָּה בָא־שָׁמָּה לְרִשְׁתָּהּ:

64 *Hashem* will scatter you among all the peoples from one end of the earth to the other, and there you shall serve other gods, wood and stone, whom neither you nor your ancestors have experienced.

סד וֶהֱפִיצְךָ יְהֹוָה בְּכָל־הָעַמִּים מִקְצֵה הָאָרֶץ וְעַד־קְצֵה הָאָרֶץ וְעָבַדְתָּ שָּׁם אֱלֹהִים אֲחֵרִים אֲשֶׁר לֹא־יָדַעְתָּ אַתָּה וַאֲבֹתֶיךָ עֵץ וָאָבֶן:

65 Yet even among those nations you shall find no peace, nor shall your foot find a place to rest. *Hashem* will give you there an anguished heart and eyes that pine and a despondent spirit.

סה וּבַגּוֹיִם הָהֵם לֹא תַרְגִּיעַ וְלֹא־יִהְיֶה מָנוֹחַ לְכַף־רַגְלֶךָ וְנָתַן יְהֹוָה לְךָ שָׁם לֵב רַגָּז וְכִלְיוֹן עֵינַיִם וְדַאֲבוֹן נָפֶשׁ:

66 The life you face shall be precarious; you shall be in terror, night and day, with no assurance of survival.

סו וְהָיוּ חַיֶּיךָ תְּלֻאִים לְךָ מִנֶּגֶד וּפָחַדְתָּ לַיְלָה וְיוֹמָם וְלֹא תַאֲמִין בְּחַיֶּיךָ:

67 In the morning you shall say, "If only it were evening!" and in the evening you shall say, "If only it were morning!" – because of what your heart shall dread and your eyes shall see.

סז בַּבֹּקֶר תֹּאמַר מִי־יִתֵּן עֶרֶב וּבָעֶרֶב תֹּאמַר מִי־יִתֵּן בֹּקֶר מִפַּחַד לְבָבְךָ אֲשֶׁר תִּפְחָד וּמִמַּרְאֵה עֵינֶיךָ אֲשֶׁר תִּרְאֶה:

68 *Hashem* will send you back to Egypt in galleys, by a route which I told you you should not see again. There you shall offer yourselves for sale to your enemies as male and female slaves, but none will buy.

סח וֶהֱשִׁיבְךָ יְהֹוָה מִצְרַיִם בָּאֳנִיּוֹת בַּדֶּרֶךְ אֲשֶׁר אָמַרְתִּי לְךָ לֹא־תֹסִיף עוֹד לִרְאֹתָהּ וְהִתְמַכַּרְתֶּם שָׁם לְאֹיְבֶיךָ לַעֲבָדִים וְלִשְׁפָחוֹת וְאֵין קֹנֶה:

69 These are the terms of the covenant which *Hashem* commanded *Moshe* to conclude with the Israelites in the land of Moab, in addition to the covenant which He had made with them at Horeb.

סט אֵלֶּה דִבְרֵי הַבְּרִית אֲשֶׁר־צִוָּה יְהֹוָה אֶת־מֹשֶׁה לִכְרֹת אֶת־בְּנֵי יִשְׂרָאֵל בְּאֶרֶץ מוֹאָב מִלְּבַד הַבְּרִית אֲשֶׁר־כָּרַת אִתָּם בְּחֹרֵב:

Deuteronomy

29 ¹ *Moshe* summoned all *Yisrael* and said to them: You have seen all that *Hashem* did before your very eyes in the land of Egypt, to Pharaoh and to all his courtiers and to his whole country:

כט א וַיִּקְרָא מֹשֶׁה אֶל־כָּל־יִשְׂרָאֵל וַיֹּאמֶר אֲלֵהֶם אַתֶּם רְאִיתֶם אֵת כָּל־אֲשֶׁר עָשָׂה יְהֹוָה לְעֵינֵיכֶם בְּאֶרֶץ מִצְרַיִם לְפַרְעֹה וּלְכָל־עֲבָדָיו וּלְכָל־אַרְצוֹ:

² the wondrous feats that you saw with your own eyes, those prodigious signs and marvels.

ב הַמַּסּוֹת הַגְּדֹלֹת אֲשֶׁר רָאוּ עֵינֶיךָ הָאֹתֹת וְהַמֹּפְתִים הַגְּדֹלִים הָהֵם:

³ Yet to this day *Hashem* has not given you a mind to understand or eyes to see or ears to hear.

ג וְלֹא־נָתַן יְהֹוָה לָכֶם לֵב לָדַעַת וְעֵינַיִם לִרְאוֹת וְאָזְנַיִם לִשְׁמֹעַ עַד הַיּוֹם הַזֶּה:

⁴ I led you through the wilderness forty years; the clothes on your back did not wear out, nor did the sandals on your feet;

ד וָאוֹלֵךְ אֶתְכֶם אַרְבָּעִים שָׁנָה בַּמִּדְבָּר לֹא־בָלוּ שַׂלְמֹתֵיכֶם מֵעֲלֵיכֶם וְנַעַלְךָ לֹא־בָלְתָה מֵעַל רַגְלֶךָ:

⁵ you had no bread to eat and no wine or other intoxicant to drink – that you might know that I *Hashem* am your God.

ה לֶחֶם לֹא אֲכַלְתֶּם וְיַיִן וְשֵׁכָר לֹא שְׁתִיתֶם לְמַעַן תֵּדְעוּ כִּי אֲנִי יְהֹוָה אֱלֹהֵיכֶם:

⁶ When you reached this place, King Sihon of Heshbon and King Og of Bashan came out to engage us in battle, but we defeated them.

ו וַתָּבֹאוּ אֶל־הַמָּקוֹם הַזֶּה וַיֵּצֵא סִיחֹן מֶלֶךְ־חֶשְׁבּוֹן וְעוֹג מֶלֶךְ־הַבָּשָׁן לִקְרָאתֵנוּ לַמִּלְחָמָה וַנַּכֵּם:

⁷ We took their land and gave it to the Reubenites, the Gadites, and the half-tribe of *Menashe* as their heritage.

ז וַנִּקַּח אֶת־אַרְצָם וַנִּתְּנָהּ לְנַחֲלָה לָראוּבֵנִי וְלַגָּדִי וְלַחֲצִי שֵׁבֶט הַמְנַשִּׁי:

⁸ Therefore observe faithfully all the terms of this covenant, that you may succeed in all that you undertake.

ח וּשְׁמַרְתֶּם אֶת־דִּבְרֵי הַבְּרִית הַזֹּאת וַעֲשִׂיתֶם אֹתָם לְמַעַן תַּשְׂכִּילוּ אֵת כָּל־אֲשֶׁר תַּעֲשׂוּן:

⁹ You stand this day, all of you, before *Hashem* your God – your tribal heads, your elders and your officials, all the men of *Yisrael*,

ט אַתֶּם נִצָּבִים הַיּוֹם כֻּלְּכֶם לִפְנֵי יְהֹוָה אֱלֹהֵיכֶם רָאשֵׁיכֶם שִׁבְטֵיכֶם זִקְנֵיכֶם וְשֹׁטְרֵיכֶם כֹּל אִישׁ יִשְׂרָאֵל:

¹⁰ your children, your wives, even the stranger within your camp, from woodchopper to water drawer

י טַפְּכֶם נְשֵׁיכֶם וְגֵרְךָ אֲשֶׁר בְּקֶרֶב מַחֲנֶיךָ מֵחֹטֵב עֵצֶיךָ עַד שֹׁאֵב מֵימֶיךָ:

¹¹ to enter into the covenant of *Hashem* your God, which *Hashem* your God is concluding with you this day, with its sanctions;

יא לְעָבְרְךָ בִּבְרִית יְהֹוָה אֱלֹהֶיךָ וּבְאָלָתוֹ אֲשֶׁר יְהֹוָה אֱלֹהֶיךָ כֹּרֵת עִמְּךָ הַיּוֹם:

l'-av-r'-KHA biv-REET a-do-NAI e-lo-HE-kha uv-a-la-TO a-SHER a-do-NAI e-lo-HE-kha ko-RAYT i-m'-KHA ha-YOM

Rabbi Shlomo Riskin
(b. 1940)

29:11 To enter into the covenant of *Hashem* your God As the People of Israel stand at the plains of Moab, ready to enter the Promised Land, *Moshe* leads them in reaffirming their covenant with *Hashem* for all generations. The Hebrew name for 'plains of Moab,' *Arvot Moav* (ערבות מואב), has a dual meaning, as the word *Arvot* is related to the term *areivut* (ערבות),

which means 'mutual responsibility.' Rabbi Shlomo Riskin explains the significance: "I would submit that this covenant is that of mutuality, interdependent co-signership, but not necessarily between Jew and Jew – that was already incorporated into the previous covenants – but rather between Israel and the other nations of the world. After all, when *Avraham* was originally elected, God com-

12 to the end that He may establish you this day as His people and be your God, as He promised you and as He swore to your fathers, *Avraham, Yitzchak*, and *Yaakov*.

יב לְמַעַן הָקִים־אֹתְךָ הַיּוֹם לוֹ לְעָם וְהוּא יִהְיֶה־לְּךָ לֵאלֹהִים כַּאֲשֶׁר דִּבֶּר־לָךְ וְכַאֲשֶׁר נִשְׁבַּע לַאֲבֹתֶיךָ לְאַבְרָהָם לְיִצְחָק וּלְיַעֲקֹב:

13 I make this covenant, with its sanctions, not with you alone,

יג וְלֹא אִתְּכֶם לְבַדְּכֶם אָנֹכִי כֹּרֵת אֶת־הַבְּרִית הַזֹּאת וְאֶת־הָאָלָה הַזֹּאת:

14 but both with those who are standing here with us this day before *Hashem* our God and with those who are not with us here this day.

יד כִּי אֶת־אֲשֶׁר יֶשְׁנוֹ פֹּה עִמָּנוּ עֹמֵד הַיּוֹם לִפְנֵי יְהוָֹה אֱלֹהֵינוּ וְאֵת אֲשֶׁר אֵינֶנּוּ פֹּה עִמָּנוּ הַיּוֹם:

15 Well you know that we dwelt in the land of Egypt and that we passed through the midst of various other nations through which you passed;

טו כִּי־אַתֶּם יְדַעְתֶּם אֵת אֲשֶׁר־יָשַׁבְנוּ בְּאֶרֶץ מִצְרָיִם וְאֵת אֲשֶׁר־עָבַרְנוּ בְּקֶרֶב הַגּוֹיִם אֲשֶׁר עֲבַרְתֶּם:

16 and you have seen the detestable things and the fetishes of wood and stone, silver and gold, that they keep.

טז וַתִּרְאוּ אֶת־שִׁקּוּצֵיהֶם וְאֵת גִּלֻּלֵיהֶם עֵץ וָאֶבֶן כֶּסֶף וְזָהָב אֲשֶׁר עִמָּהֶם:

17 Perchance there is among you some man or woman, or some clan or tribe, whose heart is even now turning away from *Hashem* our God to go and worship the gods of those nations – perchance there is among you a stock sprouting poison weed and wormwood.

יז פֶּן־יֵשׁ בָּכֶם אִישׁ אוֹ־אִשָּׁה אוֹ מִשְׁפָּחָה אוֹ־שֵׁבֶט אֲשֶׁר לְבָבוֹ פֹנֶה הַיּוֹם מֵעִם יְהוָֹה אֱלֹהֵינוּ לָלֶכֶת לַעֲבֹד אֶת־אֱלֹהֵי הַגּוֹיִם הָהֵם פֶּן־יֵשׁ בָּכֶם שֹׁרֶשׁ פֹּרֶה רֹאשׁ וְלַעֲנָה:

18 When such a one hears the words of these sanctions, he may fancy himself immune, thinking, "I shall be safe, though I follow my own willful heart" – to the utter ruin of moist and dry alike.

יח וְהָיָה בְּשָׁמְעוֹ אֶת־דִּבְרֵי הָאָלָה הַזֹּאת וְהִתְבָּרֵךְ בִּלְבָבוֹ לֵאמֹר שָׁלוֹם יִהְיֶה־לִּי כִּי בִּשְׁרִרוּת לִבִּי אֵלֵךְ לְמַעַן סְפוֹת הָרָוָה אֶת־הַצְּמֵאָה:

19 *Hashem* will never forgive him; rather will *Hashem's* anger and passion rage against that man, till every sanction recorded in this book comes down upon him, and *Hashem* blots out his name from under heaven.

יט לֹא־יֹאבֶה יְהוָֹה סְלֹחַ לוֹ כִּי אָז יֶעְשַׁן אַף־יְהוָֹה וְקִנְאָתוֹ בָּאִישׁ הַהוּא וְרָבְצָה בּוֹ כָּל־הָאָלָה הַכְּתוּבָה בַּסֵּפֶר הַזֶּה וּמָחָה יְהוָֹה אֶת־שְׁמוֹ מִתַּחַת הַשָּׁמָיִם:

20 *Hashem* will single them out from all the tribes of *Yisrael* for misfortune, in accordance with all the sanctions of the covenant recorded in this book of Teaching.

כ וְהִבְדִּילוֹ יְהוָֹה לְרָעָה מִכֹּל שִׁבְטֵי יִשְׂרָאֵל כְּכֹל אָלוֹת הַבְּרִית הַכְּתוּבָה בְּסֵפֶר הַתּוֹרָה הַזֶּה:

---

manded that (Genesis 12:3) 'through you all the families of the world will be blessed' – through the message of ethical monotheism, the vision of a God who demands justice, compassion and peace, which *Avraham's* descen- dants must convey to the world. This is the true mission of Israel… This third covenant is the covenant of Israel's responsibility to the world."

Deuteronomy

²¹ And later generations will ask – the children who succeed you, and foreigners who come from distant lands and see the plagues and diseases that *Hashem* has inflicted upon that land,

כא וְאָמַר הַדּוֹר הָאַחֲרוֹן בְּנֵיכֶם אֲשֶׁר יָקוּמוּ מֵאַחֲרֵיכֶם וְהַנָּכְרִי אֲשֶׁר יָבֹא מֵאֶרֶץ רְחוֹקָה וְרָאוּ אֶת־מַכּוֹת הָאָרֶץ הַהִוא וְאֶת־תַּחֲלֻאֶיהָ אֲשֶׁר־חִלָּה יְהוָֹה בָּהּ:

²² all its soil devastated by sulfur and salt, beyond sowing and producing, no grass growing in it, just like the upheaval of Sodom and Gomorrah, Admah and Zeboiim, which *Hashem* overthrew in His fierce anger

כב גָּפְרִית וָמֶלַח שְׂרֵפָה כָל־אַרְצָהּ לֹא תִזָּרַע וְלֹא תַצְמִחַ וְלֹא־יַעֲלֶה בָהּ כָּל־עֵשֶׂב כְּמַהְפֵּכַת סְדֹם וַעֲמֹרָה אַדְמָה וּצְבֹיִים [וּצְבוֹיִם] אֲשֶׁר הָפַךְ יְהוָֹה בְּאַפּוֹ וּבַחֲמָתוֹ:

²³ all nations will ask, "Why did *Hashem* do thus to this land? Wherefore that awful wrath?"

כג וְאָמְרוּ כָּל־הַגּוֹיִם עַל־מֶה עָשָׂה יְהוָֹה כָּכָה לָאָרֶץ הַזֹּאת מֶה חֳרִי הָאַף הַגָּדוֹל הַזֶּה:

²⁴ They will be told, "Because they forsook the covenant that *Hashem*, God of their fathers, made with them when He freed them from the land of Egypt;

כד וְאָמְרוּ עַל אֲשֶׁר עָזְבוּ אֶת־בְּרִית יְהוָֹה אֱלֹהֵי אֲבֹתָם אֲשֶׁר כָּרַת עִמָּם בְּהוֹצִיאוֹ אֹתָם מֵאֶרֶץ מִצְרָיִם:

²⁵ they turned to the service of other gods and worshiped them, gods whom they had not experienced and whom He had not allotted to them.

כה וַיֵּלְכוּ וַיַּעַבְדוּ אֱלֹהִים אֲחֵרִים וַיִּשְׁתַּחֲווּ לָהֶם אֱלֹהִים אֲשֶׁר לֹא־יְדָעוּם וְלֹא חָלַק לָהֶם:

²⁶ So *Hashem* was incensed at that land and brought upon it all the curses recorded in this book.

כו וַיִּחַר־אַף יְהוָֹה בָּאָרֶץ הַהִוא לְהָבִיא עָלֶיהָ אֶת־כָּל־הַקְּלָלָה הַכְּתוּבָה בַּסֵּפֶר הַזֶּה:

²⁷ *Hashem* uprooted them from their soil in anger, fury, and great wrath, and cast them into another land, as is still the case."

כז וַיִּתְּשֵׁם יְהוָֹה מֵעַל אַדְמָתָם בְּאַף וּבְחֵמָה וּבְקֶצֶף גָּדוֹל וַיַּשְׁלִכֵם אֶל־אֶרֶץ אַחֶרֶת כַּיּוֹם הַזֶּה:

²⁸ Concealed acts concern *Hashem* our God; but with overt acts, it is for us and our children ever to apply all the provisions of this Teaching.

כח הַנִּסְתָּרֹת לַיהוָֹה אֱלֹהֵינוּ וְהַנִּגְלֹת לָנוּ וּלְבָנֵינוּ עַד־עוֹלָם לַעֲשׂוֹת אֶת־כָּל־דִּבְרֵי הַתּוֹרָה הַזֹּאת:

30 ¹ When all these things befall you – the blessing and the curse that I have set before you – and you take them to heart amidst the various nations to which *Hashem* your God has banished you,

ל א וְהָיָה כִי־יָבֹאוּ עָלֶיךָ כָּל־הַדְּבָרִים הָאֵלֶּה הַבְּרָכָה וְהַקְּלָלָה אֲשֶׁר נָתַתִּי לְפָנֶיךָ וַהֲשֵׁבֹתָ אֶל־לְבָבֶךָ בְּכָל־הַגּוֹיִם אֲשֶׁר הִדִּיחֲךָ יְהוָֹה אֱלֹהֶיךָ שָׁמָּה:

² and you return to *Hashem* your God, and you and your children heed His command with all your heart and soul, just as I enjoin upon you this day,

ב וְשַׁבְתָּ עַד־יְהוָֹה אֱלֹהֶיךָ וְשָׁמַעְתָּ בְקֹלוֹ כְּכֹל אֲשֶׁר־אָנֹכִי מְצַוְּךָ הַיּוֹם אַתָּה וּבָנֶיךָ בְּכָל־לְבָבְךָ וּבְכָל־נַפְשֶׁךָ:

Deuteronomy

³ then *Hashem* your God will restore your fortunes and take you back in love. He will bring you together again from all the peoples where *Hashem* your God has scattered you.

ג וְשָׁב יְהֹוָה אֱלֹהֶיךָ אֶת־שְׁבוּתְךָ וְרִחֲמֶךָ וְשָׁב וְקִבֶּצְךָ מִכָּל־הָעַמִּים אֲשֶׁר הֱפִיצְךָ יְהֹוָה אֱלֹהֶיךָ שָׁמָּה:

v'-SHAV a-do-NAI e-lo-HE-kha et sh'-vu-t'-KHA v'-ri-kha-ME-kha
v'-SHAV v'-ki-betz-KHA mi-kol HA-a-MEEM a-SHER
he-fitz-KHA a-do-NAI e-lo-HE-kha SHA-mah

⁴ Even if your outcasts are at the ends of the world, from there *Hashem* your God will gather you, from there He will fetch you.

ד אִם־יִהְיֶה נִדַּחֲךָ בִּקְצֵה הַשָּׁמָיִם מִשָּׁם יְקַבֶּצְךָ יְהֹוָה אֱלֹהֶיךָ וּמִשָּׁם יִקָּחֶךָ:

⁵ And *Hashem* your God will bring you to the land that your fathers possessed, and you shall possess it; and He will make you more prosperous and more numerous than your fathers.

ה וֶהֱבִיאֲךָ יְהֹוָה אֱלֹהֶיךָ אֶל־הָאָרֶץ אֲשֶׁר־ יָרְשׁוּ אֲבֹתֶיךָ וִירִשְׁתָּהּ וְהֵיטִבְךָ וְהִרְבְּךָ מֵאֲבֹתֶיךָ:

ve-he-vee-a-KHA a-do-NAI e-lo-HE-kha el ha-A-retz a-sher ya-r'-SHU a-vo-TE-kha
vee-rish-TA v'-hay-tiv-KHA v'-hir-b'-KHA ear-be-KHA may-a-vo-TE-kha

⁶ Then *Hashem* your God will open up your heart and the hearts of your offspring to love *Hashem* your God with all your heart and soul, in order that you may live.

ו וּמָל יְהֹוָה אֱלֹהֶיךָ אֶת־לְבָבְךָ וְאֶת־לְבַב זַרְעֶךָ לְאַהֲבָה אֶת־יְהֹוָה אֱלֹהֶיךָ בְּכָל־ לְבָבְךָ וּבְכָל־נַפְשְׁךָ לְמַעַן חַיֶּיךָ:

⁷ *Hashem* your God will inflict all those curses upon the enemies and foes who persecuted you.

ז וְנָתַן יְהֹוָה אֱלֹהֶיךָ אֵת כָּל־הָאָלוֹת הָאֵלֶּה עַל־אֹיְבֶיךָ וְעַל־שֹׂנְאֶיךָ אֲשֶׁר רְדָפוּךָ:

⁸ You, however, will again heed *Hashem* and obey all His commandments that I enjoin upon you this day.

ח וְאַתָּה תָשׁוּב וְשָׁמַעְתָּ בְּקוֹל יְהֹוָה וְעָשִׂיתָ אֶת־כָּל־מִצְוֺתָיו אֲשֶׁר אָנֹכִי מְצַוְּךָ הַיּוֹם:

30:3 Then *Hashem* your God will restore your fortunes In his book *Meshech Chochma*, Rabbi Meir Simcha of Dvinsk (1843–1926) clarifies that this verse, foretelling the ingathering of the exiles, refers to two distinct groups of people. "God will restore your fortunes" alludes to the Jews who yearn to return to the Land of Israel. This group will be brought to *Eretz Yisrael* first. Subsequently, "He will bring you together again," and even those Jews who have become comfortable on foreign soil and lost their connection with Israel will be brought back. We are privileged to witness the first part of the verse being fulfilled, as thousands of Jews choose to make *aliyah* each year. In 2015, more than 31,000 Jewish immigrants left their homes worldwide and moved to the Land of Israel. Why do so many Jews choose to make *Eretz Yisrael* their home? According to Natan Sharansky, former Soviet "refusenik" and chairman of the Jewish Agency for Israel, "The high number of immigrants, particularly from western countries, attests to the drawing power of the Zionist idea. The fact that immigrants choose to come to Israel is a sign that Israel invests their lives with meaning that they cannot find elsewhere."

30:5 The land that your fathers possessed Customarily, this passage is read in synagogue every year prior to *Rosh Hashana*, the Jewish New Year and the first of the High Holidays. It describes the redemption of the Jewish people and their physical return to the Land of Israel. What is the connection between the return to the land and the High Holidays? One of the central themes of *Rosh Hashana* is the recognition of *Hashem*'s dominion over the whole world. Only at the time of the complete return of the People of Israel to *Eretz Yisrael* will all the world recognize *Hashem* as the King of the world. As it says "And *Hashem* shall be king over all the earth; in that day there shall be one *Hashem* with one name" (Zechariah 14:9).

Natan Sharansky
(b. 1948)

New immigrants arrive at Ben Gurion airport

9 And *Hashem* your God will grant you abounding prosperity in all your undertakings, in the issue of your womb, the offspring of your cattle, and the produce of your soil. For *Hashem* will again delight in your well-being, as He did in that of your fathers,

ט וְהוֹתִֽירְךָ֤ יְהֹוָ֣ה אֱלֹהֶ֨יךָ֙ בְּכֹ֣ל ׀ מַעֲשֵׂ֣ה יָדֶ֗ךָ בִּפְרִ֨י בִטְנְךָ֜ וּבִפְרִ֧י בְהֶמְתְּךָ֛ וּבִפְרִ֥י אַדְמָתְךָ֖ לְטֹבָ֑ה כִּ֣י ׀ יָשׁ֣וּב יְהֹוָ֗ה לָשׂ֤וּשׂ עָלֶ֨יךָ֙ לְט֔וֹב כַּאֲשֶׁר־שָׂ֖שׂ עַל־אֲבֹתֶֽיךָ:

10 since you will be heeding *Hashem* your God and keeping His commandments and laws that are recorded in this book of the Teaching – once you return to *Hashem* your God with all your heart and soul.

י כִּ֣י תִשְׁמַ֗ע בְּקוֹל֙ יְהֹוָ֣ה אֱלֹהֶ֔יךָ לִשְׁמֹ֤ר מִצְוֺתָיו֙ וְחֻקֹּתָ֔יו הַכְּתוּבָ֕ה בְּסֵ֖פֶר הַתּוֹרָ֣ה הַזֶּ֑ה כִּ֤י תָשׁוּב֙ אֶל־יְהֹוָ֣ה אֱלֹהֶ֔יךָ בְּכָל־לְבָבְךָ֖ וּבְכָל־נַפְשֶֽׁךָ:

11 Surely, this Instruction which I enjoin upon you this day is not too baffling for you, nor is it beyond reach.

יא כִּ֚י הַמִּצְוָ֣ה הַזֹּ֔את אֲשֶׁ֛ר אָנֹכִ֥י מְצַוְּךָ֖ הַיּ֑וֹם לֹא־נִפְלֵ֥את הִוא֙ מִמְּךָ֔ וְלֹ֥א רְחֹקָ֖ה הִֽוא:

12 It is not in the heavens, that you should say, "Who among us can go up to the heavens and get it for us and impart it to us, that we may observe it?"

יב לֹ֥א בַשָּׁמַ֖יִם הִ֑וא לֵאמֹ֗ר מִ֣י יַעֲלֶה־לָּ֤נוּ הַשָּׁמַ֨יְמָה֙ וְיִקָּחֶ֣הָ לָּ֔נוּ וְיַשְׁמִעֵ֥נוּ אֹתָ֖הּ וְנַעֲשֶֽׂנָּה:

13 Neither is it beyond the sea, that you should say, "Who among us can cross to the other side of the sea and get it for us and impart it to us, that we may observe it?"

יג וְלֹֽא־מֵעֵ֥בֶר לַיָּ֖ם הִ֑וא לֵאמֹ֗ר מִ֣י יַעֲבָר־לָ֜נוּ אֶל־עֵ֤בֶר הַיָּם֙ וְיִקָּחֶ֣הָ לָּ֔נוּ וְיַשְׁמִעֵ֥נוּ אֹתָ֖הּ וְנַעֲשֶֽׂנָּה:

14 No, the thing is very close to you, in your mouth and in your heart, to observe it.

יד כִּֽי־קָר֥וֹב אֵלֶ֛יךָ הַדָּבָ֖ר מְאֹ֑ד בְּפִ֥יךָ וּבִלְבָבְךָ֖ לַעֲשֹׂתֽוֹ:

15 See, I set before you this day life and prosperity, death and adversity.

טו רְאֵ֨ה נָתַ֤תִּי לְפָנֶ֨יךָ֙ הַיּ֔וֹם אֶת־הַֽחַיִּ֖ים וְאֶת־הַטּ֑וֹב וְאֶת־הַמָּ֖וֶת וְאֶת־הָרָֽע:

16 For I command you this day, to love *Hashem* your God, to walk in His ways, and to keep His commandments, His laws, and His rules, that you may thrive and increase, and that *Hashem* your God may bless you in the land that you are about to enter and possess.

טז אֲשֶׁ֨ר אָנֹכִ֣י מְצַוְּךָ֮ הַיּוֹם֒ לְאַהֲבָ֞ה אֶת־ יְהֹוָ֤ה אֱלֹהֶ֨יךָ֙ לָלֶ֣כֶת בִּדְרָכָ֔יו וְלִשְׁמֹ֛ר מִצְוֺתָ֥יו וְחֻקֹּתָ֖יו וּמִשְׁפָּטָ֑יו וְחָיִ֣יתָ וְרָבִ֔יתָ וּבֵרַכְךָ֙ יְהֹוָ֣ה אֱלֹהֶ֔יךָ בָּאָ֕רֶץ אֲשֶׁר־אַתָּ֥ה בָא־שָׁ֖מָּה לְרִשְׁתָּֽהּ:

a-SHER a-no-KHEE m'-tza-v'-KHA ha-YOM l'-a-ha-VAH et a-do-NAI
e-lo-HE-kha la-LE-khet bid-ra-KHAV v'-lish-MOR mitz-vo-TAV v'khu-ko-TAV
u-mish-pa-TAV v'-kha-YEE-ta v'-ra-VEE-ta u-vay-ra-kh'-KHA a-do-NAI
e-lo-HE-kha ba-A-retz a-sher a-TAH va SHA-mah l'-rish-TAH

17 But if your heart turns away and you give no heed, and are lured into the worship and service of other gods,

יז וְאִם־יִפְנֶ֤ה לְבָֽבְךָ֙ וְלֹ֣א תִשְׁמָ֔ע וְנִדַּחְתָּ֗ וְהִֽשְׁתַּחֲוִ֛יתָ לֵאלֹהִ֥ים אֲחֵרִ֖ים וַעֲבַדְתָּֽם:

18 I declare to you this day that you shall certainly perish; you shall not long endure on the soil that you are crossing the *Yarden* to enter and possess.

יח הִגַּ֤דְתִּי לָכֶם֙ הַיּ֔וֹם כִּ֥י אָבֹ֖ד תֹּאבֵד֑וּן לֹֽא־ תַאֲרִיכֻ֤ן יָמִים֙ עַל־הָ֣אֲדָמָ֔ה אֲשֶׁ֨ר אַתָּ֜ה עֹבֵ֧ר אֶת־הַיַּרְדֵּ֛ן לָבֹ֥א שָׁ֖מָּה לְרִשְׁתָּֽהּ:

19 I call heaven and earth to witness against you this day: I have put before you life and death, blessing and curse. Choose life – if you and your offspring would live

יט הַעִדֹ֨תִי בָכֶ֜ם הַיּ֗וֹם אֶת־הַשָּׁמַ֨יִם֙ וְאֶת־ הָאָ֔רֶץ הַֽחַיִּ֤ים וְהַמָּ֨וֶת֙ נָתַ֣תִּי לְפָנֶ֔יךָ הַבְּרָכָ֖ה וְהַקְּלָלָ֑ה וּבָֽחַרְתָּ֙ בַּֽחַיִּ֔ים לְמַ֨עַן תִּֽחְיֶ֖ה אַתָּ֥ה וְזַרְעֶֽךָ:

Deuteronomy

20 by loving *Hashem* your God, heeding His commands, and holding fast to Him. For thereby you shall have life and shall long endure upon the soil that *Hashem* swore to your ancestors, *Avraham*, *Yitzchak*, and *Yaakov*, to give to them.

כ לְאַהֲבָה אֶת־יְהֹוָה אֱלֹהֶיךָ לִשְׁמֹעַ
בְּקֹלוֹ וּלְדָבְקָה־בוֹ כִּי הוּא חַיֶּיךָ וְאֹרֶךְ
יָמֶיךָ לָשֶׁבֶת עַל־הָאֲדָמָה אֲשֶׁר נִשְׁבַּע
יְהֹוָה לַאֲבֹתֶיךָ לְאַבְרָהָם לְיִצְחָק
וּלְיַעֲקֹב לָתֵת לָהֶם:

l'-a-ha-VAH et a-do-NAI e-lo-HE-kha lish-MO-a b'-ko-LO ul-dav-kah
VO KEE HU kha-YE-kha v'-O-rekh ya-ME-kha la-SHE-vet
al ha-a-da-MAH a-SHER nish-BA a-do-NAI la-a-vo-TE-kha
l'-av-ra-HAM l'-yitz-KHAK ul-ya-a-KOV la-TAYT la-HEM

31 ¹ *Moshe* went and spoke these things to all *Yisrael*.

לא א וַיֵּלֶךְ מֹשֶׁה וַיְדַבֵּר אֶת־הַדְּבָרִים הָאֵלֶּה
אֶל־כָּל־יִשְׂרָאֵל:

² He said to them: I am now one hundred and twenty years old, I can no longer be active. Moreover, *Hashem* has said to me, "You shall not go across yonder *Yarden*."

ב וַיֹּאמֶר אֲלֵהֶם בֶּן־מֵאָה וְעֶשְׂרִים שָׁנָה
אָנֹכִי הַיּוֹם לֹא־אוּכַל עוֹד לָצֵאת וְלָבוֹא
וַיהֹוָה אָמַר אֵלַי לֹא תַעֲבֹר אֶת־הַיַּרְדֵּן
הַזֶּה:

³ *Hashem* your God Himself will cross over before you; and He Himself will wipe out those nations from your path and you shall dispossess them. – *Yehoshua* is the one who shall cross before you, as *Hashem* has spoken.

ג יְהֹוָה אֱלֹהֶיךָ הוּא עֹבֵר לְפָנֶיךָ הוּא־
יַשְׁמִיד אֶת־הַגּוֹיִם הָאֵלֶּה מִלְּפָנֶיךָ
וִירִשְׁתָּם יְהוֹשֻׁעַ הוּא עֹבֵר לְפָנֶיךָ
כַּאֲשֶׁר דִּבֶּר יְהֹוָה:

⁴ *Hashem* will do to them as He did to Sihon and Og, kings of the Amorites, and to their countries, when He wiped them out.

ד וְעָשָׂה יְהֹוָה לָהֶם כַּאֲשֶׁר עָשָׂה לְסִיחוֹן
וּלְעוֹג מַלְכֵי הָאֱמֹרִי וּלְאַרְצָם אֲשֶׁר
הִשְׁמִיד אֹתָם:

⁵ *Hashem* will deliver them up to you, and you shall deal with them in full accordance with the Instruction that I have enjoined upon you.

ה וּנְתָנָם יְהֹוָה לִפְנֵיכֶם וַעֲשִׂיתֶם לָהֶם
כְּכָל־הַמִּצְוָה אֲשֶׁר צִוִּיתִי אֶתְכֶם:

⁶ Be strong and resolute, be not in fear or in dread of them; for *Hashem* your God Himself marches with you: He will not fail you or forsake you.

ו חִזְקוּ וְאִמְצוּ אַל־תִּירְאוּ וְאַל־תַּעַרְצוּ
מִפְּנֵיהֶם כִּי יְהֹוָה אֱלֹהֶיךָ הוּא הַהֹלֵךְ
עִמָּךְ לֹא יַרְפְּךָ וְלֹא יַעַזְבֶךָּ:

khiz-KU v'-im-TZOO al tee-r'-U v'-al ta-ar-TZOO mi-p'-nay-HEM KEE a-do-NAI
e-lo-HE-kha HU ha-ho-LAYKH i-MAKH LO yar-p'-KHA ve-LO ya-az-VE-ka

⁷ Then *Moshe* called *Yehoshua* and said to him in the sight of all *Yisrael*: "Be strong and resolute, for it is you who shall go with this people into the land that *Hashem* swore to their fathers to give them, and it is you who shall apportion it to them.

ז וַיִּקְרָא מֹשֶׁה לִיהוֹשֻׁעַ וַיֹּאמֶר אֵלָיו
לְעֵינֵי כָל־יִשְׂרָאֵל חֲזַק וֶאֱמָץ כִּי אַתָּה
תָּבוֹא אֶת־הָעָם הַזֶּה אֶל־הָאָרֶץ אֲשֶׁר
נִשְׁבַּע יְהֹוָה לַאֲבֹתָם לָתֵת לָהֶם וְאַתָּה
תַּנְחִילֶנָּה אוֹתָם:

va-yik-RA mo-SHEH lee-ho-SHU-ah va-YO-mer ay-LAV l'-ay-NAY
khol yis-ra-AYL kha-ZAK ve-eh-MATZ KEE a-TAH ta-VO et ha-AM
ha-ZEH el ha-A-retz a-SHER nish-BA a-do-NAI la-a-vo-TAM
la-TAYT la-HEM ve-a-TAH tan-khee-LE-na o-TAM

31:7 Be strong and resolute In this verse, *Moshe* encourages *Yehoshua* to be "strong and reso-lute" in settling the Land of Israel. Rabbi Naftali Tzvi Yehuda Berlin, known as the *Netziv*, ex-plains the double language used in this verse. *Yehoshua* will need to be "strong" to

IDF soldier with the Israeli flag

Deuteronomy

8 And *Hashem* Himself will go before you. He will be with you; He will not fail you or forsake you. Fear not and be not dismayed!"

ח וַיהוָה הוּא הַהֹלֵךְ לְפָנֶיךָ הוּא יִהְיֶה עִמָּךְ לֹא יַרְפְּךָ וְלֹא יַעַזְבֶךָּ לֹא תִירָא וְלֹא תֵחָת:

9 *Moshe* wrote down this Teaching and gave it to the *Kohanim*, sons of *Levi*, who carried the *Aron* Brit *Hashem*, and to all the elders of *Yisrael*.

ט וַיִּכְתֹּב מֹשֶׁה אֶת־הַתּוֹרָה הַזֹּאת וַיִּתְּנָהּ אֶל־הַכֹּהֲנִים בְּנֵי לֵוִי הַנֹּשְׂאִים אֶת־אֲרוֹן בְּרִית יְהוָה וְאֶל־כָּל־זִקְנֵי יִשְׂרָאֵל:

10 And *Moshe* instructed them as follows: Every seventh year, the year set for remission, at the festival of *Sukkot*,

י וַיְצַו מֹשֶׁה אוֹתָם לֵאמֹר מִקֵּץ שֶׁבַע שָׁנִים בְּמֹעֵד שְׁנַת הַשְּׁמִטָּה בְּחַג הַסֻּכּוֹת:

11 when all *Yisrael* comes to appear before *Hashem* your God in the place that He will choose, you shall read this Teaching aloud in the presence of all *Yisrael*.

יא בְּבוֹא כָל־יִשְׂרָאֵל לֵרָאוֹת אֶת־פְּנֵי יְהוָה אֱלֹהֶיךָ בַּמָּקוֹם אֲשֶׁר יִבְחָר תִּקְרָא אֶת־הַתּוֹרָה הַזֹּאת נֶגֶד כָּל־יִשְׂרָאֵל בְּאָזְנֵיהֶם:

12 Gather the people – men, women, children, and the strangers in your communities – that they may hear and so learn to revere *Hashem* your God and to observe faithfully every word of this Teaching.

יב הַקְהֵל אֶת־הָעָם הָאֲנָשִׁים וְהַנָּשִׁים וְהַטַּף וְגֵרְךָ אֲשֶׁר בִּשְׁעָרֶיךָ לְמַעַן יִשְׁמְעוּ וּלְמַעַן יִלְמְדוּ וְיָרְאוּ אֶת־יְהוָה אֱלֹהֵיכֶם וְשָׁמְרוּ לַעֲשׂוֹת אֶת־כָּל־דִּבְרֵי הַתּוֹרָה הַזֹּאת:

13 Their children, too, who have not had the experience, shall hear and learn to revere *Hashem* your God as long as they live in the land that you are about to cross the *Yarden* to possess.

יג וּבְנֵיהֶם אֲשֶׁר לֹא־יָדְעוּ יִשְׁמְעוּ וְלָמְדוּ לְיִרְאָה אֶת־יְהוָה אֱלֹהֵיכֶם כָּל־הַיָּמִים אֲשֶׁר אַתֶּם חַיִּים עַל־הָאֲדָמָה אֲשֶׁר אַתֶּם עֹבְרִים אֶת־הַיַּרְדֵּן שָׁמָּה לְרִשְׁתָּהּ:

14 *Hashem* said to *Moshe*: The time is drawing near for you to die. Call *Yehoshua* and present yourselves in the Tent of Meeting, that I may instruct him. *Moshe* and *Yehoshua* went and presented themselves in the Tent of Meeting.

יד וַיֹּאמֶר יְהוָה אֶל־מֹשֶׁה הֵן קָרְבוּ יָמֶיךָ לָמוּת קְרָא אֶת־יְהוֹשֻׁעַ וְהִתְיַצְּבוּ בְּאֹהֶל מוֹעֵד וַאֲצַוֶּנּוּ וַיֵּלֶךְ מֹשֶׁה וִיהוֹשֻׁעַ וַיִּתְיַצְּבוּ בְּאֹהֶל מוֹעֵד:

15 *Hashem* appeared in the Tent, in a pillar of cloud, the pillar of cloud having come to rest at the entrance of the tent.

טו וַיֵּרָא יְהוָה בָּאֹהֶל בְּעַמּוּד עָנָן וַיַּעֲמֹד עַמּוּד הֶעָנָן עַל־פֶּתַח הָאֹהֶל:

16 *Hashem* said to *Moshe*: You are soon to lie with your fathers. This people will thereupon go astray after the alien gods in their midst, in the land that they are about to enter; they will forsake Me and break My covenant that I made with them.

טז וַיֹּאמֶר יְהוָה אֶל־מֹשֶׁה הִנְּךָ שֹׁכֵב עִם־אֲבֹתֶיךָ וְקָם הָעָם הַזֶּה וְזָנָה אַחֲרֵי אֱלֹהֵי נֵכַר־הָאָרֶץ אֲשֶׁר הוּא בָא־שָׁמָּה בְּקִרְבּוֹ וַעֲזָבַנִי וְהֵפֵר אֶת־בְּרִיתִי אֲשֶׁר כָּרַתִּי אִתּוֹ:

---

face the Canaanite enemy, and he will need to be "resolute" when dividing the land among the people. Though the battle for Israel might not be easy, it is well worth the fight. Three thousand years later, *Yehoshua's* spiritual heirs can be found among the ranks of the Israel Defense Forces, men and women who demonstrate strength and courage every day in serving their country and their nation.

17 Then My anger will flare up against them, and I will abandon them and hide My countenance from them. They shall be ready prey; and many evils and troubles shall befall them. And they shall say on that day, "Surely it is because our God is not in our midst that these evils have befallen us."

יז וְחָרָה אַפִּי בוֹ בַיּוֹם־הַהוּא וַעֲזַבְתִּים וְהִסְתַּרְתִּי פָנַי מֵהֶם וְהָיָה לֶאֱכֹל וּמְצָאֻהוּ רָעוֹת רַבּוֹת וְצָרוֹת וְאָמַר בַּיּוֹם הַהוּא הֲלֹא עַל כִּי־אֵין אֱלֹהַי בְּקִרְבִּי מְצָאוּנִי הָרָעוֹת הָאֵלֶּה:

18 Yet I will keep My countenance hidden on that day, because of all the evil they have done in turning to other gods.

יח וְאָנֹכִי הַסְתֵּר אַסְתִּיר פָּנַי בַּיּוֹם הַהוּא עַל כָּל־הָרָעָה אֲשֶׁר עָשָׂה כִּי פָנָה אֶל־אֱלֹהִים אֲחֵרִים:

19 Therefore, write down this poem and teach it to the people of *Yisrael*; put it in their mouths, in order that this poem may be My witness against the people of *Yisrael*.

יט וְעַתָּה כִּתְבוּ לָכֶם אֶת־הַשִּׁירָה הַזֹּאת וְלַמְּדָהּ אֶת־בְּנֵי־יִשְׂרָאֵל שִׂימָהּ בְּפִיהֶם לְמַעַן תִּהְיֶה־לִּי הַשִּׁירָה הַזֹּאת לְעֵד בִּבְנֵי יִשְׂרָאֵל:

20 When I bring them into the land flowing with milk and honey that I promised on oath to their fathers, and they eat their fill and grow fat and turn to other gods and serve them, spurning Me and breaking My covenant,

כ כִּי־אֲבִיאֶנּוּ אֶל־הָאֲדָמָה אֲשֶׁר־נִשְׁבַּעְתִּי לַאֲבֹתָיו זָבַת חָלָב וּדְבַשׁ וְאָכַל וְשָׂבַע וְדָשֵׁן וּפָנָה אֶל־אֱלֹהִים אֲחֵרִים וַעֲבָדוּם וְנִאֲצוּנִי וְהֵפֵר אֶת־בְּרִיתִי:

21 and the many evils and troubles befall them – then this poem shall confront them as a witness, since it will never be lost from the mouth of their offspring. For I know what plans they are devising even now, before I bring them into the land that I promised on oath.

כא וְהָיָה כִּי־תִמְצֶאןָ אֹתוֹ רָעוֹת רַבּוֹת וְצָרוֹת וְעָנְתָה הַשִּׁירָה הַזֹּאת לְפָנָיו לְעֵד כִּי לֹא תִשָּׁכַח מִפִּי זַרְעוֹ כִּי יָדַעְתִּי אֶת־יִצְרוֹ אֲשֶׁר הוּא עֹשֶׂה הַיּוֹם בְּטֶרֶם אֲבִיאֶנּוּ אֶל־הָאָרֶץ אֲשֶׁר נִשְׁבָּעְתִּי:

22 That day, *Moshe* wrote down this poem and taught it to the Israelites.

כב וַיִּכְתֹּב מֹשֶׁה אֶת־הַשִּׁירָה הַזֹּאת בַּיּוֹם הַהוּא וַיְלַמְּדָהּ אֶת־בְּנֵי יִשְׂרָאֵל:

23 And He charged *Yehoshua* son of *Nun*: "Be strong and resolute: for you shall bring the Israelites into the land that I promised them on oath, and I will be with you."

כג וַיְצַו אֶת־יְהוֹשֻׁעַ בִּן־נוּן וַיֹּאמֶר חֲזַק וֶאֱמָץ כִּי אַתָּה תָּבִיא אֶת־בְּנֵי יִשְׂרָאֵל אֶל־הָאָרֶץ אֲשֶׁר־נִשְׁבַּעְתִּי לָהֶם וְאָנֹכִי אֶהְיֶה עִמָּךְ:

24 When *Moshe* had put down in writing the words of this Teaching to the very end,

כד וַיְהִי כְּכַלּוֹת מֹשֶׁה לִכְתֹּב אֶת־דִּבְרֵי הַתּוֹרָה־הַזֹּאת עַל־סֵפֶר עַד תֻּמָּם:

25 *Moshe* charged the *Leviim* who carried the *Aron Brit Hashem*, saying:

כה וַיְצַו מֹשֶׁה אֶת־הַלְוִיִּם נֹשְׂאֵי אֲרוֹן בְּרִית־יְהוָה לֵאמֹר:

26 Take this book of Teaching and place it beside the *Aron Brit Hashem* your God, and let it remain there as a witness against you.

כו לָקֹחַ אֵת סֵפֶר הַתּוֹרָה הַזֶּה וְשַׂמְתֶּם אֹתוֹ מִצַּד אֲרוֹן בְּרִית־יְהוָה אֱלֹהֵיכֶם וְהָיָה־שָׁם בְּךָ לְעֵד:

27 Well I know how defiant and stiffnecked you are: even now, while I am still alive in your midst, you have been defiant toward *Hashem*; how much more, then, when I am dead!

כז כִּי אָנֹכִי יָדַעְתִּי אֶת־מֶרְיְךָ וְאֶת־עָרְפְּךָ הַקָּשֶׁה הֵן בְּעוֹדֶנִּי חַי עִמָּכֶם הַיּוֹם מַמְרִים הֱיִתֶם עִם־יְהוָה וְאַף כִּי־אַחֲרֵי מוֹתִי:

Deuteronomy

28 Gather to me all the elders of your tribes and your officials, that I may speak all these words to them and that I may call heaven and earth to witness against them.

כח הַקְהִ֣ילוּ אֵלַ֗י אֶת־כָּל־זִקְנֵ֤י שִׁבְטֵיכֶם֙ וְשֹׁטְרֵיכֶ֔ם וַאֲדַבְּרָ֣ה בְאָזְנֵיהֶ֔ם אֵ֖ת הַדְּבָרִ֣ים הָאֵ֑לֶּה וְאָעִ֣ידָה בָּ֔ם אֶת־הַשָּׁמַ֖יִם וְאֶת־הָאָֽרֶץ׃

29 For I know that, when I am dead, you will act wickedly and turn away from the path that I enjoined upon you, and that in time to come misfortune will befall you for having done evil in the sight of *Hashem* and vexed Him by your deeds.

כט כִּ֣י יָדַ֗עְתִּי אַחֲרֵ֤י מוֹתִי֙ כִּֽי־הַשְׁחֵ֣ת תַּשְׁחִת֔וּן וְסַרְתֶּ֣ם מִן־הַדֶּ֔רֶךְ אֲשֶׁ֥ר צִוִּ֖יתִי אֶתְכֶ֑ם וְקָרָ֤את אֶתְכֶם֙ הָֽרָעָה֙ בְּאַחֲרִ֣ית הַיָּמִ֔ים כִּֽי־תַעֲשׂ֤וּ אֶת־הָרַע֙ בְּעֵינֵ֣י יְהֹוָ֔ה לְהַכְעִיס֖וֹ בְּמַעֲשֵׂ֥ה יְדֵיכֶֽם׃

30 Then *Moshe* recited the words of this poem to the very end, in the hearing of the whole congregation of *Yisrael*:

ל וַיְדַבֵּ֣ר מֹשֶׁ֗ה בְּאָזְנֵי֙ כָּל־קְהַ֣ל יִשְׂרָאֵ֔ל אֶת־דִּבְרֵ֥י הַשִּׁירָ֖ה הַזֹּ֑את עַ֖ד תֻּמָּֽם׃

32 1 Give ear, O heavens, let me speak; Let the earth hear the words I utter!

ב ⬛ א הַאֲזִ֥ינוּ הַשָּׁמַ֖יִם וַאֲדַבֵּ֑רָה וְתִשְׁמַ֥ע הָאָ֖רֶץ אִמְרֵי־פִֽי׃

ha-a-ZEE-nu ha-sha-MA-yim va-a-da-BAY-ra v'-tish-MA ha-A-retz im-ray FEE

2 May my discourse come down as the rain, My speech distill as the dew, Like showers on young growth, Like droplets on the grass.

ב יַעֲרֹ֤ף כַּמָּטָר֙ לִקְחִ֔י תִּזַּ֥ל כַּטַּ֖ל אִמְרָתִ֑י כִּשְׂעִירִ֣ם עֲלֵי־דֶ֔שֶׁא וְכִרְבִיבִ֖ים עֲלֵי־עֵֽשֶׂב׃

3 For the name of *Hashem* I proclaim; Give glory to our God!

ג כִּ֥י שֵׁ֥ם יְהֹוָ֖ה אֶקְרָ֑א הָב֥וּ גֹ֖דֶל לֵאלֹהֵֽינוּ׃

4 The Rock! – His deeds are perfect, Yea, all His ways are just; A faithful *Hashem*, never false, True and upright is He.

ד הַצּוּר֙ תָּמִ֣ים פׇּעֳל֔וֹ כִּ֥י כׇל־דְּרָכָ֖יו מִשְׁפָּ֑ט אֵ֤ל אֱמוּנָה֙ וְאֵ֣ין עָ֔וֶל צַדִּ֥יק וְיָשָׁ֖ר הֽוּא׃

5 Children unworthy of Him – That crooked, perverse generation – Their baseness has played Him false.

ה שִׁחֵ֣ת ל֗וֹ לֹ֚א בָּנָ֣יו מוּמָ֔ם דּ֥וֹר עִקֵּ֖שׁ וּפְתַלְתֹּֽל׃

6 Do you thus requite *Hashem*, O dull and witless people? Is not He the Father who created you, Fashioned you and made you endure!

ו הֲ־לַיְהֹוָה֙ תִּגְמְלוּ־זֹ֔את עַ֥ם נָבָ֖ל וְלֹ֣א חָכָ֑ם הֲלוֹא־הוּא֙ אָבִ֣יךָ קָּנֶ֔ךָ ה֥וּא עָֽשְׂךָ֖ וַֽיְכֹנְנֶֽךָ׃

7 Remember the days of old, Consider the years of ages past; Ask your father, he will inform you, Your elders, they will tell you:

ז זְכֹר֙ יְמ֣וֹת עוֹלָ֔ם בִּ֖ינוּ שְׁנ֣וֹת דֹּר־וָדֹ֑ר שְׁאַ֤ל אָבִ֙יךָ֙ וְיַגֵּ֔דְךָ זְקֵנֶ֖יךָ וְיֹ֥אמְרוּ לָֽךְ׃

"Heaven and Earth" in the Golan Heights

32:1 Give ear, O heavens *Devarim* 32 contains the song that *Moshe* teaches to the Israelites before his passing. In it, he reminds the people that if they sin in *Eretz Yisrael* they will be punished with exile. However, the song concludes with the promise that God will redeem His people and exact retribution from their enemies. *Moshe* starts his song by addressing heaven and earth, calling upon them as his witnesses for this covenant. Unlike humans who come and go, heaven and earth exist for eternity. Though it may take thousands of years, *Hashem* will keep His promise to redeem the entire Jewish people and return them to their land, and heaven and earth will be the loyal witnesses who see the process through to its complete fulfillment.

8 When the Most High gave nations their homes And set the divisions of man, He fixed the boundaries of peoples In relation to *Yisrael*'s numbers.

ח בְּהַנְחֵל עֶלְיוֹן גּוֹיִם בְּהַפְרִידוֹ בְּנֵי אָדָם יַצֵּב גְּבֻלֹת עַמִּים לְמִסְפַּר בְּנֵי יִשְׂרָאֵל:

9 For *Hashem*'s portion is His people, *Yaakov* His own allotment.

ט כִּי חֵלֶק יְהוָה עַמּוֹ יַעֲקֹב חֶבֶל נַחֲלָתוֹ:

10 He found him in a desert region, In an empty howling waste. He engirded him, watched over him, Guarded him as the pupil of His eye.

י יִמְצָאֵהוּ בְּאֶרֶץ מִדְבָּר וּבְתֹהוּ יְלֵל יְשִׁמֹן יְסֹבְבֶנְהוּ יְבוֹנְנֵהוּ יִצְּרֶנְהוּ כְּאִישׁוֹן עֵינוֹ:

11 Like an eagle who rouses his nestlings, Gliding down to his young, So did He spread His wings and take him, Bear him along on His pinions;

יא כְּנֶשֶׁר יָעִיר קִנּוֹ עַל־גּוֹזָלָיו יְרַחֵף יִפְרֹשׂ כְּנָפָיו יִקָּחֵהוּ יִשָּׂאֵהוּ עַל־אֶבְרָתוֹ:

12 *Hashem* alone did guide him, No alien god at His side.

יב יְהוָה בָּדָד יַנְחֶנּוּ וְאֵין עִמּוֹ אֵל נֵכָר:

13 He set him atop the highlands, To feast on the yield of the earth; He fed him honey from the crag, And oil from the flinty rock,

יג יַרְכִּבֵהוּ עַל־במותי [בָּמֳתֵי] אָרֶץ וַיֹּאכַל תְּנוּבֹת שָׂדָי וַיֵּנִקֵהוּ דְבַשׁ מִסֶּלַע וְשֶׁמֶן מֵחַלְמִישׁ צוּר:

14 Curd of kine and milk of flocks; With the best of lambs, And rams of Bashan, and he-goats; With the very finest wheat – And foaming grape-blood was your drink.

יד חֶמְאַת בָּקָר וַחֲלֵב צֹאן עִם־חֵלֶב כָּרִים וְאֵילִים בְּנֵי־בָשָׁן וְעַתּוּדִים עִם־חֵלֶב כִּלְיוֹת חִטָּה וְדַם־עֵנָב תִּשְׁתֶּה־חָמֶר:

15 So Jeshurun grew fat and kicked – You grew fat and gross and coarse – He forsook the God who made him And spurned the Rock of his support.

טו וַיִּשְׁמַן יְשֻׁרוּן וַיִּבְעָט שָׁמַנְתָּ עָבִיתָ כָּשִׂיתָ וַיִּטֹּשׁ אֱלוֹהַּ עָשָׂהוּ וַיְנַבֵּל צוּר יְשֻׁעָתוֹ:

16 They incensed Him with alien things, Vexed Him with abominations.

טז יַקְנִאֻהוּ בְּזָרִים בְּתוֹעֵבֹת יַכְעִיסֻהוּ:

17 They sacrificed to demons, no-gods, *Hashems* they had never known, New ones, who came but lately, Who stirred not your fathers' fears.

יז יִזְבְּחוּ לַשֵּׁדִים לֹא אֱלֹהַ אֱלֹהִים לֹא יְדָעוּם חֲדָשִׁים מִקָּרֹב בָּאוּ לֹא שְׂעָרוּם אֲבֹתֵיכֶם:

18 You neglected the Rock that begot you, Forgot the God who brought you forth.

יח צוּר יְלָדְךָ תֶּשִׁי וַתִּשְׁכַּח אֵל מְחֹלְלֶךָ:

19 *Hashem* saw and was vexed And spurned His sons and His daughters.

יט וַיַּרְא יְהוָה וַיִּנְאָץ מִכַּעַס בָּנָיו וּבְנֹתָיו:

20 He said: I will hide My countenance from them, And see how they fare in the end. For they are a treacherous breed, Children with no loyalty in them.

כ וַיֹּאמֶר אַסְתִּירָה פָנַי מֵהֶם אֶרְאֶה מָה אַחֲרִיתָם כִּי דוֹר תַּהְפֻּכֹת הֵמָּה בָּנִים לֹא־אֵמֻן בָּם:

21 They incensed Me with no-gods, Vexed Me with their futilities; I'll incense them with a no-folk, Vex them with a nation of fools.

כא הֵם קִנְאוּנִי בְלֹא־אֵל כִּעֲסוּנִי בְּהַבְלֵיהֶם וַאֲנִי אַקְנִיאֵם בְּלֹא־עָם בְּגוֹי נָבָל אַכְעִיסֵם:

22 For a fire has flared in My wrath And burned to the bottom of Sheol, Has consumed the earth and its increase, Eaten down to the base of the hills.

כב כִּי־אֵשׁ קָדְחָה בְאַפִּי וַתִּיקַד עַד־שְׁאוֹל תַּחְתִּית וַתֹּאכַל אֶרֶץ וִיבֻלָהּ וַתְּלַהֵט מוֹסְדֵי הָרִים:

23 I will sweep misfortunes on them, Use up My arrows on them:

כג אַסְפֶּ֤ה עָלֵ֙ימוֹ֙ רָע֔וֹת חִצַּ֖י אֲכַלֶּה־בָּֽם׃

24 Wasting famine, ravaging plague, Deadly pestilence, and fanged beasts Will I let loose against them, With venomous creepers in dust.

כד מְזֵ֥י רָעָ֛ב וּלְחֻ֥מֵי רֶ֖שֶׁף וְקֶ֣טֶב מְרִירִ֑י וְשֶׁן־בְּהֵמֹת֙ אֲשַׁלַּח־בָּ֔ם עִם־חֲמַ֖ת זֹחֲלֵ֥י עָפָֽר׃

25 The sword shall deal death without, As shall the terror within, To youth and maiden alike, The suckling as well as the aged.

כה מִח֣וּץ תְּשַׁכֶּל־חֶ֗רֶב וּמֵחֲדָרִים֙ אֵימָ֔ה גַּם־בָּחוּר֙ גַּם־בְּתוּלָ֔ה יוֹנֵ֖ק עִם־אִ֥ישׁ שֵׂיבָֽה׃

26 I might have reduced them to naught, Made their memory cease among men,

כו אָמַ֖רְתִּי אַפְאֵיהֶ֑ם אַשְׁבִּ֥יתָה מֵאֱנ֖וֹשׁ זִכְרָֽם׃

27 But for fear of the taunts of the foe, Their enemies who might misjudge And say "Our own hand has prevailed; None of this was wrought by *Hashem*!"

כז לוּלֵ֗י כַּ֤עַס אוֹיֵב֙ אָג֔וּר פֶּֽן־יְנַכְּר֖וּ צָרֵ֑ימוֹ פֶּן־יֹֽאמְרוּ֙ יָדֵ֣נוּ רָ֔מָה וְלֹ֥א יְהֹוָ֖ה פָּעַ֥ל כָּל־זֹֽאת׃

28 For they are a folk void of sense, Lacking in all discernment.

כח כִּי־ג֛וֹי אֹבַ֥ד עֵצ֖וֹת הֵ֑מָּה וְאֵ֥ין בָּהֶ֖ם תְּבוּנָֽה׃

29 ere they wise, they would think upon this, Gain insight into their future:

כט ל֥וּ חָכְמ֖וּ יַשְׂכִּ֣ילוּ זֹ֑את יָבִ֖ינוּ לְאַחֲרִיתָֽם׃

30 "How could one have routed a thousand, Or two put ten thousand to flight, Unless their Rock had sold them, *Hashem* had given them up?"

ל אֵיכָ֞ה יִרְדֹּ֤ף אֶחָד֙ אֶ֔לֶף וּשְׁנַ֖יִם יָנִ֣יסוּ רְבָבָ֑ה אִם־לֹא֙ כִּי־צוּרָ֣ם מְכָרָ֔ם וַֽיהֹוָ֖ה הִסְגִּירָֽם׃

31 For their rock is not like our Rock, In our enemies' own estimation.

לא כִּ֛י לֹ֥א כְצוּרֵ֖נוּ צוּרָ֑ם וְאֹיְבֵ֖ינוּ פְּלִילִֽים׃

32 Ah! The vine for them is from Sodom, From the vineyards of Gomorrah; The grapes for them are poison, A bitter growth their clusters.

לב כִּֽי־מִגֶּ֤פֶן סְדֹם֙ גַּפְנָ֔ם וּמִשַּׁדְמֹ֖ת עֲמֹרָ֑ה עֲנָבֵ֙מוֹ֙ עִנְּבֵי־ר֔וֹשׁ אַשְׁכְּלֹ֥ת מְרֹרֹ֖ת לָֽמוֹ׃

33 Their wine is the venom of asps, The pitiless poison of vipers.

לג חֲמַ֥ת תַּנִּינִ֖ם יֵינָ֑ם וְרֹ֥אשׁ פְּתָנִ֖ים אַכְזָֽר׃

34 Lo, I have it all put away, Sealed up in My storehouses,

לד הֲלֹא־ה֖וּא כָּמֻ֣ס עִמָּדִ֑י חָתֻ֖ם בְּאוֹצְרֹתָֽי׃

35 To be My vengeance and recompense, At the time that their foot falters. Yea, their day of disaster is near, And destiny rushes upon them.

לה לִ֤י נָקָם֙ וְשִׁלֵּ֔ם לְעֵ֖ת תָּמ֣וּט רַגְלָ֑ם כִּ֤י קָרוֹב֙ י֣וֹם אֵידָ֔ם וְחָ֖שׁ עֲתִדֹ֥ת לָֽמוֹ׃

36 For *Hashem* will vindicate His people And take revenge for His servants, When He sees that their might is gone, And neither bond nor free is left.

לו כִּֽי־יָדִ֤ין יְהֹוָה֙ עַמּ֔וֹ וְעַל־עֲבָדָ֖יו יִתְנֶחָ֑ם כִּ֤י יִרְאֶה֙ כִּי־אָ֣זְלַת יָ֔ד וְאֶ֖פֶס עָצ֥וּר וְעָזֽוּב׃

37 He will say: Where are their gods, The rock in whom they sought refuge,

לז וְאָמַ֖ר אֵ֣י אֱלֹהֵ֑ימוֹ צ֖וּר חָסָ֥יוּ בֽוֹ׃

38 Who ate the fat of their offerings And drank their libation wine? Let them rise up to your help, And let them be a shield unto you!

לח אֲשֶׁ֨ר חֵ֤לֶב זְבָחֵ֙ימוֹ֙ יֹאכֵ֔לוּ יִשְׁתּ֖וּ יֵ֣ין נְסִיכָ֑ם יָק֙וּמוּ֙ וְיַעְזְרֻכֶ֔ם יְהִ֥י עֲלֵיכֶ֖ם סִתְרָֽה׃

39 See, then, that I, I am He; There is no god beside Me. I deal death and give life; I wounded and I will heal: None can deliver from My hand.

לט רְאוּ עַתָּה כִּי אֲנִי אֲנִי הוּא וְאֵין אֱלֹהִים עִמָּדִי אֲנִי אָמִית וַאֲחַיֶּה מָחַצְתִּי וַאֲנִי אֶרְפָּא וְאֵין מִיָּדִי מַצִּיל:

40 Lo, I raise My hand to heaven And say: As I live forever,

מ כִּי־אֶשָּׂא אֶל־שָׁמַיִם יָדִי וְאָמַרְתִּי חַי אָנֹכִי לְעֹלָם:

41 When I whet My flashing blade And My hand lays hold on judgment, Vengeance will I wreak on My foes, Will I deal to those who reject Me.

מא אִם־שַׁנּוֹתִי בְּרַק חַרְבִּי וְתֹאחֵז בְּמִשְׁפָּט יָדִי אָשִׁיב נָקָם לְצָרָי וְלִמְשַׂנְאַי אֲשַׁלֵּם:

42 I will make My arrows drunk with blood – As My sword devours flesh – Blood of the slain and the captive From the long-haired enemy chiefs.

מב אַשְׁכִּיר חִצַּי מִדָּם וְחַרְבִּי תֹּאכַל בָּשָׂר מִדַּם חָלָל וְשִׁבְיָה מֵרֹאשׁ פַּרְעוֹת אוֹיֵב:

43 O nations, acclaim His people! For He'll avenge the blood of His servants, Wreak vengeance on His foes, And cleanse the land of His people.

מג הַרְנִינוּ גוֹיִם עַמּוֹ כִּי דַם־עֲבָדָיו יִקּוֹם וְנָקָם יָשִׁיב לְצָרָיו וְכִפֶּר אַדְמָתוֹ עַמּוֹ:

44 *Moshe* came, together with *Hoshea* son of *Nun*, and recited all the words of this poem in the hearing of the people.

מד וַיָּבֹא מֹשֶׁה וַיְדַבֵּר אֶת־כָּל־דִּבְרֵי הַשִּׁירָה־הַזֹּאת בְּאָזְנֵי הָעָם הוּא וְהוֹשֵׁעַ בִּן־נוּן:

45 And when *Moshe* finished reciting all these words to all *Yisrael*,

מה וַיְכַל מֹשֶׁה לְדַבֵּר אֶת־כָּל־הַדְּבָרִים הָאֵלֶּה אֶל־כָּל־יִשְׂרָאֵל:

46 he said to them: Take to heart all the words with which I have warned you this day. Enjoin them upon your children, that they may observe faithfully all the terms of this Teaching.

מו וַיֹּאמֶר אֲלֵהֶם שִׂימוּ לְבַבְכֶם לְכָל־הַדְּבָרִים אֲשֶׁר אָנֹכִי מֵעִיד בָּכֶם הַיּוֹם אֲשֶׁר תְּצַוֻּם אֶת־בְּנֵיכֶם לִשְׁמֹר לַעֲשׂוֹת אֶת־כָּל־דִּבְרֵי הַתּוֹרָה הַזֹּאת:

47 For this is not a trifling thing for you: it is your very life; through it you shall long endure on the land that you are to possess upon crossing the *Yarden*.

מז כִּי לֹא־דָבָר רֵק הוּא מִכֶּם כִּי־הוּא חַיֵּיכֶם וּבַדָּבָר הַזֶּה תַּאֲרִיכוּ יָמִים עַל־הָאֲדָמָה אֲשֶׁר אַתֶּם עֹבְרִים אֶת־הַיַּרְדֵּן שָׁמָּה לְרִשְׁתָּהּ:

KEE lo da-VAR RAYK HU mi-KEM kee HU kha-yay-KHEM u-va-da-VAR ha-ZEH ta-a-REE-khu ya-MEEM al ha-a-da-MAH a-SHER a-TEM o-v'-REEM et ha-yar-DAYN SHA-mah l'-rish-TAH

48 That very day *Hashem* spoke to *Moshe*:

מח וַיְדַבֵּר יְהֹוָה אֶל־מֹשֶׁה בְּעֶצֶם הַיּוֹם הַזֶּה לֵאמֹר:

49 Ascend these heights of Abarim to Mount Nebo, which is in the land of Moab facing *Yericho*, and view the land of Canaan, which I am giving the Israelites as their holding.

מט עֲלֵה אֶל־הַר הָעֲבָרִים הַזֶּה הַר־נְבוֹ אֲשֶׁר בְּאֶרֶץ מוֹאָב אֲשֶׁר עַל־פְּנֵי יְרֵחוֹ וּרְאֵה אֶת־אֶרֶץ כְּנַעַן אֲשֶׁר אֲנִי נֹתֵן לִבְנֵי יִשְׂרָאֵל לַאֲחֻזָּה:

50 You shall die on the mountain that you are about to ascend, and shall be gathered to your kin, as your brother *Aharon* died on Mount Hor and was gathered to his kin;

נ וּמֻת בָּהָר אֲשֶׁר אַתָּה עֹלֶה שָׁמָּה וְהֵאָסֵף אֶל־עַמֶּיךָ כַּאֲשֶׁר־מֵת אַהֲרֹן אָחִיךָ בְּהֹר הָהָר וַיֵּאָסֶף אֶל־עַמָּיו:

51 for you both broke faith with Me among *B'nei Yisrael*, at the waters of Meribath-kadesh in the wilderness of Zin, by failing to uphold My sanctity among *B'nei Yisrael*.

נא עַל אֲשֶׁר מְעַלְתֶּם בִּי בְּתוֹךְ בְּנֵי יִשְׂרָאֵל בְּמֵי־מְרִיבַת קָדֵשׁ מִדְבַּר־צִן עַל אֲשֶׁר לֹא־קִדַּשְׁתֶּם אוֹתִי בְּתוֹךְ בְּנֵי יִשְׂרָאֵל:

52 You may view the land from a distance, but you shall not enter it – the land that I am giving to *B'nei Yisrael*.

נב כִּי מִנֶּגֶד תִּרְאֶה אֶת־הָאָרֶץ וְשָׁמָּה לֹא תָבוֹא אֶל־הָאָרֶץ אֲשֶׁר־אֲנִי נֹתֵן לִבְנֵי יִשְׂרָאֵל:

33 ¹ This is the blessing with which *Moshe*, the man of *Hashem*, bade the Israelites farewell before he died.

לג א וְזֹאת הַבְּרָכָה אֲשֶׁר בֵּרַךְ מֹשֶׁה אִישׁ הָאֱלֹהִים אֶת־בְּנֵי יִשְׂרָאֵל לִפְנֵי מוֹתוֹ:

² He said: *Hashem* came from Sinai; He shone upon them from Seir; He appeared from Mount Paran, And approached from Riboth-kodesh, Lightning flashing at them from His right.

ב וַיֹּאמַר יְהֹוָה מִסִּינַי בָּא וְזָרַח מִשֵּׂעִיר לָמוֹ הוֹפִיעַ מֵהַר פָּארָן וְאָתָה מֵרִבְבֹת קֹדֶשׁ מִימִינוֹ אשדת [אֵשׁ] [דָּת] לָמוֹ:

³ Lover, indeed, of the people, Their hallowed are all in Your hand. They followed in Your steps, Accepting Your pronouncements,

ג אַף חֹבֵב עַמִּים כָּל־קְדֹשָׁיו בְּיָדֶךָ וְהֵם תֻּכּוּ לְרַגְלֶךָ יִשָּׂא מִדַּבְּרֹתֶיךָ:

⁴ When *Moshe* charged us with the Teaching As the heritage of the congregation of *Yaakov*.

ד תּוֹרָה צִוָּה־לָנוּ מֹשֶׁה מוֹרָשָׁה קְהִלַּת יַעֲקֹב:

⁵ Then He became King in Jeshurun, When the heads of the people assembled, The tribes of *Yisrael* together.

ה וַיְהִי בִישֻׁרוּן מֶלֶךְ בְּהִתְאַסֵּף רָאשֵׁי עָם יַחַד שִׁבְטֵי יִשְׂרָאֵל:

⁶ May *Reuven* live and not die, Though few be his numbers.

ו יְחִי רְאוּבֵן וְאַל־יָמֹת וִיהִי מְתָיו מִסְפָּר:

⁷ And this he said of *Yehuda*: Hear, *Hashem* the voice of *Yehuda* And restore him to his people. Though his own hands strive for him, Help him against his foes.

ז וְזֹאת לִיהוּדָה וַיֹּאמַר שְׁמַע יְהֹוָה קוֹל יְהוּדָה וְאֶל־עַמּוֹ תְּבִיאֶנּוּ יָדָיו רָב לוֹ וְעֵזֶר מִצָּרָיו תִּהְיֶה:

⁸ And of *Levi* he said: Let Your Thummim and Urim Be with Your faithful one, Whom You tested at Massah, Challenged at the waters of Meribah;

ח וּלְלֵוִי אָמַר תֻּמֶּיךָ וְאוּרֶיךָ לְאִישׁ חֲסִידֶךָ אֲשֶׁר נִסִּיתוֹ בְּמַסָּה תְּרִיבֵהוּ עַל־מֵי מְרִיבָה:

⁹ Who said of his father and mother, "I consider them not." His brothers he disregarded, Ignored his own children. Your precepts alone they observed, And kept Your covenant.

ט הָאֹמֵר לְאָבִיו וּלְאִמּוֹ לֹא רְאִיתִיו וְאֶת־אֶחָיו לֹא הִכִּיר וְאֶת־בָּנָו [בָּנָיו] לֹא יָדָע כִּי שָׁמְרוּ אִמְרָתֶךָ וּבְרִיתְךָ יִנְצֹרוּ:

¹⁰ They shall teach Your laws to *Yaakov* And Your instructions to *Yisrael*. They shall offer You incense to savor And whole-offerings on Your *Mizbayach*.

י יוֹרוּ מִשְׁפָּטֶיךָ לְיַעֲקֹב וְתוֹרָתְךָ לְיִשְׂרָאֵל יָשִׂימוּ קְטוֹרָה בְּאַפֶּךָ וְכָלִיל עַל־מִזְבְּחֶךָ:

¹¹ Bless, *Hashem*, his substance, And favor his undertakings. Smite the loins of his foes; Let his enemies rise no more.

יא בָּרֵךְ יְהֹוָה חֵילוֹ וּפֹעַל יָדָיו תִּרְצֶה מְחַץ מָתְנַיִם קָמָיו וּמְשַׂנְאָיו מִן־יְקוּמוּן:

Deuteronomy

12 Of *Binyamin* he said: Beloved of *Hashem*, He rests securely beside Him; Ever does He protect him, As he rests between His shoulders.

יב לְבִנְיָמִן אָמַר יְדִיד יְהֹוָה יִשְׁכֹּן לָבֶטַח עָלָיו חֹפֵף עָלָיו כָּל־הַיּוֹם וּבֵין כְּתֵיפָיו שָׁכֵן:

l'-vin-ya-MIN a-MAR y'-DEED a-do-NAI yish-KON la-VE-takh a-LAV kho-FAYF a-LAV kol ha-YOM u-VAYN k'-tay-FAV sha-KHAYN

13 And of *Yosef* he said: Blessed of *Hashem* be his land With the bounty of dew from heaven, And of the deep that couches below;

יג וּלְיוֹסֵף אָמַר מְבֹרֶכֶת יְהֹוָה אַרְצוֹ מִמֶּגֶד שָׁמַיִם מִטָּל וּמִתְּהוֹם רֹבֶצֶת תָּחַת:

14 With the bounteous yield of the sun, And the bounteous crop of the moons;

יד וּמִמֶּגֶד תְּבוּאֹת שָׁמֶשׁ וּמִמֶּגֶד גֶּרֶשׁ יְרָחִים:

15 With the best from the ancient mountains, And the bounty of hills immemorial;

טו וּמֵרֹאשׁ הַרְרֵי־קֶדֶם וּמִמֶּגֶד גִּבְעוֹת עוֹלָם:

16 With the bounty of earth and its fullness, And the favor of the Presence in the Bush. May these rest on the head of *Yosef*, On the crown of the elect of his brothers.

טז וּמִמֶּגֶד אֶרֶץ וּמְלֹאָהּ וּרְצוֹן שֹׁכְנִי סְנֶה תָּבוֹאתָה לְרֹאשׁ יוֹסֵף וּלְקָדְקֹד נְזִיר אֶחָיו:

17 Like a firstling bull in his majesty, He has horns like the horns of the wild-ox; With them he gores the peoples, The ends of the earth one and all. These are the myriads of *Efraim*, Those are the thousands of *Menashe*.

יז בְּכוֹר שׁוֹרוֹ הָדָר לוֹ וְקַרְנֵי רְאֵם קַרְנָיו בָּהֶם עַמִּים יְנַגַּח יַחְדָּו אַפְסֵי־אָרֶץ וְהֵם רִבְבוֹת אֶפְרַיִם וְהֵם אַלְפֵי מְנַשֶּׁה:

18 And of *Zevulun* he said: Rejoice, O *Zevulun*, on your journeys, And *Yissachar*, in your tents.

יח וְלִזְבוּלֻן אָמַר שְׂמַח זְבוּלֻן בְּצֵאתֶךָ וְיִשָּׂשכָר בְּאֹהָלֶיךָ:

19 They invite their kin to the mountain, Where they offer sacrifices of success. For they draw from the riches of the sea And the hidden hoards of the sand.

יט עַמִּים הַר־יִקְרָאוּ שָׁם יִזְבְּחוּ זִבְחֵי־צֶדֶק כִּי שֶׁפַע יַמִּים יִינָקוּ וּשְׂפֻנֵי טְמוּנֵי חוֹל:

20 And of *Gad* he said: Blessed be He who enlarges *Gad*! Poised is he like a lion To tear off arm and scalp.

כ וּלְגָד אָמַר בָּרוּךְ מַרְחִיב גָּד כְּלָבִיא שָׁכֵן וְטָרַף זְרוֹעַ אַף־קָדְקֹד:

21 He chose for himself the best, For there is the portion of the revered chieftain, Where the heads of the people come. He executed *Hashem*'s judgments And His decisions for *Yisrael*.

כא וַיַּרְא רֵאשִׁית לוֹ כִּי־שָׁם חֶלְקַת מְחֹקֵק סָפוּן וַיֵּתֵא רָאשֵׁי עָם צִדְקַת יְהֹוָה עָשָׂה וּמִשְׁפָּטָיו עִם־יִשְׂרָאֵל:

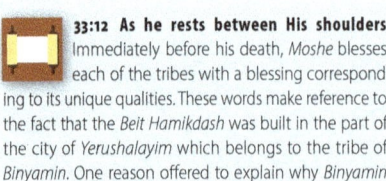

33:12 As he rests between His shoulders Immediately before his death, *Moshe* blesses each of the tribes with a blessing corresponding to its unique qualities. These words make reference to the fact that the *Beit Hamikdash* was built in the part of the city of *Yerushalayim* which belongs to the tribe of *Binyamin*. One reason offered to explain why *Binyamin* merited the *Beit Hamikdash* in his portion is that while all the other sons of *Yaakov* were born outside Israel, the youngest son, *Binyamin*, was born in the land (see Genesis 35:18). Therefore, he merited the special privilege of having the Temple in his territory.

Model of the Second *Beit Hamikdash*

88

Deuteronomy

22 And of *Dan* he said: *Dan* is a lion's whelp That leaps forth from Bashan.

כב וּלְדָן אָמַר דָּן גּוּר אַרְיֵה יְזַנֵּק מִן־הַבָּשָׁן:

23 And of *Naftali* he said: O *Naftali,* sated with favor And full of *Hashem*'s blessing, Take possession on the west and south.

כג וּלְנַפְתָּלִי אָמַר נַפְתָּלִי שְׂבַע רָצוֹן וּמָלֵא בִּרְכַּת יְהוָה יָם וְדָרוֹם יְרָשָׁה:

24 And of *Asher* he said: Most blessed of sons be *Asher*; May he be the favorite of his brothers, May he dip his foot in oil.

כד וּלְאָשֵׁר אָמַר בָּרוּךְ מִבָּנִים אָשֵׁר יְהִי רְצוּי אֶחָיו וְטֹבֵל בַּשֶּׁמֶן רַגְלוֹ:

25 May your doorbolts be iron and copper, And your security last all your days.

כה בַּרְזֶל וּנְחֹשֶׁת מִנְעָלֶיךָ וּכְיָמֶיךָ דָּבְאֶךָ:

26 O Jeshurun, there is none like *Hashem*, Riding through the heavens to help you, Through the skies in His majesty.

כו אֵין כָּאֵל יְשֻׁרוּן רֹכֵב שָׁמַיִם בְּעֶזְרֶךָ וּבְגַאֲוָתוֹ שְׁחָקִים:

27 The ancient *Hashem* is a refuge, A support are the arms everlasting. He drove out the enemy before you By His command: Destroy!

כז מְעֹנָה אֱלֹהֵי קֶדֶם וּמִתַּחַת זְרֹעֹת עוֹלָם וַיְגָרֶשׁ מִפָּנֶיךָ אוֹיֵב וַיֹּאמֶר הַשְׁמֵד:

28 Thus *Yisrael* dwells in safety, Untroubled is *Yaakov*'s abode, In a land of grain and wine, Under heavens dripping dew.

כח וַיִּשְׁכֹּן יִשְׂרָאֵל בֶּטַח בָּדָד עֵין יַעֲקֹב אֶל־אֶרֶץ דָּגָן וְתִירוֹשׁ אַף־שָׁמָיו יַעַרְפוּ טָל:

29 O happy *Yisrael*! Who is like you, A people delivered by *Hashem*, Your protecting Shield, your Sword triumphant! Your enemies shall come cringing before you, And you shall tread on their backs.

כט אַשְׁרֶיךָ יִשְׂרָאֵל מִי כָמוֹךָ עַם נוֹשַׁע בַּיהוָה מָגֵן עֶזְרֶךָ וַאֲשֶׁר־חֶרֶב גַּאֲוָתֶךָ וְיִכָּחֲשׁוּ אֹיְבֶיךָ לָךְ וְאַתָּה עַל־בָּמוֹתֵימוֹ תִדְרֹךְ:

34 1 *Moshe* went up from the steppes of Moab to Mount Nebo, to the summit of Pisgah, opposite *Yericho,* and *Hashem* showed him the whole land: Gilad as far as *Dan*;

לד א וַיַּעַל מֹשֶׁה מֵעַרְבֹת מוֹאָב אֶל־הַר נְבוֹ רֹאשׁ הַפִּסְגָּה אֲשֶׁר עַל־פְּנֵי יְרֵחוֹ וַיַּרְאֵהוּ יְהוָה אֶת־כָּל־הָאָרֶץ אֶת־הַגִּלְעָד עַד־דָּן:

*va-YA-al mo-SHEH may-ar-VOT mo-AV el HAR n'-VO ROSH
ha-pis-GAH a-SHER al p'-NAY y'-ray-KHO va-yar-AY-hu
a-do-NAI et kol ha-A-retz et ha-gil-AD ad DAN*

The Temple Mount at sunset

34:1 And *Hashem* showed him the whole land As the leader of the Jewish people, *Moshe* involved himself with all matters of concern to the nation. Yet, his final activity in this world was devoted to one area alone: *Moshe* ascends the mountain of *Nevo* and gazes upon the Land of Israel. The Talmud (*Sotah* 14a)

asks: Why did *Moshe* desire to enter *Eretz Yisrael*? Was it to enjoy its fruits or to satiate himself of its bounty? The Talmud answers that *Moshe*'s desire was a spiritual one; he craved an opportunity to keep the commandments unique to the Land of Israel. While he was not permitted to enter, being allowed to view the land was a comfort to *Moshe,* as he understood that even just seeing it propels a person to new spiritual heights. Similarly, there are people today who access high balconies in the Old City of *Yerushalayim* in order to view *Har Habayit,* the Temple Mount. They appreciate the spiritual benefit they can get just from seeing this holy sight.

2 all *Naftali*; the land of *Efraim* and *Menashe*; the whole land of *Yehuda* as far as the Western Sea;

3 the *Negev*; and the Plai n– the Valley of *Yericho*, the city of palm trees – as far as Zoar.

4 And *Hashem* said to him, "This is the land of which I swore to *Avraham*, *Yitzchak*, and *Yaakov*, 'I will assign it to your offspring.' I have let you see it with your own eyes, but you shall not cross there."

5 So *Moshe* the servant of *Hashem* died there, in the land of Moab, at the command of *Hashem*.

6 He buried him in the valley in the land of Moab, near Beth-peor; and no one knows his burial place to this day.

7 *Moshe* was a hundred and twenty years old when he died; his eyes were undimmed and his vigor unabated.

8 And the Israelites bewailed *Moshe* in the steppes of Moab for thirty days. The period of wailing and mourning for *Moshe* came to an end.

9 Now *Yehoshua* son of *Nun* was filled with the spirit of wisdom because *Moshe* had laid his hands upon him; and the Israelites heeded him, doing as *Hashem* had commanded *Moshe*.

10 Never again did there arise in *Yisrael* a *navi* like *Moshe* – whom *Hashem* singled out, face to face,

11 for the various signs and portents that *Hashem* sent him to display in the land of Egypt, against Pharaoh and all his courtiers and his whole country,

12 and for all the great might and awesome power that *Moshe* displayed before all *Yisrael*.

ב וְאֵת כָּל־נַפְתָּלִי וְאֶת־אֶרֶץ אֶפְרַיִם וּמְנַשֶּׁה וְאֵת כָּל־אֶרֶץ יְהוּדָה עַד הַיָּם הָאַחֲרוֹן:

ג וְאֶת־הַנֶּגֶב וְאֶת־הַכִּכָּר בִּקְעַת יְרֵחוֹ עִיר הַתְּמָרִים עַד־צֹעַר:

ד וַיֹּאמֶר יְהֹוָה אֵלָיו זֹאת הָאָרֶץ אֲשֶׁר נִשְׁבַּעְתִּי לְאַבְרָהָם לְיִצְחָק וּלְיַעֲקֹב לֵאמֹר לְזַרְעֲךָ אֶתְּנֶנָּה הֶרְאִיתִיךָ בְעֵינֶיךָ וְשָׁמָּה לֹא תַעֲבֹר:

ה וַיָּמָת שָׁם מֹשֶׁה עֶבֶד־יְהֹוָה בְּאֶרֶץ מוֹאָב עַל־פִּי יְהֹוָה:

ו וַיִּקְבֹּר אֹתוֹ בַגַּיְ בְּאֶרֶץ מוֹאָב מוּל בֵּית פְּעוֹר וְלֹא־יָדַע אִישׁ אֶת־קְבֻרָתוֹ עַד הַיּוֹם הַזֶּה:

ז וּמֹשֶׁה בֶּן־מֵאָה וְעֶשְׂרִים שָׁנָה בְּמֹתוֹ לֹא־כָהֲתָה עֵינוֹ וְלֹא־נָס לֵחֹה:

ח וַיִּבְכּוּ בְנֵי יִשְׂרָאֵל אֶת־מֹשֶׁה בְּעַרְבֹת מוֹאָב שְׁלֹשִׁים יוֹם וַיִּתְּמוּ יְמֵי בְכִי אֵבֶל מֹשֶׁה:

ט וִיהוֹשֻׁעַ בִּן־נוּן מָלֵא רוּחַ חָכְמָה כִּי־סָמַךְ מֹשֶׁה אֶת־יָדָיו עָלָיו וַיִּשְׁמְעוּ אֵלָיו בְּנֵי־יִשְׂרָאֵל וַיַּעֲשׂוּ כַּאֲשֶׁר צִוָּה יְהֹוָה אֶת־מֹשֶׁה:

י וְלֹא־קָם נָבִיא עוֹד בְּיִשְׂרָאֵל כְּמֹשֶׁה אֲשֶׁר יְדָעוֹ יְהֹוָה פָּנִים אֶל־פָּנִים:

יא לְכָל־הָאֹתֹת וְהַמּוֹפְתִים אֲשֶׁר שְׁלָחוֹ יְהֹוָה לַעֲשׂוֹת בְּאֶרֶץ מִצְרָיִם לְפַרְעֹה וּלְכָל־עֲבָדָיו וּלְכָל־אַרְצוֹ:

יב וּלְכֹל הַיָּד הַחֲזָקָה וּלְכֹל הַמּוֹרָא הַגָּדוֹל אֲשֶׁר עָשָׂה מֹשֶׁה לְעֵינֵי כָּל־יִשְׂרָאֵל:

List of Transliterated Words in *The Israel Bible*

The following is a list of nouns which have been transliterated into Hebrew in the English translation and commentary of *The Israel Bible*:

Hebrew Name	English Name	Pronunciation	Hebrew
Achan	Achan	a-KHAN	עָכָן
Achav	Ahab	akh-AV	אַחְאָב
Achaz	Ahaz	a-KHAZ	אָחָז
Achazyahu	Ahaziah	a-khaz-YA-hu	אֲחַזְיָהוּ
Achiezer	Ahiezer	a-khee-E-zer	אֲחִיעֶזֶר
Achihud	Ahihud	a-khee-HUD	אֲחִיהוּד
Achikam	Ahikam	a-khee-KAM	אֲחִיקָם
Achilud	Ahilud	a-khee-LUD	אֲחִילוּד
Achimelech	Ahimelech	a-khee-ME-lekh	אֲחִימֶלֶךְ
Achira	Ahira	a-khee-RA	אֲחִירַע
Achisamach	Ahisamach	a-khee-sa-MAKH	אֲחִיסָמָךְ
Achitofel	Ahithophel	a-khee-TO-fel	אֲחִיתֹפֶל
Achituv	Ahitub	a-khee-TUV	אֲחִיטוּב
Achiya	Ahijah	a-khi-YAH	אֲחִיָּה
Adam	Adam	a-DAM	אָדָם
Adar	Adar	a-DAR	אֲדָר
Adoniyahu	Adonijah	a-do-ni-YA-hu	אֲדֹנִיָּהוּ
Adulam	Adullam	a-du-LAM	עֲדֻלָּם
Agur	Agur	a-GUR	אָגוּר
Aharon	Aaron	a-ha-RON	אַהֲרֹן
Amasa	Amasa	a-ma-SA	עֲמָשָׂא
Amatzya	Amaziah	a-matz-YAH	אֲמַצְיָה
Amen	Amen	a-MAYN	אָמֵן
Amiel	Ammiel	a-mee-AYL	עַמִּיאֵל
Aminadav	Amminadab	a-mee-na-DAV	עַמִּינָדָב
Amitai	Amittai	a-mi-TAI	אֲמִתַּי
Amnon	Amnon	am-NON	אַמְנֹן

91

Hebrew Name	English Name	Pronunciation	Hebrew
Amon	Amon	a-MON	אָמוֹן
Amos	Amos	a-MOS	עָמוֹס
Amotz	Amoz	a-MOTZ	אָמוֹץ
Amram	Amram	am-RAM	עַמְרָם
Anatot	Anathoth	a-na-TOT	עֲנָתוֹת
Aron	Ark	a-RON	אָרוֹן
Aron HaBrit	Ark of the Covenant	a-RON ha-b'-REET	אָרוֹן הַבְּרִית
Arpachshad	Arpachshad	ar-pakh-SHAD	אַרְפַּכְשַׁד
Asa	Asa	a-SA	אָסָא
Asael	Asahel	a-sah-AYL	עֲשָׂהאֵל
Asaf	Asaph	a-SAF	אָסָף
Ashdod	Ashdod	ash-DOD	אַשְׁדּוֹד
Asher	Asher	a-SHAYR	אָשֵׁר
Ashkelon	Ashkelon	ash-k'-LON	אַשְׁקְלוֹן
Atalya	Athaliah	a-tal-YAH	עֲתַלְיָה
Avdon	Abdon	av-DON	עַבְדּוֹן
Avichayil	Abihail	a-vee-KHA-yil	אֲבִיחַיִל
Avidan	Abidan	a-vee-DAN	אֲבִידָן
Avigail	Abigail	a-vee-GA-yil	אֲבִיגַיִל
Avihu	Abihu	a-vee-HU	אֲבִיהוּא
Avimelech	Abimelech	a-vee-ME-lekh	אֲבִימֶלֶךְ
Avinadav	Abinadab	a-vee-na-DAV	אֲבִינָדָב
Aviram	Abiram	a-vee-RAM	אֲבִירָם
Avishai	Abishai	a-vee-SHAI	אֲבִישַׁי
Aviya	Abijah	a-vi-YAH	אֲבִיָּה
Aviyam	Abijam	a-vi-YAM	אֲבִיָּם
Avner	Abner	av-NAYR	אַבְנֵר
Avraham	Abraham	av-ra-HAM	אַבְרָהָם
Avram	Abram	av-RAM	אַבְרָם
Avshalom	Absalom	av-sha-LOM	אַבְשָׁלוֹם
Azarya	Azariah	a-zar-YAH	עֲזַרְיָה
Azeika	Azekah	a-zay-KAH	עֲזֵקָה
Azza	Gaza	a-ZAH	עַזָּה

Hebrew Name	English Name	Pronunciation	Hebrew
B'nei Yisrael	The Children of Israel	b'-NAY yis-ra-AYL	בְּנֵי יִשְׂרָאֵל
Barak	Barak	ba-rakh-AYL	בָּרָק
Baruch	Baruch	ba-RUKH	בָּרוּךְ
Barzilai	Barzillai	bar-zi-LAI	בַּרְזִלַּי
Basha	Baasa	ba-SHA	בַּעְשָׁא
Batsheva	Bath-sheba	bat-SHE-va	בַּת־שֶׁבַע
Be'er Sheva	Beer-sheba	b'-AYR SHE-va	בְּאֵר שֶׁבַע
Be'eri	Beeri	b'-ay-REE	בְּאֵרִי
Beit Aven	Beth-aven	bayt A-ven	בֵּית אָוֶן
Beit El	Beth-el	bayt el	בֵּית אֵל
Beit Hamikdash	Temple	bayt ha-mik-DASH	בֵּית הַמִּקְדָּשׁ
Beit Lechem	Beth-lehem	bayt LE-khem	בֵּית לָחֶם
Beit Shean	Beth-shean	bayt sh'-AN	בֵּית שְׁאָן
Beit Shemesh	Beth-shemesh	bayt SHE-mesh	בֵּית שָׁמֶשׁ
Berechya	Berechiah	be-rekh-YAH	בֶּרֶכְיָה
Betzalel	Bezalel	b'-tzal-AYL	בְּצַלְאֵל
Bilha	Bilhah	bil-HAH	בִּלְהָה
Binyamin	Benjamin	bin-ya-MIN	בִּנְיָמִין
Boaz	Boaz	BO-az	בֹּעַז
Buki	Bukki	bu-KEE	בֻּקִּי
Buzi	Buzi	bu-ZEE	בּוּזִי
Carmel	Carmel	kar-MEL	כַּרְמֶל
Chachalya	Hacaliah	kha-khal-YAH	חֲכַלְיָה
Chagai	Haggai	kha-GAI	חַגַּי
Chana	Hannah	kha-NAH	חַנָּה
Chanamel	Hanamel	kha-nam-AYL	חֲנַמְאֵל
Chanani	Hanani	kha-NA-nee	חֲנָנִי
Chananya	Hananiah	kha-nan-YAH	חֲנַנְיָה
Chaniel	Hanniel	kha-nee-AYL	חַנִּיאֵל
Chanoch	Enoch	kha-NOKH	חֲנוֹךְ
Chava	Eve	kha-VAH	חַוָּה
Chavakuk	Habakkuk	kha-va-KUK	חֲבַקּוּק
Chermon	Hermon	kher-MON	חֶרְמוֹן

Hebrew Name	English Name	Pronunciation	Hebrew
Chetzron	Hezron	khetz-RON	חֶצְרוֹן
Chever	Heber	KHE-ver	חֶבֶר
Chevron	Hebron	khev-RON	חֶבְרוֹן
Chilkiyahu	Hilkiah	khil-ki-YA-hu	חִלְקִיָהוּ
Chizkiyahu	Hezekiah	khiz-ki-YA-hu	חִזְקִיָהוּ
Chofni	Hophni	khof-NEE	חָפְנִי
Chogla	Hoglah	khog-LAH	חָגְלָה
Chulda	Hulda	khul-DAH	חֻלְדָה
Chur	Hur	Khur	חוּר
Dan	Dan	Dan	דָן
Daniel	Daniel	da-ni-YAYL	דָנִיֵאל
Datan	Dathan	da-TAN	דָתָן
David	David	da-VID	דָוִד
Devora	Deborah	d'-vo-RAH	דְבוֹרָה
Dina	Dinah	DEE-nah	דִינָה
Doeg Ha'adomi	Doeg the Edomite	do-AYG ha-a-do-MEE	דוֹאֵג הָאֲדֹמִי
Efraim	Ephraim	ef-RA-yim	אֶפְרַיִם
Efrat	Ephrat	ef-RAT	אֶפְרָתָה
Efrat	Ephrathah	ef-RA-tah	אֶפְרָתָה
Ehud	Ehud	ay-HUD	אֵהוּד
Eila	Elah	AY-lah	אֵלָה
Eilon	Elon	ay-LON	אֵילוֹן
Ein Gedi	En-gedi	ayn GE-dee	עֵין גֶּדִי
Elazar	Eleazar	el-a-ZAR	אֶלְעָזָר
Elchanan	Elhanan	el-kha-NAN	אֶלְחָנָן
Eli	Eli	ay-LEE	עֵלִי
Eliav	Eliab	e-lee-AV	אֱלִיאָב
Elidad	Elidad	e-lee-DAD	אֱלִידָד
Eliezer	Eliezer	e-lee-E-zer	אֱלִיעֶזֶר
Elimelech	Elimelech	e-lee-ME-lekh	אֱלִימֶלֶךְ
Elisha	Elisha	e-lee-SHA	אֱלִישָׁע
Elishama	Elishama	e-lee-sha-MA	אֱלִישָׁמָע

Hebrew Name	English Name	Pronunciation	Hebrew
Elisheva	Elisheba	e-lee-SHE-va	אֱלִישֶׁבַע
Elitzafan	Eli-zaphan	e-lee-tza-FAN	אֱלִיצָפָן
Elitzur	Elizur	e-lee-TZUR	אֱלִיצוּר
Eliyahu	Elijah	ay-li-YA-hu	אֵלִיָּהוּ
Elkana	Elkanah	el-ka-NAH	אֶלְקָנָה
Elyasaf	Eliasaph	el-ya-SAF	אֶלְיָסָף
Elyashiv	Eliashib	el-ya-SHEEV	אֶלְיָשִׁיב
Enosh	Enosh	e-NOSH	אֱנוֹשׁ
Er	Er	ayr	עֵר
Eshtaol	Eshtaol	esh-ta-OL	אֶשְׁתָּאֹל
Esther	Esther	es-TAYR	אֶסְתֵּר
Eved Melech	Ebed-melech	E-ved ME-lekh	עֶבֶד־מֶלֶךְ
Even Ha-Ezer	Eben-Ezer	E-ven ha-E-zer	אֶבֶן הָעֶזֶר
Ever	Eber	AY-ver	עֵבֶר
Evyatar	Abiathar	ev-ya-TAR	אֶבְיָתָר
Ezra	Ezra	ez-RA	עֶזְרָא
Gad	Gad	gad	גָּד
Gadi	Gaddi	ga-DEE	גַּדִּי
Gadiel	Gaddiel	ga-dee-AYL	גַּדִּיאֵל
Gamliel	Gamaliel	gam-lee-AYL	גַּמְלִיאֵל
Gedalia	Gedaliah	g'-dal-YA (hu)	גְּדַלְיָהוּ
Gedera	Gederah	g'-day-RAH	גְּדֵרָה
Gershom	Gershom	gay-r'-SHOM	גֵּרְשׁוֹם
Gershon	Gershon	gay-r'-SHON	גֵּרְשׁוֹן
Geshem	Geshem	GE-shem	גֶּשֶׁם
Geuel	Geuel	g'-u-AYL	גְּאוּאֵל
Gidon	Gideon	gid-ON	גִּדְעוֹן
Gilad	Gilead	gil-AD	גִּלְעָד
Gilgal	Gilgal	gil-GAL	גִּלְגָּל
Giva	Gibeah	giv-AH	גִּבְעָה
Givon	Gibeon	giv-ON	גִּבְעוֹן
Hadassa	Hadassah	ha-da-SAH	הֲדַסָּה

Hebrew Name	English Name	Pronunciation	Hebrew
Har Eival	Mount Ebal	ay-VAL	הַר עֵיבָל
Har Gerizim	Mount Gerizim	g'-ri-ZEEM	הַר גְּרִזִים
Har HaBayit	Temple Mount	har ha-BA-yit	הַר הַבַּיִת
Har HaZeitim	the Mount of Olives	har ha-zay-TEEM	הַר הַזֵּיתִים
Hashem	Lord/God		
Hayman	Heman	hay-MAN	הֵימָן
Hoshea	Hosea	ho-SHAY-a	הוֹשֵׁעַ
Ido	Iddo	i-DO	עִדּוֹ
Imanu-El	Immanuel	i-MA-nu ayl	עִמָּנוּ אֵל
Ish-boshet	Ish-bosheth	eesh BO-shet	אִישׁ־בֹּשֶׁת
Itamar	Ithamar	ee-ta-MAR	אִיתָמָר
Itiel	Ithiel	ee-tee-AYL	אִיתִיאֵל
Ivtzan	Ibzan	iv-TZAN	אִבְצָן
Iyov	Job	i-YOV	אִיּוֹב
Kadmiel	Kadmiel	kad-mee-AYL	קַדְמִיאֵל
Kalev	Caleb	ka-LAYV	כָּלֵב
Keesh	Kish	keesh	קִישׁ
Kehat	Kohath	k'-HAT	קְהָת
Keinan	Kenan	kay-NAN	קֵינָן
Kemuel	Kemuel	k'-mu-AYL	קְמוּאֵל
Keruvim	Cherubim	k'-ru-VEEM	כְּרוּבִים
Kilyon	Chilion	kil-YON	כִּלְיוֹן
Kiryat Arba	Kiriath-arba	keer-YAT AR-bah	קִרְיַת אַרְבַּע
Kiryat Sefer	Kiriath-sepher	keer-YAT SAY-fer	קִרְיַת־סֵפֶר
Kiryat Ye'arim	Kiriath-jearim	keer-YAT y'-a-REEM	קִרְיַת יְעָרִים
Kislev	Chislev	kis-LAYV	כִּסְלֵו
Kohanim	Priests	ko-ha-NEEM	כֹּהֲנִים
Kohelet	Koheleth	ko-HE-let	קֹהֶלֶת
Kohen	Priest	ko-HAYN	כֹּהֵן
Kohen Gadol	High Priest	ko-HAYN ga-DOL	כֹּהֵן גָּדוֹל
Korach	Korah	KO-rakh	קֹרַח
Kushi	Cushi	ku-SHEE	כּוּשִׁי

96

Hebrew Name	English Name	Pronunciation	Hebrew
Lachish	Lachish	la-KHEESH	לָכִיש
Leah	Leah	lay-AH	לֵאָה
Lemech	Lamech	LE-mekh	לֶמֶךְ
Lemuel	Lemuel	l'-mu-AYL	לְמוֹאֵל
Levi	Levi	lay-VEE	לֵוִי
Leviim	Levites	l'-vee-IM	לְוִים
Machla	Mahlah	makh-LAH	מַחְלָה
Machlon	Mahlon	makh-LON	מַחְלוֹן
Machseya	Mahseiah	makh-say-YAH	מַחְסֵיָה
Malachi	Malachi	mal-a-KHEE	מַלְאָכִי
Manoach	Manoah	ma-NO-akh	מָנוֹחַ
Mashiach	Messiah	ma-SHEE-akh	מָשִׁיחַ
Mefiboshet	Mephibosheth	m'-fee-VO-shet	מְפִיבֹשֶׁת
Mehalalel	Mahalalel	ma-ha-lal-AYL	מַהֲלַלְאֵל
Menachem	Menahem	m'-na-KHAYM	מְנַחֵם
Menashe	Menasseh	m'-na-SHEH	מְנַשֶּׁה
Menorah	Candlestick	m'-no-RAH	מְנֹרָה
Merari	Merari	m'-ra-REE	מְרָרִי
Metushelach	Methusaleh	m'-tu-SHE-lakh	מְתוּשֶׁלָח
Micha	Micah	mee-KHAH	מִיכָה
Michael	Michael	mee-kha-AYL	מִיכָאֵל
Michaihu	Micaiah	mee-KHAI-hu	מִיכָיְהוּ
Michal	Michal	mee-KHAL	מִיכַל
Milka	Milcah	mil-KAH	מִלְכָּה
Miriam	Miriam	mir-YAM	מִרְיָם
Mishael	Mishael	mee-sha-AYL	מִישָׁאֵל
Mishkan	Tabernacle	mish-KAN	מִשְׁכַּן
Mitzpa	Mizpah	mitz-PAH	מִצְפָּה
Mizbayach	Altar	miz-BAY-akh	מִזְבֵּחַ
Mordechai	Mordecai	mor-d'-KHAI	מָרְדְּכַי
Moriah	Moriah	mo-ri-YAH	מוֹרִיָּה
Moshe	Moses	mo-SHEH	מֹשֶׁה

Hebrew Name	English Name	Pronunciation	Hebrew
Nachbi	Nahbi	nakh-BEE	נַחְבִּי
Nachor	Nahor	na-KHOR	נָחוֹר
Nachshon	Nahshon	nakh-SHON	נַחְשׁוֹן
Nachum	Nahum	na-KHUM	נַחוּם
Nadav	Nadab	na-DAV	נָדָב
Naftali	Naphtali	naf-ta-LEE	נַפְתָּלִי
Naomi	Naomi	na-o-MEE	נָעֳמִי
Natan	Nathan	na-TAN	נָתָן
Naval	Nabal	na-VAL	נָבָל
Navi	Prophet	na-VEE	נָבִיא
Navot	Naboth	na-VAL	נָבֵל
Nechemya	Nehemiah	n'-khem-YAH	נְחֶמְיָה
Negev	Negeb	NE-gev	נֶגֶב
Nerya	Neriah	nay-ri-YAH	נֵרִיָּה
Netanel	Nethanel	n'-tan-AYL	נְתַנְאֵל
Neviah	Prophetess	n'-vee-AH	נְבִיאָה
Neviim	Prophets	n'-vee-EEM	נְבִיאִים
Nisan	Nisan	nee-SAN	נִיסָן
Noa	Noah	no-AH	נֹעָה
Noach	Noah	NO-akh	נֹחַ
Nov	Nob	nov	נֹב
Nun	Nun	nun	נוּן
Oded	Oded	o-DAYD	עוֹדֵד
Ohola	Oholah	a-ho-LAH	אָהֳלָה
Oholiav	Oholiab	o-ha-lee-AV	אָהֳלִיאָב
Oholiva	Oholibah	a-ho-lee-VAH	אָהֳלִיבָה
Omri	Omri	om-REE	עָמְרִי
Onan	Onan	o-NAN	אוֹנָן
Otniel	Othniel	ot-nee-AYL	עָתְנִיאֵל
Ovadya	Obadiah	o-vad-YAH	עֹבַדְיָה
Oved	Obed	o-VAYD	עוֹבֵד
Oved Edom	Obed Edom	o-VAYD e-DOM	עוֹבֵד אֱדוֹם

98

Hebrew Name	English Name	Pronunciation	Hebrew
Pagiel	Pagiel	pag-ee-AYL	פַּגְעִיאֵל
Palti	Palti	pal-TEE	פַּלְטִי
Paltiel	Paltiel	pal-tee-AYL	פַּלְטִיאֵל
Pekach	Pekah	PE-kakh	פֶּקַח
Pedael	Pedahel	p'-da-AYL	פְּדַהְאֵל
Pekachya	Pekahiah	p'-kakh-YAH	פְּקַחְיָה
Peleg	Peleg	PE-leg	פֶּלֶג
Penina	Peninnah	p'-ni-NAH	פְּנִנָּה
Peretz	Perez	PE-retz	פֶּרֶץ
Petuel	Pethuel	p'-tu-AYL	פְּתוּאֵל
Pinchas	Phinehas	peen-KHAS	פִּינְחָס
Rachel	Rachel	ra-KHAYL	רָחֵל
Ram	Ram	ram	רָם
Rama	Ramah	ra-MAH	רָמָה
Re'u	Reu	r'-U	רְעוּ
Rechovam	Rehoboam	r'-khav-AM	רְחַבְעָם
Reuven	Reuben	r'-u-VAYN	רְאוּבֵן
Rivka	Rebecca	riv-KAH	רִבְקָה
Rut	Ruth	rut	רוּת
Salma	Salmon/Salmah	sal-MAH	שַׂלְמָה
Salmon	Salmon	sal-MON	שַׂלְמוֹן
Sara	Sarah	sa-RAH	שָׂרָה
Sarai	Sarai	sa-RAI	שָׂרַי
Selah	Selah	SE-lah	סֶלָה
Seraya	Seraiah	s'-ra-YAH	שְׂרָיָה
Serug	Serug	s'-RUG	שְׂרוּג
Setur	Sethur	s'-TUR	סְתוּר
Shaarayim	Shaaraim	sha-a-RA-yim	שַׁעֲרַיִם
Shabbat	Sabbath	sha-BAT	שַׁבָּת
Shabbatot	Sabbaths	sha-ba-TOT	שַׁבָּתוֹת
Shafan	Shaphan	sha-FAN	שָׁפָן
Shafat	Shaphat	sha-FAT	שָׁפָט

Hebrew Name	English Name	Pronunciation	Hebrew
Shalem	Salem	sha-LAYM	שָׁלֵם
Shalum	Shallum	sha-LUM	שַׁלּוּם
Shamgar	Shamgar	sham-GAR	שַׁמְגַּר
Shamua	Shammua	sha-MU-a	שַׁמּוּעַ
Shaul	Saul	sha-UL	שָׁאוּל
Shealtiel	Shealtiel	sh'-al-tee-AYL	שְׁאַלְתִּיאֵל
Shear Yashuv	Shear-Jashub	sh'-AR ya-SHUV	שְׁאָר יָשׁוּב
Shechanya	Shecaniah	sh'-khan-YAH	שְׁכַנְיָה
Shechem	Shechem	sh'-KHEM	שְׁכֶם
Sheila	Shelah	shay-LAH	שֵׁלָה
Shelach	Shelah	SHE-lakh	שֶׁלַח
Shelumiel	Shelumiel	sh'-lu-mee-AYL	שְׁלֻמִיאֵל
Shem	Shem	Shaym	שֵׁם
Shemaya	Shemaiah	sh'-ma-YAH	שְׁמַעְיָה
Sheshbatzar	Sheshbazzar	shaysh-ba-TZAR	שֵׁשְׁבַּצַּר
Shet	Seth	Shayt	שֵׁת
Shevat	Shebat	sh'-VAT	שְׁבָט
Shilo	Shiloh	shi-LOH	שִׁלֹה
Shim'i	Shimei	shim-EE	שִׁמְעִי
Shimon	Simeon	shim-ON	שִׁמְעוֹן
Shimshon	Samson	shim-SHON	שִׁמְשׁוֹן
Shlomo	Solomon	sh'-lo-MOH	שְׁלֹמֹה
Shmuel	Samuel	sh'-mu-AYL	שְׁמוּאֵל
Shofar	Horn	sho-FAR	שׁוֹפָר
Shofarot	Horns	sho-fa-ROT	שׁוֹפָרוֹת
Shomron	Samaria	sho-m'-RON	שֹׁמְרוֹן
Sivan	Sivan	see-VAN	סִיוָן
Tamar	Tamar	ta-MAR	תָּמָר
Tanakh	Hebrew Bible	ta-NAKH	תָּנַ"ךְ
Tapuach	Tappuah	ta-PU-akh	תַּפּוּחַ
Tavor	Tabor	ta-VOR	תָּבוֹר
Tekoa	Tekoa	t'-KO-a	תְּקוֹעָה

100

Hebrew Name	English Name	Pronunciation	Hebrew
Terach	Terah	TE-rakh	תֶּרַח
Teveria	Tiberias	t'-ver-YAH	טְבֶרְיָה
Tevet	Tebeth	tay-VAYT	טֵבֵת
Tirtza	Tirzah	tir-TZAH	תִּרְצָה
Tola	Tola	to-LA	תּוֹלָע
Tzadok	Zadok	tza-DOK	צָדוֹק
Tzefanya	Zephaniah	tz'-fan-YAH	צְפַנְיָה
Tzelofchad	Zelophehad	tz'-la-f'-KHAD	צְלָפְחָד
Tzeruya	Zeruiah	tz'-ru-YAH	צְרוּיָה
Tzfat	Safed	tz'-FAT	צְפַת
Tzidkiyahu	Zedekiah	tzid-ki-YA-hu	צִדְקִיָּהוּ
Tziklag	Ziklag	tzi-k'-LAG	צִקְלַג
Tzion	Zion	tzi-YON	צִיּוֹן
Tzipora	Zipporah	tzi-po-RAH	צִפֹּרָה
Tzora	Zorah	tzor-AH	צָרְעָה
Tzuriel	Zuriel	tzu-ree-AYL	צוּרִיאֵל
Ukal	Ucal	u-KAL	אֻכָל
Uri	Uri	u-REE	אוּרִי
Uriya	Uriah	u-ri-YAH	אוּרִיָּה
Utz	Uz	Utz	עוּץ
Uzziyahu	Uzziah	u-zi-YA-hu	עֻזִּיָּהוּ
Yaakov	Jacob	ya-a-KOV	יַעֲקֹב
Yachaziel	Jahaziel	ya-kha-zee-AYL	יַחֲזִיאֵל
Yael	Jael	ya-AYL	יָעֵל
Yaffo	Joppa/Jaffa	ya-FO	יָפוֹ
Yair	Jair	ya-EER	יָאִיר
Yakeh	Jakeh	ya-KEH	יָקֶה
Yarden	Jordan	yar-DAYN	יַרְדֵּן
Yarmut	Jarmuth	yar-MUT	יַרְמוּת
Yechezkel	Ezekiel	y'-khez-KAYL	יְחֶזְקֵאל
Yechiel	Jehiel	y'-khee-AYL	יְחִיאֵל
Yechonya	Jeconiah	y'-khon-YAH	יְכָנְיָה

Hebrew Name	English Name	Pronunciation	Hebrew
Yedutun	Jeduthun	y'-du-TUN	יְדוּתוּן
Yehoachaz	Jehoahaz	y'-ho-a-KHAZ	יְהוֹאָחָז
Yehoash	Jehoash	y'-ho-ASH	יְהוֹאָשׁ
Yehochanan	Jehohanan	y'-ho-kha-NAN	יְהוֹחָנָן
Yehonatan	Jonathan	y'-ho-na-TAN	יְהוֹנָתָן
Yehoram	Jehoram	y'-ho-RAM	יְהוֹרָם
Yehoshafat	Jehoshaphat	y'-ho-sha-FAT	יְהוֹשָׁפָט
Yehoshavat	Jehoshabeath	y'-ho-shav-AT	יְהוֹשַׁבְעַת
Yehosheva	Jehosheba	y-ho-SHE-va	יְהוֹשֶׁבַע
Yehoshua	Joshua	y'-ho-SHU-a	יְהוֹשֻׁעַ
Yehotzadak	Jehozadak	y'-ho-tza-DAK	יְהוֹצָדָק
Yehoyachin	Jehoiachin	y'-ho-ya-KHEEN	יְהוֹיָכִין
Yehoyada	Jehoiada	y'-ho-ya-DA	יְהוֹיָדָע
Yehoyakim	Jehoiakim	y'-ho-ya-KEEM	יְהוֹיָקִים
Yehu	Jehu	yay-HU	יֵהוּא
Yehuda	Judah	y'-hu-DAH	יְהוּדָה
Yehudi	Jew	y'-hu-DEE	יְהוּדִי
Yehudim	Jews	y'-hu-DEEM	יְהוּדִים
Yered	Jared	YE-red	יֶרֶד
Yericho	Jericho	y'-ree-KHO	יְרִיחוֹ
Yerovam	Jeroboam	ya-rov-AM	יָרָבְעָם
Yerubaal	Jerubbaal	y'-ru-BA-al	יְרֻבַּעַל
Yerushalayim	Jerusalem	y'-ru-sha-LA-yim	יְרוּשָׁלַיִם
Yeshayahu	Isaiah	y'-sha-YA-hu	יְשַׁעְיָהוּ
Yeshua	Jeshua	yay-SHU-a	יֵשׁוּעַ
Yiftach	Jephthah	yif-TAKH	יִפְתָּח
Yigal	Igal	yig-AL	יִגְאָל
Yirmiyahu	Jeremiah	yir-m'-YA-hu	יִרְמְיָהוּ
Yishai	Jesse	yi-SHAI	יִשַׁי
Yisrael	Israel	yis-ra-AYL	יִשְׂרָאֵל
Yissachar	Issachar	yi-sa-KHAR	יִשָּׂשכָר
Yitzchak	Issac	yitz-KHAK	יִצְחָק

Hebrew Name	English Name	Pronunciation	Hebrew
Yizrael	Jezreel	yiz-r'-EL	יִזְרְעֶאל
Yoash	Joash	yo-ASH	יוֹאָשׁ
Yoav	Joab	yo-AV	יוֹאָב
Yochanan	Johanan	yo-kha-NAN	יוֹחָנָן
Yocheved	Jochebed	yo-KHE-ved	יוֹכֶבֶד
Yoel	Joel	yo-AYL	יוֹאֵל
Yona	Jonah	yo-NAH	יוֹנָה
Yonadav	Jonadab	yo-na-DAV	יוֹנָדָב
Yonatan	Jonathan	yo-na-TAN	יוֹנָתָן
Yoram	Joram	yo-RAM	יוֹרָם
Yosef	Joseph	yo-SAYF	יוֹסֵף
Yoshiyahu	Josiah	yo-shi-YA-hu	יֹאשִׁיָּהוּ
Yotam	Jotham	yo-TAM	יוֹתָם
Yotzadak	Jozadak	yo-tza-DAK	יוֹצָדָק
Yozavad	Jozabad	yo-za-VAD	יוֹזָבָד
Zanoach	Zanoah	za-NO-akh	זָנוֹחַ
Zecharya	Zechariah	z'-khar-YAH	זְכַרְיָה
Zerach	Zerah	ZE-rakh	זֶרַח
Zerubavel	Zerubbabel	z'-ru-ba-VEL	זְרֻבָּבֶל
Zevulun	Zebulun	z'-vu-LUN	זְבוּלֻן
Zilpa	Zilpah	zil-PAH	זִלְפָּה
Zimri	Zimri	zim-REE	זִמְרִי

Jewish Holidays

Chanukah	Hanukkah	kha-nu-KAH	חֲנוּכָּה
Pesach	Passover	PE-sakh	פֶּסַח
Purim	Purim	pu-REEM	פּוּרִים
Rosh Hashana	Jewish New Year	rosh ha-sha-NAH	רֹאשׁ הַשָּׁנָה
Shavuot	Feast of Weeks	sha-vu-OT	שָׁבוּעוֹת
Shemini Atzeret	Eight Day of Assembly	sh'-mee-NEE a-TZE-ret	שְׁמִינִי עֲצֶרֶת
Sukkot	Feast of Tabernacles	su-KOT	סֻכּוֹת
Yom Kippur	Day of Atonement	yom kee-PUR	יוֹם כִּיפּוּר

Hebrew Name	English Name	Pronunciation	Hebrew
Biblical Measurements			
Amah	Cubit	a-MAH	אַמָה
Amot	Cubits	a-MOT	אַמוֹת
Bat	Bath	bat	בַּת
Batim	Baths	ba-TEEM	בָּתִּים
Beka	half-shekel	BE-ka	בֶּקַע
Chomarim	Homers	kho-ma-REEM	חֳמָרִים
Chomer	Homer	KHO-mer	חֹמֶר
Efah	Ephah	ay-FAH	אֵיפָה
Geira	Gerah	gay-RAH	גֵּרָה
Gomed	Gomed	GO- med	גֹּמֶד
Hin	Hin	heen	הִין
Kav	kab	kav	קַב
Kesita	kesitah	k'-see-TAH	קְשִׂיטָה
Kikar	talent	ki-KAR	כִּכָּר
Kikarim	talents	ki-ka-RIM	כִּכָּרִים
Kor	kor	kor	כֹּר
Letek	lethech	LE-tek	לֶתֶךְ
Log	Log	log	לֹג
Maneh	Mina	ma-NEH	מָנֶה
Manim	Minas	ma-NEEM	מָנִים
Omer	Omer	O-mer	עֹמֶר
Pim	Pim	peem	פִּים
Se'ah	Seah	say-AH	סְאָה
Se'eem	Seahs	s'-EEM	סְאִים
Shekalim	Shekels	sh'-ka-LEEM	שְׁקָלִים
Shekel	Shekel	SHE-kel	שֶׁקֶל
Tefach	Handbreadth	TE-fakh	טֶפַח
Zeret	Span	ZE-ret	זֶרֶת

Photo Credits

1:1 Inna Reznik/Shutterstock.com, 1:25 Avi Ohayon / GPO, 2:9 MoLarjung/ Shutterstock.com, 3:18 David 1 / Wikimedia Commons, 3:25 RnDmS / Shutterstock.com, 4:35 Liron-Afuta/Shutterstock.com, 5:28 Yair Aronshtam / Shutterstock.com, 6:6 Boris Diakovsky/Shutterstock.com, 7:12 Guy Zidel / Shutterstock.com, 7:22 Alexander Ingerman / Shutterstock.com, 8:8 Wikimedia Commons, 9:1 dnaveh / Shutterstock.com, 10:19 Courtesy of Israel365, 11:12 Alexey Stiop / Shutterstock.com, 12:5 Avi Ohayon / GPO, 12:10 Alexandre Rotenberg / Shutterstock, 13:5 Israel Defense Forces / Wikimedia Commons, 14:1 / John Theodor / Shutterstock.com, 15:4 Itay.G / Shutterstock.com, 15:11 Daria Nor/Shutterstock.com, 16:16 kavram/Shutterstock.com, 16:16 Wikimedia Commons, 17:20 John Theodor / Shutterstock.com, 18:9 Meirav Ben Izhak / Shutterstock.com, 19:14 Eli Schwartz/Shutterstock. com, 20:10 Inna Reznik / Shutterstock.com, 22:7 max shamota/Shutterstock. com, 23:8 Kobi Gideon / GPO, 24:20 Mark Neyman / GPO, 26:1 Zoltan Kluger / GPO, 26:6 courtesy of Israel365, 26:15 blueeyes/Shutterstock.com, 27:5 Yuval Y / Wikimedia Commons, 28:12 Emma Grimberg / Shutterstock.com, 30:3 Mark Neyman / GPO, 31:7 Max Zalevsky / Shutterstock.com, 32:1 Mark Neyman / GPO, 33:12 Flik47 / Shutterstock.com, 34:1 SJ Travel Photo and Video / Shutterstock.com

Map of Modern-Day Israel and its Neighbors

The following is a map of modern-day Israel and the surrounding countries

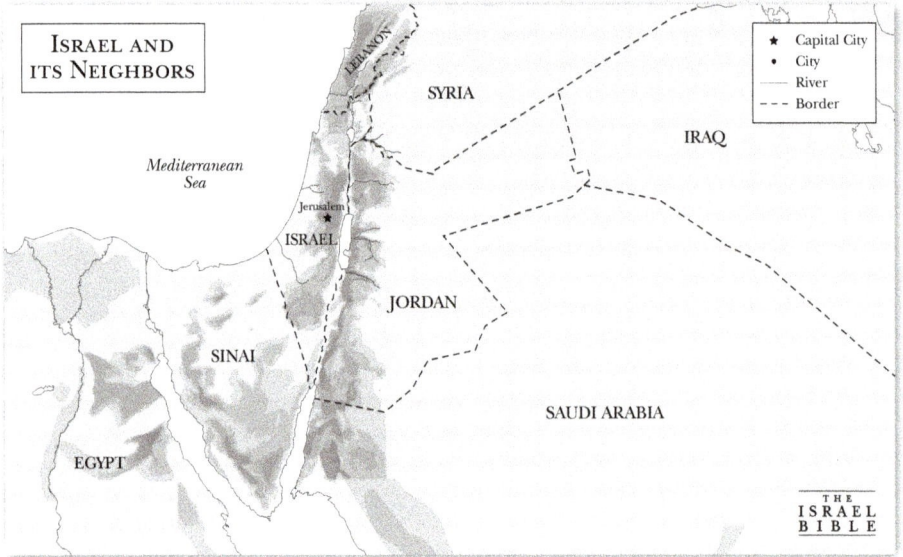

NOTES

NOTES

NOTES

NOTES

NOTES

For more inspiring commentary,
interactive maps, educational videos,
vivid photographs and more,
please visit our website

www.TheIsraelBible.com

THE
ISRAEL
BIBLE